SUPERCOMPUTERS OF TODAY AND TOMORROW

THE PARALLEL PROCESSING REVOLUTION

RICHARD A. JENKINS

TAB BOOKS Inc.
Blue Ridge Summit, PA 17214

To Susan
Without you, life itself
would be impossible

FIRST EDITION
FIRST PRINTING

Printed in the United States of America

Library of Congress Cataloging in Publication Data

Jenkins, Richard A.
Supercomputers of today and tomorrow.

Includes index.
1. Supercomputers. 2. Parallel processing
(Electronic computers) I. Title.
QA76.5.J445 1986 004.1′1 85-27639
ISBN 0-8306-0422-7
ISBN 0-8306-0322-0 (pbk.)

Front cover photograph courtesy of Lawrence Livermore National Laboratory.

Contents

Acknowledgments

I would like to acknowledge the help of several individuals who took time away from their research to assist me in presenting their achievements as simply and accurately as possible. They include: Geoffrey Fox at California Institute of Technology; David Shaw, Columbia University; Allan Gottlieb, New York University; Creve Maples, Lawrence Berkeley Laboratories; and Thomas Nash, Fermilab.

Especially helpful in ensuring the accuracy of technical portions of the book were three researchers at the Information Sciences Institute of the University of Southern California. Joel Goldberger, Bill Brackenridge, and Paul Mockapetris checked this material in several sections and helped to clarify its presentation.

I would also like to thank the Lawrence Livermore National Laboratory, Control Data Corp., Bell Laboratories, and IBM Corp. for generously providing suggestions, technical material, and information on their latest research.

Finally, I would like to thank my father, Albion U. Jenkins, a man with no training in the computer field, who served both as editor and test subject, compelling me to write simply and make sense. And my mother, Marguerite, who provided moral support.

Introduction

Two profound changes in the way that computers have been built and used for the past four decades have spurred a revolution in the field of computer science that is just beginning to be felt in the world at large. Both developments have roots that can be traced to the machine's earliest years, but for a variety of reasons, they are only now coming into being. This book focuses on new computer architectures and artificial intelligence, two parallel lines of inquiry that are turning mere calculating engines into "superbrains."

Physiological studies of the human brain have revealed an organ of astonishing complexity and unexpected power. At the tasks it does well, the brain is unsurpassed. What has surprised many researchers, however, is that the brain does best the things that seem to us almost absurdly easy. Its capacity to see, direct motion and understand language far exceeds that of any computer now and for the foreseeable future. The brain's 100 billion neurons, each with as many as 1,000 connections to other nerve cells, form circuitry that is 1,400 times more complex than the global telephone network. In the act of seeing, the brain's visual circuitry processes information at the rate of 10 billion operations per second; yet the fastest nerve impulses travel only 250 miles per hour, and the entire brain consumes no more energy than a 20-watt lightbulb.

The world's fastest computer processes data one-tenth as fast as the brain with circuitry one-millionth as complex. It consumes enough energy to power a small town and generates so much heat that its circuits must be immersed in a bath of liquid fluorocarbons. But the computer has its advantages, too. It can outperform the brain by a wide margin in doing what it does best: calculation. The Cray 2 supercomputer, undergoing initial testing and software development as this book goes to press, is said to be capable of peak calculation rates of 1 billion arithmetic operations per second. If an individual sat down to add a billion pairs of numbers, and could work at a rate of one per second, 24 hours a day, seven days a week, it would take 31 years, 259 days to complete 1 billion.

Discoveries about the functioning of the brain at the cellular level, that of the neuron, have pointed computer researchers in a new direction. It was the observation of the brain's tremendous processing power that piqued the curiosity of researchers. How could a processor with a "switch" as slow as the neuron, firing 100 times per second, perform at the astonishing rate of 10 billion calculations per second? The answer seemed to be "parallelism." By combining the processing might of many computers, they reasoned, it should be possible to build machines with almost unlimited power. Before the end of the decade, several mainframe computer manufacturers plan to have machines that will perform at peak rates of 10 billion operations per second.

Some people will surely wonder what possible use could be found for such incredible speed. Surprisingly, there are many scientific fields in which further discovery is restrained primarily by the limited power of even the fastest of modern supercomputers. In most cases, the problem arises not from the complexity of calculations to be performed but from their astronomical numbers. In nuclear physics, aerodynamics, seismology, fluid dynamics, and the stress mechanics of solid objects, researchers know how to ask questions larger than the most powerful computers can solve. In addition, supercomputers have given rise to a new form of scientific inquiry—computer modeling—which allows phenomena that are unobservable in a laboratory or field setting to be "created" by computer for direct study and manipulation.

More powerful computers are also needed for the second line of inquiry based on the study of the human brain: artificial intelligence. Studies of how the brain's complex circuitry functions to perform the many complex tasks that are popularly lumped together as "thinking" have given researchers new ideas about how to organize the computer's processing elements. The importance of knowledge to the thinking process has emerged as paramount in artificial intelligence research, and new machines that process knowledge instead of numbers are already entering the marketplace. These "expert systems" are expected to have an impact on white-collar work in the coming decades as significant as that of robots on blue-collar work.

The industrialized nations have recognized the importance of both parallel supercomputers and artificial intelligence to economic life in the Information Age. Japan, Europe, and the United States have entered into an intense competition, comparable to the space race of the 1960s. Billions of dollars have been earmarked for advanced computer research in an effort to dominate the computer field and seize the spoils of the new era.

The purpose of this book is to chart the progress of the new computer revolution and assess its impact in a variety of fields. An examination of the electronic and mechanical ancestry of these new technologies will show that they arise from innovative combinations of simple elements, making even the most complex machines comprehensible at a basic level.

Chapter 1

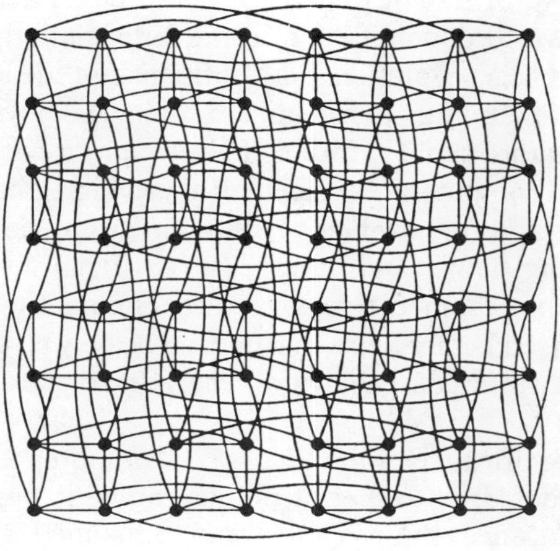

The Computer Jet Age

We're at a pivotal point in computer history. Fifty years from now people will look back on this transition with almost mystical respect.

Salvatore Stolfo
Computer Scientist
Columbia University

In its broadest sense, the computer revolution encompasses the 40 years or so since the invention of the electronic computer. But in the past few years, a conceptual upheaval has swept the world of computer science, calling into question the traditional way of building computers. A machine dynasty based on the ideas of the mathematician John von Neumann and others is being overturned. In its place is a new concept—*parallel processing*. The basic idea behind parallel processing is a simple one: if one processor is fast, 10 working together would be faster and 1,000 would be superfast. This revolutionary change in thinking about computer design promises equally dramatic changes in the world at large during the 1990s and beyond. Dozens of different designs for parallel computers are being tested at research facilities in the United States, Japan, and Europe. The outcome of this race to the future, some experts believe, could mean nothing less than world denomination in the Information Age.

Behind this revolution is a confluence of ideas in three areas: the functioning of the human brain, the physical laws that govern the miniaturization of electronic circuits, and the structure of computers. Possibilities beyond imagination even a few years ago are now being realized in prototype machines of surprising power and versatility. Artificial intelligence, quantum physics, medicine, structural engineering, mineral exploration, and other fields that depend heavily on computers may be transformed by this new generation of parallel supercomputers.

The significance of parallelism in computer technology could be compared to that of the jet engine in aeronautics. For four decades, the propeller was to manned flight what sequential, von Neumann-style processing is to computation. Then one day in 1943, the German Luftwaffe thrust the airplane into the Jet Age. American soldiers on the battlefield stared up in awe at the machine that streaked across the sky trailing smoke and belching thunder. The world is standing now on the threshold of the computer's Jet Age. And while there's no smoke or thunder to announce their arrival, these powerful new machines still inspire awe.

EVOLUTION OF THE REVOLUTION

Few would argue that the computer revolution, which was born in the fires of World War II, has brought with it changes in virtually every aspect of life. We're long familiar with the monthly harassment of billing computers, and even the once-novel automated teller machine has become merely another piece of machinery. But the number-crunching power of modern supercomputers is remote and inaccessible, emanating from a mere hundred machines locked away in heavily guarded laboratories. These supersystems are opening new worlds to the vision of science. Aerodynamics, particle physics, deep space exploration, and genetic engineering all depend on supercomputers to manipulate vast volumes of information or perform trillions of calculations. In some cases, supercomputers have been direct agents of discovery, modeling phenomena that would otherwise be unobservable. The key to the computer's success in so many fields is its ability to handle complexity on a scale inconceivable in the precomputer era.

There have been three great technological revolutions in the history of modern man. The first was the scientific revolution, which opened the way to systematic exploration of the physical world. The second, the industrial revolution, turned that scientific knowledge to the service of man, producing food and goods in abundance. The third, the computer revolution, has enabled man to systematically and efficiently quantify and manipulate information. Computers give man the power to gather and codify knowledge from the scientific and industrial revolutions, multiplying and manipulating it into new forms of wealth and new understanding.

From another perspective, it could be said that mankind first developed means to expand the power of his senses, then his hands, and finally his brain. Each epoch has brought with it new tools and a new way of looking at the world. The impact of the industrial revolution, for example, extended well beyond the factories into the homes of the workers. It influenced art and language, philosophy and government. Some would argue that the industrial revolution extended even into the mind and still governs our thoughts today. There's evidence that the computer's impact has been equally significant. Already it has added dozens of new words and phrases to the language: *glitch, input, hacker,* and *garbage in garbage out*, among others. Its effect on culture has been just as pervasive.

Yet, despite the power of scientific instruments, machinery, and computers, there are some things that are beyond the reach of even the most powerful technology. Scientific instruments are blind to beauty. No one has ever invented a gauge that can measure love, and only a minority would call the polygraph a reliable detector of truth. Machinery has proven far too coarse, thus far, for the kind of fine-textured and delicate movements of which the human hand is capable. No machine has ever successfully carved a statue or given a soothing massage. The computer, too, has its limits. What it does well, it does so well that it far exceeds human capacities. What it does poorly it does so poorly that a child can outperform it. There's never been a computer that can recognize a human face or make casual conversation.

When computer science was in its infancy, it was believed that teaching computers to see, to understand language, and even to think as humans do would be comparatively easy. After all, these machines could perform difficult mathematical calculations with amazing speed and accuracy. They ought to be able to do something as simple as identifying objects in a picture. But such tasks are as easy for computers as solving sixth-degree polynomial equations is for humans. The researchers soon discovered that they had underestimated the complexity of the human brain. The rude awakening that rattled computer scientists in the 1960s nearly brought research in this area to a halt. But now a new, more determined effort is underway to unravel the mysteries of the human mind.

Vision, language understanding, and "thinking" can be grouped loosely under the heading of artificial intelligence. It's often said that computers are dumb, that they can only do what they're told. They respond to a list of instructions called a program that is spoon-fed into the machine by a programmer. If, during this process, the programmer makes a single error in a program thousands of lines long, the machine will dutifully grind through the instructions and spit out an answer that makes no sense at all.

Programming errors have plagued the space shuttle, weapons systems, government, and business. One reason that these minor errors can become major catastrophes is the difficulty in locating these errors, known as *bugs*, and correcting them without creating a new bug elsewhere in the program. In some cases, when a particularly complex program—which may consist of as many as 100,000 lines—turns out to be bug-infested, it's easier to throw the whole mess away and start again than to fix it. Programming has turned out to be the computer's Achilles' heel, but efforts to automate at least part of the process are underway at research facilities around the world.

The computer's rapid evolution has been the source of its tremendous success. If the aircraft industry had evolved as spectacularly as the computer industry over the past 25 years, a new jet airliner would cost $500 today, and it would circle the globe in 20 minutes on five gallons of fuel. The speed of computation has increased 200-fold in that period. A machine that occupied an entire room in the late 1950s can now be found on a chip the size of a fingernail—and a small fingernail at that.

It could be said that the computer has evolved more rapidly than has our mastery of it. For with each successive generation, individual transistors (the basic building blocks of electronic circuits) get smaller and more numerous, and the connections among them more difficult to plan and execute. A single chip (the silicon wafer onto which these tiny transistors are etched) may contain as many as 600,000 such elements, each one small enough that 200 could be lined up in a row across this period. Designing new chips at this level of complexity is like laying out a city the size of Detroit in a space slightly less than a quarter-inch square.

It's ironic that the very machine that first enabled man to cope with complexity has compounded it beyond the boundaries of human intellectual capacity. So to aid in the process of designing the next generation of computers, the machines themselves have been enlisted as semi-intelligent assistants. They do the bookkeeping of the design process. Thousands of individual elements can be grouped into neighborhoods according to function, and it's the computer's task to remember who associates with whom and for what reason.

These intelligent assistants can perform a variety of other tasks and are generally known as *expert systems*. They occupy the cutting edge of commercially available artificial intelligence technology. Similar systems are available for medical diagnosis, diesel engine repair, oil exploration, chemical synthesis, molecular genetics, and battlefield analysis. But expert systems, as they're currently designed, require enormous amounts of computing power to achieve good results, even in a tightly restricted field of knowledge.

What has most excited researchers—and not just computer scientists—is the potential marriage of a new generation of extremely powerful computers with artificial intelligence software. But for most of us, who don't understand the arcane mysteries of quantum chromodynamics or electronic engineering, it may be easier to imagine an expert system designed with nothing more sophisticated in mind than the task of making life easier.

HOMAC, SWEET HOMAC

To anyone who's ever spent much time programming a typical personal computer, especially in the BASIC programming language, the machine takes on all the frustrating demeanor of an aging domestic servant who's grown fussy, difficult, and set in his ways. With much coaxing and coddling, he can be convinced to perform limited functions, but often such persuasion requires more work than the task itself. Anyone who's ever tried to program a computer to balance a checkbook knows what I'm talking about.

But imagine for a moment that the year is 2010 and Charlie Babbage, a successful young computer entrepreneur, has just pulled into the driveway of his home in Silicon Estates. A small camera mounted under the eaves of the house scans his license plate, and the garage door opens automatically. At the back door, another lens scans his face and the HOMAC IIe household computer greets him in a friendly, natural-sounding voice as it unlocks the door.

"Hi, Chaz, you look awful. Come on in and take a load off," the machine says.

Charlie grunts. The computer tells him to have a beer, sit down, and relax for a while. (HOMAC compiled its household inventory during the day and had a case of beer delivered, along with the rest of the week's groceries, from the store.)

As he sinks into the warm folds of a recliner, he tells the computer to put on some soothing background music, and it tunes in his favorite radio station. The volume is set automatically at a level previously defined to the computer as "soothing," and it faithfully screens out all but the music. A display screen is mounted next to the recliner, and Charlie asks for the front page of the evening paper. A headline and the first paragraph of each article appears, followed by an indication of each story's length and the number of illustrations accompanying it. He scans the headlines, thinking, "Eight billion people on this planet and there's never any news."

He asks HOMAC for a readout of the data search assigned to it this morning, and the screen is filled with a listing of all printed references to a certain little bioelectronics company that a colleague mentioned as a "hot prospect." As he scans a readout of the CEO's past convictions for securities fraud, the computer is busily monitoring a variety of household systems—regulating temperature, lighting, electricity demand—and keeping a constant watch on the perimeter scanning system.

Charlie reaches into his vest pocket, takes out a palm-size tape recorder, and inserts it into a slot in the monitor.

A variety of notes and data entered during the day is transferred to the main household computer. The computer notes all of the foods he's eaten (at least what he's confessing to), computes the calorie total for the day so far, and begins planning an evening meal that will keep him from exceeding the strictures of his diet.

The notes from the recorder are indexed with those bearing similar filenames. The computer also takes care of reminders Charlie's requested—birthdays, National Secretaries Week, phone calls to make—and it makes whatever adjustments his social calendar requires.

As he signs off the monitor and leans back in the recliner, HOMAC asks, "How was your day?"

An advanced software package he recently installed makes it possible to carry on a conversation with the computer. The machine is programmed to wait quietly until he decides to talk. It knows all the significant details of Charlie's life—who his coworkers are, the kind of stresses he faces on the job, his aspirations—and it asks appropriate questions when he mentions someone or something it doesn't know. The initial conversations were a little one-sided, but at times now he forgets that he's talking to a machine.

Hungry now, he heads for the kitchen. A readout on the refrigerator shows the computer's selection of preprepared dishes suggested for dinner. Cooking one's own is always an option, of course, but the quality of ready-made meals is such that it's hard to pass up a sure thing for the hazards of home cooking. He pulls out the small containers, removes a foil strip on the top, and pops them into the microwave. He reaches for another beer and passes it over a laser scanner inside the refrigerator door. A chocolate mousse is erased from the dessert portion of the dinner menu.

As the microwave completes its cycle, he lights the candles and sets the food on the table. In a soothing, though less than dramatic voice, the computer reads aloud another chapter of Arthur C. Clarke's *2001*. Astonishing, he thinks, how accurate Clarke's predictions were about the HAL 9000. Perhaps HOMAC will join me for a game of chess after dinner.

COMPUTER FANTASY VERSUS COMPUTER REALITY

The HAL 9000 was Arthur C. Clarke's ultimate computer fantasy. Clarke's machine could monitor the operations of a space station, engage in conversation, play chess and plot murder, all at the same time. The HOMAC domestic service system, my own computer fantasy, is considerably more benign than HAL but no less revolutionary; it's a computer that would take some of the nuisance out of life. It keeps track of the little odds and ends of daily living that can get so completely out of hand.

Most of the functions of the HOMAC system exist today, piecemeal and in prototype form. There are calorie counting programs, meal planners, and home inventory systems, would be simple enough to create. Experimental electronic newspapers, known as *videotext systems*, have been tried in several cities. Freelance information vendors earn $30 an hour or more to perform database searches for customers.

In the realm of artificial intelligence, computers have had perhaps the most success as chess players. There are several programs with Master ratings that can beat all but the best human players.

Some of the other things that HOMAC can do are closer to the cutting edge of present technology. Vision systems capable of reading a license plate under a wide range of conditions are available, though perhaps not foolproof. Machines that can understand the spoken word are also in commercial production. Their vocabulary is limited, however, and they must be trained to an individual's voice and speech patterns. Also, the speaker must make a brief but awkward pause between each word.

The processing of continuous, unbroken speech from many different speakers remains an elusive goal. It's conceivable that 2010 could come and go without that goal being reached. Similarly, a vision system that could recognize and interpret the many subtle expressions of the human face is probably 20 years or more away. The capability for intelligent conversation may also be a distant dream, although some present-day programs can do a reasonable imitation of it if the speaker sticks to a particular subject. Machines capable of limited learning have been demonstrated, but the degree to which that technology can be developed is uncertain, particularly with regard to a subject as subtle and full of nuance as the drama of daily life.

For all of its many bookkeeping features, HOMAC's computing requirements are small, but the simultaneous processing of speech and images would probably require hundreds of times the computing power available in even the most powerful of today's supercomputers. And while the speed and power of computers is expected to continue to increase rapidly, reducing cost per computation, it's difficult to conceive of two chickens in every pot and a super-supercomputer in every garage. One possibility that might make Charlie's system more affordable would be for the processing power of 100 or 1,000 smaller computers to be linked together in such a way that the muscle of all was available to each one in turn. Just such a scheme, called a *distributed processing network,* is under investigation.

THE NEXT GENERATION

What is required for the next generation of computers is not simply jamming an ever-larger number of ever-smaller components onto a piece of silicon—that line of effort is costing more and yielding proportionately less speed. What's required is a complete rethinking of the way computers are built and the way they process information. From von Neumann's first computer to the world's fastest single processor, the Cray 1 supercomputer (Fig. 1-1), computers have always done tasks essentially one at a time. The *central processing unit*, or CPU, fetches a pair of numbers from memory, adds them and replaces them in memory. Processing speed is limited not by the speed of the CPU but by the narrow pathway between the CPU and memory. Shuttling operands and results back and forth is like trying to condense all the traffic on a freeway at rush hour down to one lane. Computer scientists call the resulting traffic jam "the von Neumann bottleneck." Researchers working to build the next generation of computers are counting on parallelism (using many processors, each of which works on a piece of a larger problem) to detour around the von Neumann bottleneck and achieve revolutionary increases in speed.

The notion of parallel processing has never been entirely absent from computer science. Von Neumann himself considered it for certain kinds of problems. Periodically, proposals to build machines with more than one CPU surfaced in various technical journals, but they were largely ignored during the 1950s and 1960s. Progress in developing serial computers, and the difficulty of coordinating more than one CPU, forced parallelism to the back burner. The first truly parallel computers emerged in the 1970s.

Fig. 1-1. The Cray 1 supercomputer, from 1976 to 1982 the world's fastest and most powerful computer, is capable of performing at rates of 160 million arithmetic operations per second. Next-generation supercomputers are expected to be from 10 to 50 times faster (courtesy of Cray Research).

Two trends spurred the research forward: a need for more processing power and the revival of artificial intelligence research. Studies of the human brain determined that its neurons, numbering in the tens of billions, work together in parallel to create intelligence. By copying some of the brain's processing strategies, researchers hope to build computers capable not only of solving large scientific problems but also of reproducing human intellect.

Computer evolution is often broken up into generations

based on key advances in technology. Not everyone agrees on which generation ends where, but most would agree that the computer is near the beginning of its fourth generation. A rough description of each generation follows.

First Generation. From the first computer to the IBM 650, 1947 to 1956, computers relied on vacuum tubes as their basic switching element, and for memory, they used magnetic drums and cathode ray tubes.

These early machines were capable of processing about 10,000 instructions per second, similar to the speed of a modern personal computer, and storing 2,000 alphanumeric characters.

Second Generation. Typical machines were the IBM 7094 and the Control Data Corporation's CDC-6600. This was the era of discrete transistors and magnetic core memories, 1957 to 1963. Performance was in the neighborhood of 200,000 instructions per second with storage for 32,000 characters.

Third Generation. Stretching from 1964 to 1981, this generation marked the introduction of the computer on a chip, as well as specialized processor and memory chips for mainframe supercomputers. The IBM 360 and 370 series, the Cray 1 supercomputer, and Control Data's Cyber 205 are all third generation machines. Average performance for these machines is 5 million instructions per second with main memory capacities of at least two million characters. Peak processing speeds, often cited by the manufacturer, can be considerably higher.

Fourth Generation. The 1980s is the decade of the parallel supercomputer. Cray's X-MP, a four-processor machine, was one of the first next-generation computers, delivered in 1982. Its successor, the Cray 2, is believed to be the first machine to execute 1 billion arithmetic operations per second (Fig. 1-2). Control Data has also introduced a parallel multiprocessor system, Cyberplus, that can combine and integrate the power of as many as 64 high-performance CPU's. Such a system, Control Data claims, would be capable of peak execution rates of 44 billion instructions per second, a huge leap in processing power that won't be verified in actual tests until someone contracts to buy such a machine.

Fifth Generation. The Japanese christened their national effort to develop artificial intelligence machines, begun in 1981, "The Fifth Generation Project." Since then the term

Fig. 1-2. Testing and software development for the Cray 2 supercomputer is underway at Lawrence Livermore National Laboratory. The four-processor Cray 2 is said to be capable of peak computation rates at close to a billion operations per second, yet its densely packed circuitry occupies only half the volume of the Cray 1. Its circuits are cooled by immersion in a bath of liquid fluorocarbon. Scientists at LLL have affectionately nicknamed the Cray 2 "Bubbles" (courtesy of Cray Research).

has been applied to AI research in general, which includes speech and image processing, expert systems, and other knowledge-based computer applications.

The promises of the Fifth Generation read like science fiction: machines that can process thousands of bits of knowledge—not numbers but actual concepts, ideas, and images—per second; programs that encode encyclopedic volumes of knowledge in a particular field and thereby solve problems too complex or obscure for human specialists; computers that design and program other computers (that, in effect, have the power of reproduction); machines that learn from their mistakes and from experience; and computers that interact with humans vocally and in human language, without the need for mechanical input.

The focus of this book is to assess the present state of next-generation computer research and to outline what might realistically be expected in the next five or 10 years. Much of the book will be devoted to parallel computing strategies, which will play a role not only in conventional computers but in Fifth Generation machines as well. Artificial intelligence researchers have set the agenda, but it will require a cooperative effort on the part of scientists in many disciplines to move from present-day technology to that of *2001*.

RETHINKING THE COMPUTER

In mid-1984, the United States dominated the supercomputer field, possessing nearly three-fourths of the 140 or so most powerful machines in the non-Communist world. These are the nitro-burning dragsters of the computer world, zipping through arithmetic operations in billionths of a second. Today's supercomputers are as specialized and exotic, when compared with a typical personal computer, as a 250-mph dragster is to a Ford sedan. Supercomputers are built for speed and carry price tags as impressive as their power. A Cray 1 can perform at peak rates of 160 million arithmetic operations per second and costs between $8 million and $15 million, depending on whether you go for the standard model or want one loaded with optional memory capacity.

An hour of time on a Cray 1 leased from a commercial vendor can cost as much as $10,000. In an effort to assist financially strapped university researchers, the federal government makes a small amount of time on its supercomputers available for a fraction of the commercial rate. An hour on the Cray

1 at Los Alamos National Laboratory in New Mexico, during which roughly 360 billion operations could be performed, was selling in 1983 for as little as $636. But at such bargain basement rates, the computer's time has to be carefully rationed.

The high cost of high-performance computing has split research on the next generation of supermachines along two distinct lines. One is pragmatic and focuses on putting as much computing power into the hands of as many scientists as possible for the least amount of money. The other is the stuff that post-industrial dreams are made of. The latter line of research sees superfast computers, new architectures, and parallel processing simply as means to an end—artificial intelligence. The underlying assumption is that only an intelligent machine, capable of processing rules and facts together in a logical fashion, will be able to negotiate the vast ocean of information that is piling up faster than human beings can assimilate it. Since the knowledge explosion is being driven to a great extent by the computer itself, it will require a computer to bring it under control.

The first commercial expert systems are already on the market, and the number of possible applications for them seems limited only by the boundaries of human knowledge. Their development has been slowed, however, by the tedious process of spoon-feeding machines with the rules and observations drawn from human experts. What's needed for the information revolution to swing into high gear is a computer that can teach itself. As yet, such efforts have met with only limited success.

The biggest hurdle that artificial intelligence researchers must overcome is not the technical difficulty of designing machines that can mimic the human learning process but the problem of discerning just what that process is. And this is where optimistic projections for the Fifth Generation begin to founder. Predicting the path of technological change is difficult enough, but forecasting the progress of basic science is mostly wishful thinking. Creating genuine artificial intelligence is like curing cancer—researchers are attempting to solve a problem that they don't quite understand.

Even parallel processing, which is the *sine qua non* of all next generation machines, is still full of mystery. No one has really figured out the best way to build a parallel computer, and the result has been a plethora of prototypes with such whimsical names as the Cosmic Cube (my personal favorite, a revision of the mysterious Boolean N-cube), the Ultracomputer, Non-Von 1, PUPS, and the Connection Machine. The diversity of projects is fascinating, and at first a bit overwhelming.

Some machines are being developed for a single purpose—like analyzing radar signals, modeling aerodynamic problems, or running artificial intelligence programs—while others are designed to be general purpose machines. All of the general-purpose prototypes tested so far are highly efficient at some tasks, less so at others, depending on their design. Many believe that the next generation computer will turn out to be many different machines, each specialized for a specific task: science and engineering, artificial intelligence, vision, speech understanding, and robotics. It may turn out that developing processors that can do only one kind of calculation, but at lightning speeds, will be most effective for some applications.

The outcome of this multinational race to the future is far from certain. It may not even be possible to tell where the finish line is. But the Japanese, with the announcement of their Fifth Generation Project, have launched the Sputnik of the 1980s. The United States and Europe are responding to the challenge with an avalanche of money and rhetoric. To the winner will go the spoils of the Information Age.

Chapter 2

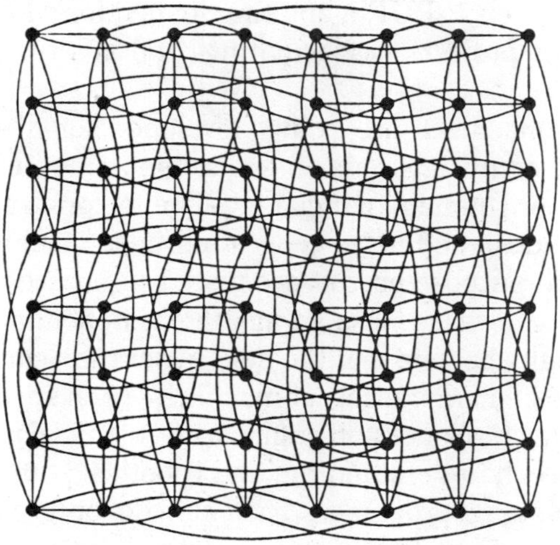

Information Über Alles

The nation that dominates this information-processing field will possess the keys to world leadership in the twenty-first century.

Robert E. Kahn
Director, Information Processing Techniques Office
Defense Advanced Research Projects Agency

In September 1981, the Japanese government announced a national plan to build intelligent machines with capabilities far beyond those of even the next generation of computers. Organized by the Ministry of International Trade and Industry, the project started with 45 of Japan's brightest young electronic and software engineers and promised funding of $430 million in the first five years. The Fifth Generation Computer Project, as they called it, would leapfrog from the current generation of computers to one that is so technologically advanced it would constitute not merely the next generation but the one beyond. The goal is audacious, the cost high, and the outcome uncertain, but the reward for success could be nothing less than dominance of the international computer market in an age when information itself will be the standard of wealth against which all other currencies are measured.

The announcement of the Fifth Generation project has come to be seen as the first salvo in an international battle to achieve supremacy in information processing technology. The industrialized nations have entered a period of intense economic competition that, according to one expert, will last the rest of this century and into the next. Victory in this one area would have a profound impact on a country's ability to compete in every sector of economic life. By handling information more effectively, a nation can respond more rapidly to consumer needs, design its products better and bring them to market more quickly than its competitors.

Artificial intelligence systems can enhance the productivity of workers—both blue collar and professional—by allowing them to cut through mountains of technical data and get rapidly to the heart of a particular problem, whether it's repairing a diesel truck engine or engineering a new, disease-resistant bean plant. In the United States, the primary patron of artificial intelligence is the Defense Department, which foresees its use in unmanned scout vehicles, smart maps for aircraft pilots, weapons development, and battlefield management.

Without land or natural resources, the Japanese have recognized that their continued prosperity depends on being able to compete effectively in the information economy. As a nation, the Japanese have demonstrated a remarkable ability to use technology culled from other societies, reengineer it, repackage it, and remarket it with tremendous success. The United States has watched as transistor radios, television sets, home electronics, steel, watches, cameras, automobiles, and a host of other products have been copied by the Japanese and made better, faster, or cheaper only to come flooding back to the American market as highly competitive imports.

A prime example of the success of the Japanese as technologists can be found in the manufacture of computer memory chips. In 1970, when Hewlett Packard first came out with a random access memory (RAM) chip, they had the market all to themselves. By 1974, the Japanese had gained a toehold with 5 percent of the market for the small, 4K memory chips, capable of storing 4,096 (4K) numerical bits of information. Four years later, they had captured 45 percent of the market share for 16K RAM chips. And by 1982, they had obtained as much as 70 percent of the world market for 64K RAMs, a market worth an estimated $3.4 billion. By 1989, according to one analyst, worldwide sales of RAM chips are expected to rise to $9.4 billion.

SUPER SPEED EQUALS SUPER COMPUTER

The Japanese drive to dominate the information processing field includes not only the Fifth Generation Project, which focuses primarily on artificial intelligence, but the National Superspeed Computer Project, as well. The six major Japanese computer manufacturers have joined with the Electro-Technical Laboratory, a government funded facility, to develop a machine far more powerful than the fastest U.S. supercomputers. Funding comes from the Ministry of International Trade and Technology (MITI), which is to Japan what the Pentagon is to the United States. The Japanese view trade as vital to national survival, in much the same way that the United States relies on military might. As a result, the prime patrons of high technology in both countries are the bureaucracies entrusted with safeguarding national security.

The primary goal of the project is a supercomputer capable of executing 10 billion floating point operations per second. *Floating point* refers to the binary version of the common method of representing unusually large or small numbers called scientific notation. A single floating point operation is the addition, subtraction, multiplication or division of two numbers in floating point notation. These operations require more computational work than fixed-point or integer operations. Most inexpensive, handheld calculators perform only integer arithmetic. The advantage of floating point arithmetic is that it allows the computer to work with extremely large numbers, up to $10^{2,466}$, which would be written out as a 1 followed by 2,466 zeroes. Equally small numbers can be manipulated just as easily.

The speed of supercomputers is often given in a unit called a *megaflop*, which represents a million (mega) floating point operations per second (flops). The Japanese Superspeed Computer would be capable of a peak execution rate of 10,000 megaflops. By comparison, the Cray 1 is about one sixty-fifth as fast at 160 megaflops. A personal computer is roughly one ten-millionth as fast, capable of a mere 1,000 floating point operations per second. To put it another way, if the Superspeed

Computer was a jet traveling at the speed of sound, 700 miles per hour, the Cray 1 would be an old man jogging at 7 miles per hour, and a personal computer would be a snail—and a slow snail at that!—moving at the rate of about 4 inches every hour.

Other goals for the Superspeed Computer include:

- One billion bytes of primary memory. Memory is measured in bytes. A byte is 8 bits, and each bit is represented in the computer by a 0 or a 1. It takes a byte of memory to represent each letter of the alphabet, punctuation mark or numeral. Even blank spaces must be stored as data bits. It takes approximately 1,400 bytes to store all of the characters, including blank spaces, on the average typed, double-spaced page. A memory capable of storing 1 billion bytes could hold up to 700,000 typed pages of text. Certain problems, such as the study of air flow over an airplane, can easily eat up that much memory and more.
- A memory bandwidth of 1.5 billion bytes per second. This means that the computer would be able to retrieve numbers from its memory at this rate. Memory bandwidth is vital to processing speed. A machine can only compute as fast as its memory can supply operands for it to work on. Bandwidth is the equivalent of the number of lanes on the von Neumann Freeway at the famed bottleneck. A narrow bandwidth restricts traffic flow and slows the machine. One of the main advantages of parallel processing is that access to memory is broadened significantly.
- The final goal is a distributed, parallel-processing architecture. What this means, in essence, is that the work of the computer is divided among many processors. The consensus among both Japanese and American researchers is that, within this century, no single processor will be capable of peak speeds much greater than 1,000 megaflops, so some form of parallel processing will be essential to meet the project's goals by 1989.

How does this compare with the next generation of American supercomputers? The Cray 2, which is already up and running at Lawrence Livermore National Laboratory in California, is said to be capable of executing at peak rates of about 1,000 megaflops. It will have up to 250 megabytes of primary memory, as many as four separate processing units working in parallel, and a memory bandwidth in excess of

1 billion bytes per second. The Cray 3 and its competitor, a supercomputer to be manufactured by ETA Systems (an offshoot of Control Data Corp.), are expected to match the performance of the Superspeed Computer and may precede it. ETA Systems expects to have its GF-10 ready for market as early as 1986.

THE SHOT HEARD ROUND THE WORLD . . . EVENTUALLY

Despite Japanese ambitions in the supercomputer arena, it was their declaration of independence from technological hand-me-downs, the announcement of the Fifth Generation Project, that put the world on notice that Japan intended to lead the world into the twenty-first century. It was more than a year, however, before the impact of that declaration was felt in this country. Only a few who attended the International Conference on Fifth Generation Technology recognized it for what it was—a Boston tea party, Japanese style. But it was stodgy American researchers, not crates of tea, who got a dunking.

By 1992, the Japanese hope to build a machine that will be able to understand continuous human speech with a vocabulary of about 10,000 words; process visual images with an acuity comparable to that of the human eye; increase the speed of present thinking machines by a factor of 10,000; reason from a memory of machine-coded knowledge far larger than that presently available, containing tens of thousands of inference rules governing 100 million objects; and contain microchips bearing 10 million transistors, 16 times the current maximum density.

The Japanese declaration of their plans for the Fifth Generation has been called, rather uncharitably, "a technological Pearl Harbor" and "a kind of Mein Kampf in electronics terms—a clear-cut statement of intentions that U.S. companies can only ignore at their peril." But ignored it was, initially. The first reaction of many researchers was to dismiss the project as hopelessly ambitious. Almost a year after the announcement, an American researcher attending a conference on software engineering in Tokyo, at which the goals of the Fifth Generation Project were reviewed, said that the reaction of many of his countrymen "was incredulity; a few were outright hostile."

It wasn't until November 1982 that the first reports of

concern on the part of American researchers reached a mass audience. In February of that year, computer researchers from Los Alamos and Lawrence Livermore National Laboratories had journeyed to Japan to assess the state of supercomputer technology. Their reaction, according to William L. Buzbee, as assistant leader of the computing division at Los Alamos, was simply: "Wow!"

Advance reports of the paper that would appear in *Science* magazine in mid-December showed up in newspapers around the country in early November. All of a sudden, it seemed, the experts were worried. Phrases like "very impressive" and "especially noteworthy," praising the Japanese program, were quoted from the report, while the researchers characterized the U.S. effort as "rather lackadaisical," a case of "leadership by default." Ironically, much of the Japanese program was based on ideas presented by American researchers who visited Japan in the late 1970s and gave seminars on artificial intelligence.

The head of the computation department at Lawrence Livermore, John Ranelletti, told one reporter: "Basically the concern we have, collectively, is that the United States is going to lose its supremacy in high-speed computers if we don't get off the ball. Do we want another major industry to go down the drain like the auto industry?"

Much of the alarm focused on supercomputers, rather than on the threat posed by the Fifth Generation Project, which had been grasped by few outside the artificial intelligence community. (In one news report, the Fifth Generation Project was summed up and dismissed with a single sentence.) The Fujitsu Vector Processor and the Hitachi M280H appeared comparable to the best U.S. supercomputers at that time, the Cray 1 and Control Data's Cyber 205. It was as if, in one giant leap, the Japanese had narrowed the once unassailable U.S. lead in supercomputer technology to the width of a microchip.

That theme was picked up and amplified in a government-sponsored report published at the end of 1982. A panel of computer experts headed by Peter D. Lax of New York University concluded that "under current conditions there is little likelihood that the United States will lead in the development and application of this new generation of machines."

And while the Japanese supercomputer program was

grabbing headlines, their intent to dominate in the artificial intelligence field was virtually ignored. The first real warning—"The Japanese are coming! The Japanese are coming!"—appeared in June 1983 in the form of a book, *The Fifth Generation: Artificial Intelligence and Japan's Computer Challenge to the World*, coauthored by Edward Feigenbaum, a pioneering researcher in the field of artificial intelligence at Stanford University, and science writer Pamela McCorduck.

The authors assert that the world is at the beginning of a second computer revolution and that ultimately applications of artificial intelligence will become more important than number-crunching. Though they studiously avoided some of the more inflammatory phrases subsequently employed by other writers, their message was clear: disaster awaits if the United States should snooze through this early warning of the computer wars. At a conference in December 1982 on the use of computers in science, Feigenbaum brought home the echoes of Pearl Harbor, saying, "At dawn we slept."

In their book, Feigenbaum and McCorduck spell out the economic relationship between value and information. "The wealth of nations, which depended upon land, labor, and capital during its agricultural and industrial phases . . . will come in the future to depend upon information, knowledge, and intelligence.

"This isn't to say that the traditional forms of wealth will be unimportant. Humans must eat, and they use up energy, and they like manufactured goods. But in the control of all these processes will reside a new form of power which will consist of facts, skills, codified experience, large amounts of easily obtained data, all accessible in fast powerful ways to anybody who wants it. . . . And it will be for sale."

Thus, even in areas such as agriculture and manufacturing, which are not directly related to information processing, intelligent machines and more efficient access to information can give the Japanese an edge over their competitors. Computer-aided manufacturing can increase productivity, thereby lowering costs, and computer-aided design can bring the latest technology to bear on a product's development, raising its information content and making it intrinsically more valuable.

Feigenbaum and McCorduck accuse the United States computer industry, and particularly IBM, of "conservatism, caution, and conventionality" in its apparent reluctance to take up the gauntlet and show those Japanese who's boss in computerland. What the United States needs, they declared, was "a kind of space shuttle program for the knowledge systems of the future." Without it, they warn, the United States is likely to become the world's largest post-industrial agrarian society.

The Japanese approach carries with it more risk than the American. Unlike the space shuttle program, a situation in which the technology was already in hand, the development of Fifth Generation computer systems will require technical breakthroughs of the kind that come along rarely, and almost never when they're needed. The Japanese have said that their research plan was left purposely vague in order to accommodate both unexpected obstacles and serendipitous discoveries. But in a nation that traditionally follows the path of consensus, it seems improbable that their research effort would stray very far from established lines of inquiry. And, as with any large bureaucracy, there is a tendency to become committed to ideas for reasons other than their technological merits.

All this is not to say that the challenge of the Fifth Generation should be ignored. The Japanese themselves have said they would be happy to achieve only 10 percent of the project's goals. But we need not be looking for Japanese submarines along the coast of California delivering Fifth Generation machines in the dead of night.

GOLIATH AWAKES

Just how serious is the Japanese threat? Is the United States rolling over like a great Goliath, ready to abandon the microchip for the plow? Is it time to unload those high-tech stocks and buy International Harvester? Hardly.

In fact, the truth of the matter is that the United States still holds a substantial lead in research on almost every aspect of high-performance computing and artificial intelligence. One source estimates that lead at two to three years, which in high technology circles is a very long time. That estimate, however, includes the sobering observation that the United States is losing that edge at the rate of about a day per day. This means that in two or three years that lead could well have evaporated if nothing is done to turn things around.

The United States has always been known for excellent fourth-quarter comebacks—and for dozing through the first three quarters. Slowly, the Sleeping Giant is awakening and responding to the Japanese challenge. A 1982 survey of universities and major corporations doing research on next generation computers turned up more than 65. At least that many smaller firms and start-ups are probably involved in some aspect of advanced computer development.

In 1982, a year after the Japanese announced their Fifth Generation project, the United States had committed $175 million from all federal agencies for computer research and training. That same year, the European Economic Community quit bickering long enough to approve a five-year, $1.25 billion computer research and development effort called the European Strategic Program for Research and Information Technology, or ESPRIT. The program is jointly funded by the EEC and twelve private computer and electronics companies. The effort focuses on development of next-generation microchip designs, parallel architectures, and artificial intelligence software.

Britain alone is committed to spending $530 million over five years for work in the same areas in their Alvey Programme. Another privately financed center, specializing in long-range research into artificial intelligence and expert systems, was set up by Europe's three largest mainframe computer manufacturers: International Computers Ltd. in the United Kingdom, Siemens in West Germany, and Bull in France. The facility, located in Munich, has an operating budget roughly equal to the Institute for New Generation Computer Technology in Japan, where the Fifth Generation Project is headquartered.

All this activity on the part of foreign governments and industry—particularly those pesky Japanese, who seem eternally unwilling to let the United States wallow in bourgeois sloth—has fed the demand for a crash program in this country. Such centralization of power in federal hands, however, is the bane of Reagan administration free marketeers. George A. Keyworth II, the president's former science adviser, had declared that the government "will not try to second-guess industry's own choice and judgment about the technologies and markets for advanced computers."

What the government has done, instead, is to throw money in the direction of anybody who has a reasonable idea about how the next generation of computers should work. The amount of money in the 1985 federal budget for all computer research doubled from the 1982 level, to $350 million. The director of the Defense Advanced Research Projects Agency, Robert S. Cooper, has announced that his agency alone plans to equal the total committed to the Japanese Fifth Generation project, roughly $600 million. The Defense Department's Strategic Computing Initiative is dedicated to building a new array of intelligent weapons and battle management systems that can help offset the larger conventional forces of the Warsaw pact.

NASA, meanwhile, is ready to spend $100 million on a network of supercomputers that would be capable of processing in parallel, yielding peak execution rates in the neighborhood of several billion operations per second. The National Science Foundation also is a substantial patron of computer research, spending somewhere in the neighborhood of $70 million. And the Department of Energy, while not heavily involved in computer research, is the world's largest buyer of supercomputers. In 1983, DOE was in possession of more than a third of the world's supercomputers, which were used primarily for nuclear power and weapons studies.

The United States computer industry has also risen to the Japanese challenge. The Microelectronics and Computer Technology Corporation, conceived by Control Data Corp. chairman William C. Norris, was created as a joint venture among 12 electronics and computer firms. Each of the companies agreed to provide top-flight researchers and at least three years' funding in one of four principal areas of investigation: computer-aided design and manufacture, computer architecture, software technology, and packaging. (Packaging is not the design of shipping cartons but the way chips are mounted on circuit boards and how those boards are connected to one another.) A staff of 250 researchers and 60 support personnel will be supported by an initial budget of $50 million annually.

The Semiconductor Research Cooperative is a similar industry-sponsored effort, but it is limited to funding the work of other organizations, primarily universities, rather than engaging directly in research. Located in North Carolina's Research Triangle, the SRC will have an annual operating budget of approximately $35 million.

IBM and Bell Laboratories are pursuing their own research paths independently of the rest of the electronics industry. The annual research and development budget for each of these giants, about $3 billion, dwarfs the expenditure of all others in the field. Not all of that money, however, is spent on advanced computer projects.

The diversity of the American research effort is impressive. Dozens of different architectures are being tried. Hundreds of software systems, microchip designs, and manufacturing techniques are under investigation. The plurality of the U.S. research effort allows for a multiplicity of strategies, which reduces the cost of failure in any one area.

For on the cutting edge of technology, early promise, even when combined with massive investment, does not necessarily lead to technological success. There have been several recent examples of catastrophic failures in the attempt to bring new computer technologies to market. One was Trilogy Ltd., which collapsed after failing to develop computers based on what's called *wafer-scale integration*. Typically, a hundred chips are etched onto a wafer simultaneously and cut apart into individual units. Wafer-scale integration, or WSI, means putting millions of microcircuits on a slice of silicon a hundred times the size of a typical chip. The total investment was estimated at $250 million. Even though a working prototype of a WSI computer was developed, it couldn't be manufactured economically and had to be abandoned.

A similar fate befell IBM's program to develop Josephson junctions, which are superfast circuits that must be cooled to the temperature of liquid nitrogen, roughly 77 degrees Kelvin—more than 273 degrees below zero on the Fahrenheit scale. At its peak, the Josephson junction project had 115 researchers working on it and a $20 million annual budget. The project began in the mid-1960s and by 1981 a working device had been built. The hope was to have a supercomputer based on Josephson junctions on the market by 1986. But the rapid progress of conventional silicon technology and certain technical difficulties with the supercooled circuits forced IBM to scale back the project dramatically and discard the notion of a Josephson junction computer for the foreseeable future.

New, equally promising technologies are on the horizon. They're being backed by the industrialized nations to the tune of several billion dollars. But what is all this money going to buy? Will it buy dominance in the world of high-powered supercomputers? Machines that think? Toys for scientists?

The plain fact of the matter is that no one can really say for sure. Not the Japanese, not the Europeans, not the United States. It is clear, however, that the computer's rapid evolution will continue well into the next century, spurred on by governments anxious for dominance in the Information Age.

Chapter 3

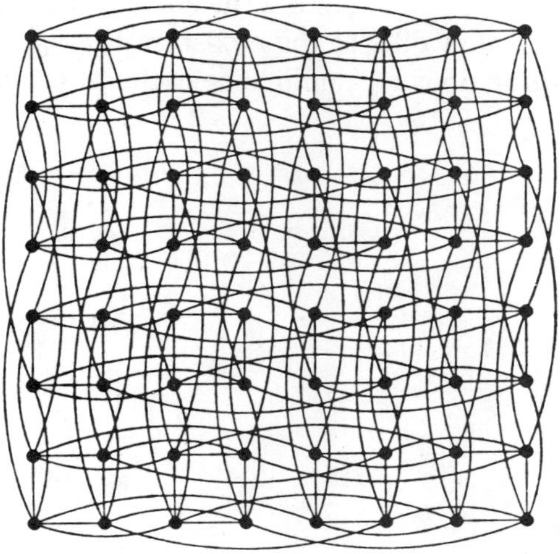

The Essential Machine

The stored program computer was not a case of independent discovery. It arose out of a background of pre-electronic computing by many people in many places.

Arthur W. Burks
Keynote Address to Conpar '81
Analysing Problem Classes and
Programming for Parallel Computing
Nuremburg, West Germany, 1981

A lot of people who are interested in computers, and quite a few who own one, know next to nothing about the long process of discovery that culminated in the development of the electronic computer. Many have only the vaguest idea of how the machine works. Generally speaking, it's no longer necessary. User programs are designed to be used, not understood. But because many of the possibilities for computation in parallel arise from the fundamental concepts on which the computer is based, it's necessary to have at least a basic awareness of how the computer performs its tasks.

A computer is, in essence, a machine that stores,

manipulates, and communicates information entered into it by the user. It performs its tasks by breaking them down into a step-by-step sequence of operations that can be carried out on binary numbers—strings of 1's and 0's. At the heart of the machine is the *central processing unit*, where basic arithmetic and logic functions are performed. The CPU also supervises the operation of the entire system: memory, input, and output. Input can come either from a keyboard, or a secondary storage device, like a disk drive, or it can be received from another computer via a telephone hookup called a modem. Output is displayed on the video monitor and can be printed out or sent by modem to another computer.

ORIGIN OF SPECIES

The modern electronic computer was never actually invented in the usual sense. It didn't suddenly spring into being at the end of World War II the way the atomic bomb did. The computing of numbers by machine goes back three centuries before a machine called ENIAC blew its first tube in 1945, at the dawn of the electronic age. The concepts that were combined to build ENIAC had evolved decades and even centuries before the machine itself. For example, the vacuum tube that was the basic switching element in ENIAC dates back to 1913, and the system of mathematical logic used to direct ENIAC's calculations dates from the mid-1800s.

Machines built of rods, ratchets, and gears were cranking out the solution to simple mathematical problems as early as 1643. With one important exception, all of the machines built before 1900 were designed to solve a single class of problems. In other words, the sequence of operations to be performed on the numbers entered was built into the machine itself, rather than the machine being programmable in the usual sense. They were, in a primitive fashion, parallel computers, in that solving a problem set all of a machine's parts in motion. Since there was no program to guide the calculation, and therefore no sequential steps to follow, it was simply a matter of gears grinding toward the eventual solution.

The first of these mechanical computers was invented by the French mathematician Blaise Pascal, who was then all of 20 years old. The machine, which he modestly called the Pascaline, could add and subtract and was built around a series of wheels, each marked off in 10 equal segments. Each time a wheel made a full revolution, the machine would carry 10 to the next wheel. Subtraction was performed by running the machine backwards.

Thirty years later, the German mathematician Gottfried Leibniz developed a machine that could not only add and subtract but also multiply and divide. Neither this machine nor the Pascaline got much notice from the world at large (although Pascal has since been recognized in the name of a modern programming language). One reason for the relative lack of interest in these machines may have been their limited speed and capacity. The operations they performed weren't particularly difficult, nor did these early machines work all that much faster than a man with pad and pencil could.

Herman H. Goldstine, author of *The Computer—from Pascal to von Neumann*, suggests that processing speed was the key factor in bringing about the computer revolution. "Without the speed made possible by electronics, our modern computerized society would have been impossible: Machines that can do as much as 10 or 20 or 30 or even 100 humans are very important but do not revolutionize society."

A MAN BEFORE HIS TIME: CHARLES BABBAGE

It was more than a century before a machine capable of doing mathematics more complex than basic arithmetic was developed. Charles Babbage, in 1823, was commissioned by the British Chancellor of the Exchequer to design a machine to solve sixth-degree polynomials—$a + bN + cN^2 + dN^3 + eN^4 + fN^5 + gN^6$—primarily for the purpose of calculating astronomical tables more accurately. Babbage had trouble constructing a working prototype and eventually abandoned the project, but it was revived by Pehr Georg Scheutz of Sweden, who built two improved Babbage-design Difference Engines with Babbage's help.

From 1833 to the end of his life in 1871, Babbage was consumed with developing a general-purpose machine, a mechanical computer with truly revolutionary speed and scope. His Analytical Engine, had it worked, would have been the world's first programmable digital computer, complete with a memory and printer. It was to have been a parallel machine as well, performing arithmetic on as many as 50 decimal digits at one time. What ultimately defeated the project was that Babbage's theory, his design, was too advanced for the technology of his day (a problem that has doomed many projects since then). It was impossible to have mechanical parts machined accurately enough for them to work together smoothly. Tiny imperfections in rods, wheels, ratchets and gears would compound as the parts were assembled into components that groaned and threatened self-destruction.

The Analytical Engine was designed as a *digital*, or *counting*, computer. Each of its inputs was accounted for by a click of the ratchet, much the same way that a clock counts seconds and compiles them into minutes and hours. Other non-electronic, digital computers were built after Babbage, but even when they functioned properly, they were slow.

THE ANALOG ERA

By the 1920s, a different kind of process was beginning to be employed in the design of computing machinery. The new machines were called *analog*, or *measuring*, computers. A familiar analog device in common use today is a microphone, which converts sound waves into electrical signals. The microphone, in effect, measures the frequency and amplitude of the sound waves and translates them into electrical pulses with similar characteristics. In an analog computer, numbers are represented as rotations of a shaft or readings on a voltage meter. Numbers are not separate quantities in the usual sense. As a result, inaccuracies in measurement can combine to produce significant errors.

In early 1927, Vannevar Bush and his associates at the Massachusetts Institute of Technology unveiled a device called the Electrical Network Analyzer that could evaluate integrals and solve simple integral equations. The purpose of the machine was primarily to sort out the complexities of electrical circuitry. Numbers were entered as current and voltage readings, but output was less-than-accurate mechanical rotations. Later versions of the machine produced an electrical output, enabling the machine to solve second-order equations.

Not satisfied with the results of his initial efforts, Bush determined to develop a more versatile and more elegant machine, a differential analyzer similar in scope and generality to Babbage's. Bush succeeded in 1931, but with a machine that was entirely mechanical in construction and operation. What had eluded Babbage was achievable with the technology of half a century later, but as an analog, not digital, device. The functioning of this early computer was based entirely on the rotation of shafts and gears. It was also a parallel computer in the most basic sense.

Analog computers proliferated and spread from university research labs into government and business offices. The 1930s marked the high-water point for the analog computer, but a fatal flaw was soon discovered. The faster it was run, the less accurately it calculated. Slipping gears and other minor electrical and mechanical problems would combine to produce ever-larger errors.

COUNTING WITHOUT FINGERS

Meanwhile, the digital machine had not been forgotten entirely. Even in the 1930s they were being built in small numbers, but instead of using purely mechanical parts, as many of the analog machines did, they were built around a simple switch—the electromechanical relay, similar to a telegraph key. This switch opened and closed gates to the flow of electrical signals in the same way that transistors do today.

In one sense, the digital computer is conceptually simpler than its analog counterpart because it mimics the human method of calculation by counting and then building variations on a theme, such as subtraction, multiplication, division, and logarithms. And unlike an analog machine, a digital computer is capable not only of doing complex mathematics but also of using logic.

Simple intuition is of little use in understanding how a digital computer turns electricity into answers, because the way it counts is far different from the way people do. Grasping the connection between electrical switching, counting, and logic is intuitively more difficult than, say, perceiving how a light bulb converts electrical energy into light energy. With the light bulb, one can see the glowing filament inside its airless chamber, feel its heat, and see its light. But a computer doesn't offer much in the way of visual clues to its operation. Electricity goes in one end, answers come out the other. The link between the physical process of switching electrical signals and the mathematical processes of computing is invisible and abstract. Understanding requires a conceptual leap from the concrete to the symbolic.

Compounding the difficulty is the unusual nature of the number system digital machines use: the binary system, which contains only 0's and 1's. The human number system is based on 10 digits, 0 through 9. It's probably no coincidence that most people also have 10 digits, so this system seems entirely natural to us. In fact, the counting numbers are often called the *natural* numbers. But numbers in the computer must be represented as either 1's or 0's, binary numbers, because the switches inside the computer—all computers are basically a collection of switches—must be either on or off. An electrical "on" usually symbolizes a 1, an "off" is 0. It also happens that the on-off states of a transistor can represent true and false, giving the digital computer its capacity to use logic. By combining logic and calculating power, a digital computer is able not only to perform arithmetic and solve sixth-degree polynomial equations, but to play chess and diagnose diseases as well.

The earliest digital machines also differed from their analog counterparts in the way that they were set up to solve a particular class of problems. The most powerful analog computers of the day had to be assembled into essentially new machines for each problem, much as the earliest calculating engines had been. The connections among different components were rearranged like building blocks to perform a particular calculation most efficiently. This machine assembly method was like an old-fashioned telephone switchboard, in which connections were made manually by an operator. The competitors of these machines, under development at IBM and Bell Laboratories, were programmed with punched paper tape—a slow but versatile process in which both numbers and instructions, encoded as holes in the tape, were fed to the machine. Machines with paper tape programs were an important step on the way to the modern computer. But victory for the digital computer still awaited one key development.

THE AGE OF THE ELECTRON

In the first half of the twentieth century, the primary reason for the success of the analog machines was their relative speed. Because of their mechanical parts, the electromechanical relays used in digital machines required from 1 second to 10 thousandths of a second to physically open or close a circuit. Similar switches in modern supercomputers are timed in billionths of a second. The difference is the mass of the switch. Relay contacts have a mass of about one gram. But in vacuum tubes, transistors, and silicon microcircuits, the elements being moved are electrons, which have a mass in the neighborhood of 9×10^{-28} grams. With virtually no inertia to overcome, an electronic switch can be said to operate almost instantaneously.

The combination of vacuum tube technology with digital processing marked the true birth of the computer revolution. But that revolution might have gotten off to a much slower start if not for the motivation provided by World War II. The British machine called Colossus, a processor specialized for cryptoanalysis, was the first to use the vacuum tube as a digital switch. Colossus was built with the help of mathematician Alan Turing, whose theories on the fundamental mechanics of computing were published in 1936 and are still influential today. The machine was turned on in December 1943 and immediately began the task of deciphering codes generated by the German Enigma machine. The Nazis believed Enigma's codes to be uncrackable. But the 2,000 tubes that formed the brain of Colossus were breaking the German codes almost as fast as Enigma was cranking them out. Some military analysts believe that the success of Colossus was the key factor in Hitler's defeat.

The Colossus project was so secret that researchers at the University of Pennsylvania who were working on ENIAC (Fig. 3-1), the first general-purpose electronic computer, were unaware of its development. Physicist John W. Mauchly and J. Presper Eckert, a 22-year-old engineer, started building their Electronic Numerical Integrator and Computor, alias ENIAC, in the same year that Colossus started unraveling Enigma. The American military needed ballistics-trajectory tables for every combination of gun, shell, and fuse that could be assembled from the U.S. armory. Trying to compile these tables using human computers—a battery of women pecking away at desktop calculating machines—proved overwhelming. A single trajectory required the solution of a large number of nonlinear differential equations in several variables that took about 12 hours to compute. Each table generally used 3,000 trajectories. Needless to say, the Ballistics Research Laboratory, where this work was being done, was falling far behind in providing firing tables for new artillery. Nancy Stern, the author of *From ENIAC to UNIVAC*, calls the wartime need

Fig. 3-1. ENIAC, the first general-purpose, electronic computer, occupied an entire room with circuitry that today can be found on a microchip. A uniformed soldier hunts for burned out tubes among ENIAC's 17,000.

for faster computing equipment "the single most important impetus to technological development in the field of electronic digital computers."

ENIAC made its initial test run in November 1945, and the researchers immediately discovered two problems that have bedeviled computer designers ever since: heat dissipation and device failure. The heat thrown off by ENIAC's 17,468 tubes sent the temperature in the room soaring to 120 degrees and the tubes to premature deaths. Whenever the computer malfunctioned, a crew of technicians had to comb through the racks searching for dead tubes before testing could begin again. Despite such difficulties, the monstrous machine did work, cost less than $500,000 and spent nearly a decade calculating trajectories and performing such civilian tasks as forecasting weather—something today's computers do little better than ENIAC.

It's not widely known outside the computing world that, when it was first built, ENIAC was a highly parallel, decentralized machine. Initially, ENIAC was divided into 27 different computing and input-output units. It had a vast plugboard-like switching system running past all the units. To structure the machine to solve a problem, the operator set switches on the program controls and manually interconnected the units to one another via the plugboard.

ENIAC's parallelism was short-lived, however. In 1948 its plugboard was reorganized in the centralized fashion of the newer, stored-program computers. After that, the plugboard was never modified, and the machine was programmed by setting switches at a central location. It seems ironic that the first general-purpose electronic computer, built with a parallel, decentralized architecture, operated for most of its life as a serial, centralized computer.

Eckert and Mauchly left the University of Pennsylvania and ENIAC behind in 1946 to begin work on the Universal Automatic Computer, also known as UNIVAC, that would eventually serve to name the computer division of the Sperry Corp. Von Neumann, who had suggested the calculations used to test ENIAC's performance (determining the feasibility of a new thermonuclear weapon code-named Super), returned to Princeton to start his own computer project. The ideas developed in the five years that followed set the course of computer development for almost the next four decades.

THE VON NEUMANN LEGACY

Though Mauchly could rightly be called the father of the electronic computer—he first proposed building ENIAC in August 1942—it was von Neumann's design for another computer that eventually became the paradigm against which all other machines are measured. The IAS Machine, built at Princeton's Institute for Advanced Study, was the first to use a program stored electronically in the machine's memory and to employ the kind of sequential processing that has characterized most computers since.

The change from ENIAC's parallelism to serial processing was a rapid one, but the roots of that change were based not on the mathematical superiority of serial processing, which is necessarily slower than its parallel equivalent, but on the available technology. Many of the first stored-program machines, including UNIVAC, relied on a storage technology called *mercury delay line memories*, which were capable of storing at most a few thousand bits of data. It was necessary with such systems to read numbers out of memory a bit at a time (a bit is a binary 1 or 0), and consequently, it was natural and economical to perform arithmetic sequentially, two bits at a time. The addition, for example, of two 32-bit numbers was performed in 32 steps.

It was von Neumann's inspiration to use cathode ray tubes as the primary storage device. The simplest way to access this memory was eight bits at a time. It then became profitable to process the bits of a number in parallel, enabling the machine to add two 32-bit numbers in only four steps. So even though the von Neumann style of programming was built on completely serial, step-by-step execution of instructions, the von Neumann architecture still employs a small degree of parallelism at its most basic level.

THE ESSENTIAL COMPUTER

In one sense, the computer has changed little from von Neumann's IAS Machine to the typical mid-1980s mainframe. Despite tremendous advances in technology, the basic ways in which sequential computers perform their tasks have remained essentially the same—and to most people, as obscure as ever. What makes the computer's operations seem so obscure is that its complexity extends both horizontally and vertically. In other words, though the switching of a single transistor can easily be read as a 1 or 0, the meaning of a thousand or a million transistors switching on or off defies understanding. Complexity derived from the sheer number of elements involved in computer processing is horizontal in nature. The computer's vertical complexity arises from its operation simultaneously on many levels.

Vertical complexity can also be found in the human brain, which must function on several levels at all times. Consider the situation of a man being challenged to a fight. At its most basic level, monitoring the body's physical functions, the brain tells the heart to beat and the lungs to breathe. At the level of instinct, it tells the adrenal gland to secrete adrenalin in response to the threatening situation. At the emotional level, the brain responds with anger toward the source of the threat. At the level of abstract thought, the brain assesses the situation to decide whether to issue a counterthreat, attack, or beat a hasty retreat.

The computer has comparable levels of operation. There are, of course, assorted exceptions that keep the analogy from fitting too neatly. But without too much quibbling, it's possible to organize the computer's vertical complexity in a multitiered hierarchy that extends from the physiological, the level of electrical signals, to the abstract, the level of user programs and high-level languages.

MACHINE LANGAUGE

The only language that computers truly understand is machine language. The on-off switching of transistors is interpreted as binary numbers, 1's and 0's, which the computer reads in strings called *bytes*. If it were possible to shrink to the size of a transistor and watch the electrical signals traveling through the machine's wires, they would look like random, staccato pulses of current. Everything that passes through the computer's CPU must be written in machine language or translated into it from another language. Numbers, letters, and program commands all can be uniquely expressed in machine language.

It's possible to program the computer in machine language, but the process is tedious and requires that every step of an operation be explicitly spelled out. To add two numbers, for example, a series of instructions must be written telling the machine to load each of two values from primary memory into an internal register (short-term, small-capacity memory) called an *accumulator*, add the two numbers and return the result to memory. The difficulty of thinking in binary digits and the step-by-step precision required by machine language increases the likelihood of errors.

For several years after ENIAC was first commissioned, there was no other language but machine language to use for programming a computer, although one early accommodation was made to the frailties of the human memory. A set of mnemonics was written that allowed instructions to be written in a more human-like form called *assembly language*. It's still necessary in assembly language to spell out exactly the sequence of steps to be taken by the CPU, but instead of writing commands in binary form, simple words are used. The instruction to load the accumulator might be LOADA, and to add two numbers, ADD. It wasn't until the mid-1950s that the first "high-level" languages were written; these freed the programmer of the necessity of specifying the CPU's every step.

THE CONTROL SYSTEM

In the computer's early years, the most difficult task in designing a computer was wiring the CPU's control system. The job of the control system is essentially to recognize commands and route signals through the CPU. A processor need recognize only a limited number of commands, but each command sends signals along a more-or-less unique pathway through the processor. Timing is critical, and so an important part of the control system is the counter, or clock. Ensuring that numbers get to the right place at the right time to execute every command in a computer's repertoire required a wiring diagram as complex as a New Jersey road map.

It should be no surprise, then, that early in the computer's development a researcher at the University of Cambridge, Maurice V. Wilkes, decided there had to be a better way. His eventual solution to the complexity of the control system was to interpose another layer of instructions between the hardware and the program commands. He called his approach *microprogramming* and borrowed many of the terms of regular programming, which caused macro-confusion. More recently, the term *firmware* has been applied to the microprogram, which denotes its intermediate status between hardware and software.

The basic idea behind microprogramming was to wire the processor in a more regular pattern (Fig. 3-2) and use *microinstructions* triggered by particular program commands to clear a specified path for the signals. The organization of the CPU at this level is like plumbing. At certain critical junctures there are valve-like electronic switches called *gates*. Each microinstruction opens a different pattern of gates at each *clock cycle*. During a clock cycle, the data moves another step along the path charted for it by the signals sent from the control system. Between clock cycles, the system is instantaneously at rest. The effect is like a motion picture that gives the illusion of movement by rapidly flashing from one still picture to the next. In other words, data and instructions don't actually flow through the machine the way water does through a pipe. Each step can be isolated and analyzed individually.

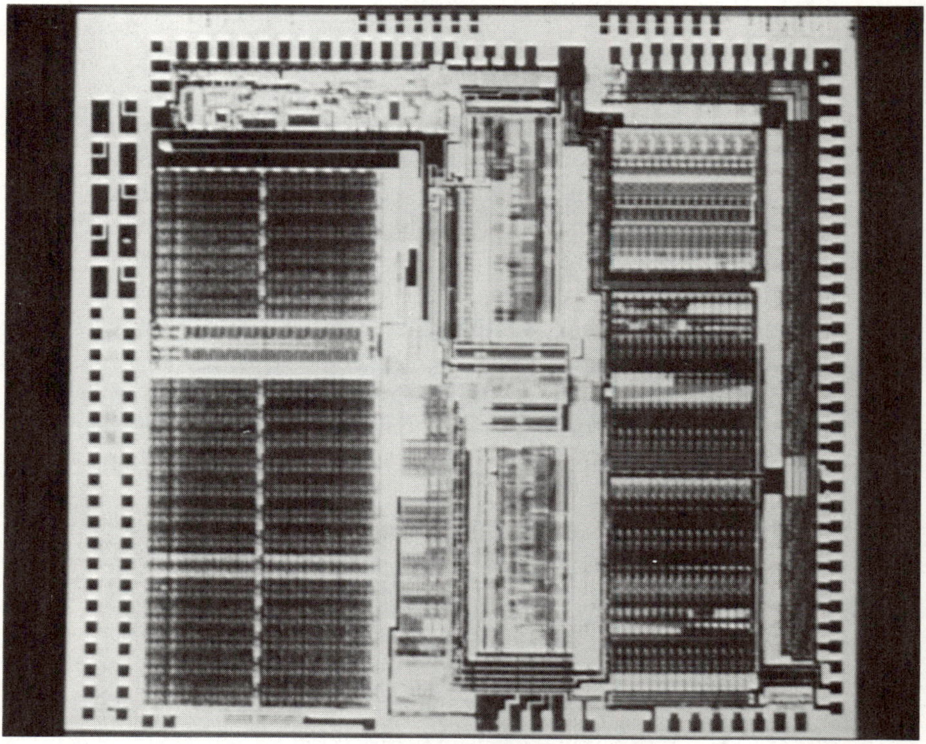

Fig. 3-2. A microprogrammed microprocessor chip shows the geometric regularity of features that is characteristic of microprogrammed integrated circuits (courtesy of Hewlett-Packard Company).

Wilkes' idea, which he published in 1949, was well ahead of the technology of his time. Microprogramming calls for fast and inexpensive memory structures that were unavailable in the 1950s. The major impetus for the development of microprogramming came from IBM. By the early 1960s, IBM had developed a line of computers that differed not only in size, speed, and price, but also in the set of program-level instructions needed to operate them. Because of the difference in these instruction sets, programs written for one class of IBM machines could not be used on another. IBM's division managers readily perceived the marketing advantages of offering a family of software-compatible computers, and in 1964 a line of microprogrammed machines was introduced that could not only run newly developed software but old IBM programs as well.

The set of instructions for the microprogram in a modern computer on a chip is stored in fast registers that, in most cases, can't be erased, and that persist even after the machine is turned off. This kind of memory is usually referred to as *read-only memory*, or ROM, to distinguish it from *random-access memory*, RAM, which is erasable and is lost when the machine is turned off. Besides the microprogram, another set of instructions is stored in ROM that tells the computer what to do after it's been switched on. An IBM PC, for example, will automatically perform a check of all its memory functions before allowing a user access to the CPU.

THE OPERATING SYSTEM

The operating system is distinct from the control system in the sense that the latter is concerned with operations within the CPU, while the former primarily involves the interaction between the CPU and the keyboard, memory, disk drives, display screen, and other parts of the system. The operating system is a software program, although it is written specifically for each type of processor. It performs a variety of housekeeping tasks as a convenience to the user. Consider the sequence of steps that must be executed to transfer data from primary memory to disk storage. First, the operating system checks to see that there is enough space on the disk to hold the entire file. Then sequential portions of the data file are called up from the RAM memory in blocks that, with slight modification, will exactly fill a sector on the disk. Each block is assigned an address and sent to the disk. Numbers called *checksums* are added in an effort to assure that errors in storage are detected, and in some cases, corrected. And finally, the operating system keeps a record in RAM of where on the disk each file is stored. The operating system enables all of those steps to be accomplished with a single command, like SAVE. Similar functions can also be performed with abbreviated operating system commands: copying and erasing files, formatting new disks to receive data, checking on the amount of space remaining on a disk, and listing a directory of the files stored on a disk.

LOGIC AND ALGORITHMS

As its most basic level, a computer program is a series of logical steps that will produce a desired result. Another name for a sequence of operations that consistently provides a correct answer is an *algorithm*. One of the most common algorithms in everyday use is long division. The process of estimating a divisor and carrying the remainder to the next digit works regardless of the numbers involved (with the exception of dividing by zero, of course). It was the mathematician Turing who first realized that any algorithm could be broken down into a sequence of simple steps that, taken together, provided a detailed model of computation. More recently, researchers have realized that certain algorithms are composed of many independent steps, which lend themselves readily to parallel processing.

Recalling the sequence of operations that the computer uses to add two numbers—fetching the numbers from memory, adding them, and replacing the sum in memory—we can see how a parallel algorithm could be employed to add 1,024 numbers in roughly one hundredth the time needed by a sequential machine. A typical von Neumann-style computer would add the first two numbers, then keep a running total as new numbers were drawn from memory and added to the sum. The entire addition sequence would require a minimum of 1,023 clock cycles.

But suppose the computer had 512 processors, instead of just one. Each processor would be sent two numbers from memory. (Completely parallel access to memory would allow this to be done in a single clock cycle.) The numbers would be added together, and then each processor and a neighbor would add their sums together, leaving 256 active processors containing the sum of four numbers each. With each clock cycle, the number of active processors is halved until there is only one processor remaining active. It contains the sum of all 1,024 numbers. The machine has used 10 clock cycles to perform the necessary addition.

This simplified example shows how closely the efficiency of parallel processing is related to the structure both of the problem and the machine. If there were fewer processors, each would have to perform several operations sequentially—though the machine itself could still be said to be operating in a parallel mode—before passing its result to a neighbor. The calculation would require several more clock cycles to complete. If there were more than 512 processors, some would be idle. The ideal parallel algorithm distributes work evenly among all available processors. But like most ideals, this one is attained only rarely. Certain classes of problems, like the simulation of events in three dimensions and image processing, lend themselves more readily to parallel processing than others. The repeated squaring of a number, for example, can only be done sequentially.

The computer uses algorithms not only to perform all kinds of mathematical calculations but also to make decisions. For example, a program intended to figure one's income taxes is based on a string of algorithms whose sequence is derived from the tax form itself. Simple decisions must be made at several points during the calculation. The computer must determine, say, whether line 17 is greater than line 18, and if so, subtract the latter from the former. If not, it enters zero and continues to the next line. This kind of simple logic is what distinguishes computers from mere adding machines.

HIGH-LEVEL LANGUAGES

Algorithms must be expressed in machine language before they can be processed by the CPU, but a number of high-level computer languages have been created to enable programmers to enter instructions in a form more comprehensible to people. Two numbers can be added, for instance, just by giving them variable names like A and B and specifying the operation $A + B$. The program has kept a record of the location of the two variables in memory. The programmed instructions are then translated by a program within a program into machine language commands, causing the two numbers to be loaded into the accumulator and added.

There are two classes of translators which are used to

transform a program written in a high-level language into machine code: interpreters and compilers. The primary difference between the two is in how the original programs are stored. A program using an interpreter is stored in high-level language and then translated command by command as the program runs. As each instruction is translated into machine language, the commands are executed. A compiled program is stored in machine language. After the program is written initially in a high-level language, the compiler works its way through the entire program before it is run, translating it into machine code. This process only has to be done once, and then the program can be stored and used again without being recompiled. An interpreted program has the advantage of allowing the user to see the result of each operation individually. Compiled programs are faster because the translation into machine language has already been done.

Since FORTRAN was developed for use with IBM mainframes in the mid-1950s, dozens of other high-level languages have been written. One of the most popular, BASIC, was created at Dartmouth College in the early 1960s as an introductory language for students of computer programming. Although scorned by serious *hackers* (a slightly pejorative term for those who live and breathe computers), it is still used for applications of all kinds.

The choice of a language is often determined by the nature of the task at hand. LISP has been favored for artificial intelligence work in this country, while European and Japanese researchers prefer a logic-based language called Prolog. The Pascal language, named after Blaise Pascal, has been gaining popularity in recent years because it is said to enable programs to be written with a clear underlying structure that can be readily understood.

The main advantage of high-level languages is that they free the programmer of the need to keep track of exactly what is happening in the CPU. A single command in BASIC may ultimately be translated into dozens of instructions in machine language that the programmer would otherwise have to laboriously enter one at a time. There is a cost, however, associated with the relative ease of high-level programming: whether interpreted or compiled, the programs run more slowly. In translating instructions into machine language, high-level languages use certain conventions that function well enough but are the result of compromises between speed and ease of use. A programmer working directly in the CPU can use shortcuts and tricks of the trade in customizing the instruction sequence for maximum speed.

In their pursuit of parallel processing, computer researchers are discovering that all the difficulties and tradeoffs associated with traditional programming are multiplied as the number of processors grows. While the notion that "many CPUs are better than one" has an appealing simplicity, its actual execution turns out to be more like computing by committee.

Chapter 4

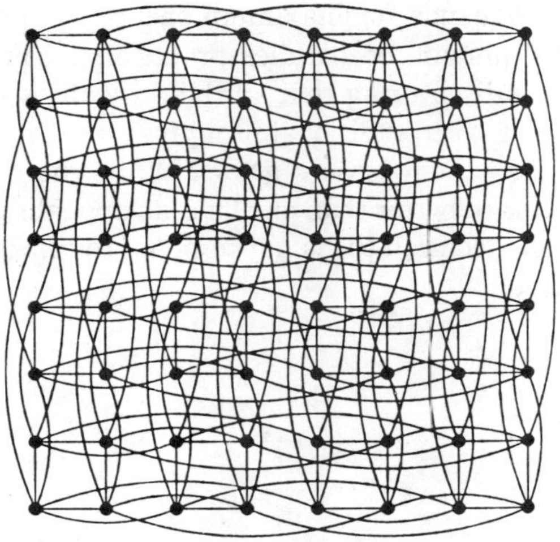

Creeping Parallelism

During the early development of any new device it is usual to find a wide range of innovative thought and design, followed by a period dominated by a heavy investment in one particular type of design. After this period, further innovation tends to be very difficult due to the extent of this investment.

David J. Hockney
Parallel Computers

Parallel processing has never been entirely absent from the field of computer research. Various proposals for parallel machines were advanced in the 1940s and 1950s, but the spectacular success of the von Neumann design inhibited the development of alternative architectures. Instead, various aspects of parallelism were incorporated in the development of serial machines, and the construction of explicitly parallel computers did not begin until the 1970s.

Since the first commercially produced computer, UNIVAC 1, appeared in 1951, computers have decreased the amount of time required to perform a single floating-point multiplication by a factor of 10 every five years. The rate of increase has slowed somewhat in recent years, but today's computers are between 10,000 and 100,000 times faster than their forebears of the early 1950s. However, the speed of basic words. Though von Neumann began designing the machine by a factor of only 1,000 to 10,000. Most of the additional speed has come from the increasing use of parallelism throughout the machine.

FIRST GENERATION

Von Neumann's IAS machine was the first to employ parallel arithmetic, the simultaneous processing of 8-bit data words. Through von Neumann began designing the machine in 1946, the year of ENIAC's introduction, it wasn't completed and fully functional until 1952. A year later, the first commercial machine to use parallel arithmetic, the IBM 701, was introduced. Perhaps the most successful of the first-generation machines was a successor to the 701, the IBM 704, which used parallel arithmetic and had the first hard-wired floating-point arithmetic unit, making it significantly faster than previous machines. Success in the vacuum tube era was measured not in millions of machines sold but in dozens. The first 704 was commissioned in 1955, and the last one was switched off in 1975—altogether, 150 had been sold.

The computer was still young enough in the 1950s that its sequential architecture did not go unchallenged. Proposals for machines with varying degrees of parallelism appeared throughout the decade, but none made it even as far as the prototype stage. Von Neumann himself investigated parallel architectures for the solution of large sets of partial differential equations, such as those for shock waves and weather prediction. He developed the concept of *cellular automata*, which were essentially simple computers capable of functioning in concert, much like the brain's neurons. The automata were connected in a flat grid that, in theory, would have been able to perform any kind of processing function. In 1959, a paper by John H. Holland described an assembly of processors that functioned in a similarly coordinated fashion, but each according to its own sequence of instructions. Some consider this influential paper to be the first design for a large-scale, parallel multiprocessor.

THE IBM DYNASTY

With the advent of the transistor, second-generation machines added another layer of parallelism that increased the computer's overall speed significantly. In a figurative sense, the IBM 704 could not walk and chew gum at the same time. Data could not be read into or out of the machine while the CPU was in operation. To solve this problem, IBM added what amounted to a separate computer whose sole job it was to transfer data to or from the main memory to much slower input-output devices, the card readers, magnetic tapes, or line printers that formed the computer's link with the outside world. Meanwhile, processing could continue in the arithmetic unit. This added parallelism actually predates the second generation and was used by IBM in a modified version of the 704 that was, in 1958, christened the IBM 709. When reliable solid-state transistors became available a year later, the system was re-engineered and its identifying number was raised by an order of magnitude, becoming the IBM 7090. An immensely popular computer, roughly 400 7090s were sold during the 1960s.

IBM lost its position of leadership in the field of ultrafast computers in the 1960s. Some say that the company was a victim of its own success. IBM's share of the high-performance, mainframe computer market was so large by the mid-1960s that the prospect of anti-trust action may have forced the company to back off. Others point to IBM's experience with STRETCH, a machine commissioned in 1956 by the Los Alamos Scientific Laboratory that was to be 100 times faster than what was then the state-of-the-art machine, the IBM 704.

Perhaps the most notable technical feature of the STRETCH design was the first use of parallelism in memory, which enabled the slow *magnetic core* memory to be matched with the faster processor. Magnetic cores were small, doughnut-shaped magnets wired together in square grids. The memory was divided into two independent banks that could send data to the arithmetic units in parallel, a strategy that has been employed on virtually all large computers since then.

It was 1961 before the first STRETCH machine was delivered to Los Alamos, but even after five years of design and development, it failed to meet the contract goals. IBM ultimately built a total of seven STRETCH systems, marketed as the IBM 7030, and lost money on all of them.

IBM rebounded with its 360 series of computers, announced in 1964, but these new machines were primarily business computers and couldn't come close to the performance of the Control Data Corporation's entry of that same year, the CDC 6600.

THE CRAY DYNASTY

With the CDC 6600, Seymour R. Cray, then vice president and leading designer at Control Data and now founder and president of Cray Research Inc., began a supercomputing dynasty that continues at the forefront of high-performance computing. The 6600 was the first machine to be capable of performing a million floating point operations per second (1 megaflop) and the first to use programmed parallelism explicitly within the CPU. The machine had 10 separate functional units that specialized in a single type of arithmetic or logic operation, such as floating point multiplication or addition. In order to make the best use of this kind of parallelism, the machine had to be able to look ahead in the instruction stream and identify operations that could be performed in parallel without altering the logic of the program. This look-ahead feature is still used in most fast serial computers.

The 6600's memory was partitioned into 32 independent banks that could feed data either to the CPU or to one of 10 peripheral processors that, in effect, executed independent programs on data in separate memories. These processors weren't strictly operating in parallel with the CPU because they all still shared the use of a single arithmetic and control unit. The dramatic improvement in performance of the 6600 over its competition, the IBM 7090, led to a *coup d'computer* in which CDC took over much of the market for large-scale scientific machines.

IBM responded, though not until three years later, with the 360/91. This machine introduced the concept of *pipelining* (Table 4-1), which has since been employed in almost all supercomputers. A pipeline is like an assembly line. Each bit of data moves through a series of stations, and all stations work in parallel on different units in different stages of completion. For example, let's say floating point addition calls for six steps that must be carried out in sequence. In previous machines, only one pair of numbers could be in the

Table 4-1. Instead of executing every step of an operation before beginning the next, a pipelined processor moves operands along an "assembly line" that allows a result to be produced with each clock cycle after the first sequence has been completed, allowing the separate steps of an operation to be performed in parallel.

Serial Processing

Clock Cycle	Step	
1	Step 1	Addition #1
2	Step 2	
3	Step 3	
4	Step 1	Addition #2
5	Step 2	
6	Step 3	
7	Step 1	Addition #3
8	Step 2	
9	Step 3	
10	Step 1	Addition #4
11	Step 2	
12	Step 3	
⋮		

Pipelined Processing

Clock Cycle	Addition #1	Addition #2	Addition #3	Addition #4
1	Step 1			
2	Step 2	Step 1		
3	Step 3	Step 2	Step 1	
4		Step 3	Step 2	Step 1
5			Step 3	Step 2
6				Step 3
7				
8				
9				
10				
⋮				

adder at a time. The addition thus required six clock cycles to complete before another pair of numbers could enter the adder. With pipelined addition, a pair of numbers enters the adder with each clock cycle, while those already in the adder advance to the next step in the sequence. In this way, the machine can produce a sum with each clock cycle.

Though the IBM 360/91 was twice as fast as the CDC 6600, its supremacy lasted only until 1969, when Control Data brought out the 7600, once again outperforming IBM's best by a factor of two. The 7600 made use of the same pipelining strategies found in the IBM machine, but its clock cycle was shortened to 27.5 nanoseconds—that's 27.5 billionths of a second—quite comparable to the 12.5 nanosecond clock period of its eventual successor, the Cray 1. IBM caught up in 1971 with a machine that equalled the 7600's performance, the 360/195, but never again bested Control Data in the high performance computer market.

In 1972 Seymour Cray left Control Data to start his own company, Cray Research, with the express purpose of producing the fastest computer in the world. In the remarkably short time of four years, the Cray 1 supercomputer was designed and built. The first model was delivered to the Los

Alamos Scientific Laboratory in 1976. The speed of the Cray 1 was astonishing. The CDC 7600 had been capable of peak execution rates in the neighborhood of 5 megaflops. The Cray 1's peak speed has been estimated at about 160 megaflops.

It should be noted that the speed of a computer is not calculated as simply as, say, the horsepower of an engine. The reason is that particular designs function more efficiently with one class of problems than with another. The peak values quoted by manufacturers are attainable only in short bursts and under conditions that arise rarely in actual practice. While a Cray 1 can reach peak speeds of 160 megaflops, its sustained performance range may actually be closer to about 20 megaflops.

The Cray was the first commercially successful machine to use a technique called *vector processing* (Table 4-2). A vector is a mathematical construct that is expressed in the computer as a related string of 64-bit numbers that can be processed in parallel as a single entity. A special set of instructions is used to process vectors, so that only one instruction need be issued to carry out the processing of the entire vector. In addition to the ten functional arithmetic units in the 7600, the Cray 1 uses three units specialized for vector operations. These units are pipelined as well, allowing the machine to produce a vector result with each clock cycle. Eight super-fast vector registers hold operands awaiting their turn to enter the pipelined processing units, and results ready for further processing or a return to the slower random access memory (Fig. 4-1).

The genius of Seymour Cray is in the science and art of arranging chips on circuit boards and plotting the interconnections among those boards in a way that minimizes the

Table 4-2. Vector processing allows operands to be strung together and treated as a single unit, rather than individually, which is known as scalar processing.

Scalar Processing	Vector Processing
Operation 1: $a_x + b_x = c_x$ Operation 2: $a_y + b_y = c_y$ Operation 3: $a_z + b_z = c_z$ Operation 4: combine results of first three operations.	Operation 1: $\begin{vmatrix} a_x \\ a_y \\ a_z \end{vmatrix} + \begin{vmatrix} b_x \\ b_y \\ b_z \end{vmatrix} = \begin{vmatrix} c_x \\ c_y \\ c_z \end{vmatrix}$
Result: $C = c_x + C_y + C_z$	Result: $C = \begin{vmatrix} c_x \\ c_y \\ c_z \end{vmatrix}$

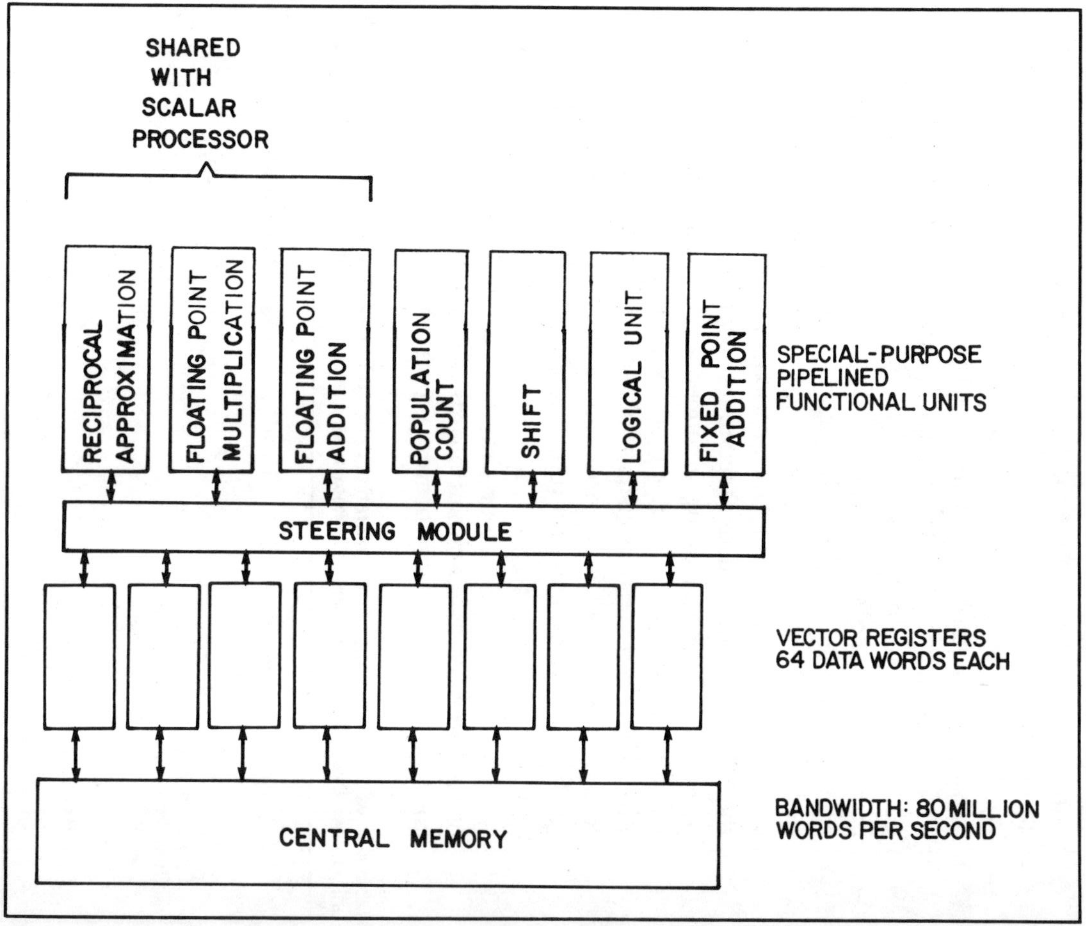

Fig. 4-1. The Cray 1's vector processor uses three specialized functional units—reciprocal approximation, floating point multiplication and floating point addition—to perform vector operations. Operands are stored in the vector registers and can be sent through one or several of the functional units via the steering module.

physical distance that electrical signals must travel along the data path. He has said that his approach is "always to use 10-year-old technology and take advantage of the unique packaging of things I'm good at." In the Cray 1, memory and processor chips are packed tightly onto layout boards that are stacked in banks, which are then grouped together in a circle roughly the size of a telephone booth.

The importance of packaging is magnified in supercomputers because the processors are so fast that one of the main constraints on speed is the time required for signals to pass through wires. Light travels about a foot per nanosecond, but due to the resistance of wiring, electrical pulses can manage only 4 to 9 inches. The longest wire in a Cray 1 is 4 feet, but in Cray's newest machine, the Cray 2, that distance has dropped to about 18 inches.

There is a price to pay for increased speed, however. The power consumption of the machine is enormous for its size and most of that is converted to that old nemesis of electronic circuitry—heat. In order to dissipate the heat generated by the 300,000 integrated circuit chips in the Cray 1, the refrigerant Freon is circulated through channels in each layout board, cooling the toes of each overworked chip. To perform the same task in the more densely packed Cray 2, the entire system must be immersed in a bath of liquid fluorocarbon.

From the introduction of the Cray 1 until 1979, a Cray-designed computer was alone at the top of the commercial supercomputer heap. By 1982, 34 systems had been sold, each at superprices ranging from $10 million to $15 million. Not one to sit on his laurels, when the competition began catching up, Cray came out with the X-MP, or Experimental Multi-Processor, in 1983. The new machine, which is essentially two or four Cray 1's combined in a single system, has a clock cycle of about 9.5 nanoseconds and allows broader, more parallel access to memory. Most often the two or four CPU's function independently, but their instruction streams can be synchronized to coordinate the two halves. The Cray 2 is similarly structured but uses a 4.5 nanosecond clock.

The Cray X-MP was one of the first commercial examples of multi-processing, which can be loosely defined as the connection of two or more von Neumann-style machines, each with separate control systems and instruction streams but capable of sharing data. The distinction between multiprocessing and parallel processing is that in the latter processors function under the direction of a single control system.

AN OLD STAR MAKES A COMEBACK

Cray's competition in the late 1970s came from the company he had abandoned, Control Data Corp. A machine that had been conceived 15 years earlier under Cray's aegis, the STAR 100, ultimately came back to haunt him. The STAR 100 was proposed in 1964 as a pipelined vector processor, much like the Cray 1 but using more primitive second-generation technology. The Lawrence Livermore National Laboratory in California signed a letter of intent to finance the development of the STAR 100, which it was believed would be capable of sustained execution rates of 100 megaflops in performing the kind of long-vector calculations common to the lab's work in high-energy physics. By the time the first fully functioning system was installed in 1975, it was a dinosaur. It used the older, slower magnetic core memory, rather than silicon memory chips, and had an 80-nanosecond clock cycle, compared with the CDC 7600 at 27.5 and the Cray 1, introduced a year later, at 12.5 nanoseconds. As a result, only three STAR 100s were ever sold, and all of those went to government laboratories. Not a single machine was ever sold to a genuine commercial customer.

But it was a re-engineered STAR 100 that, using then state-of the-art memory chips, reentered the supercomputer arena as the CYBER 203E and proved to be a highly competitive adversary to the Cray 1. An improved version, the CYBER 205, was introduced early in 1982 and proved comparable in performance to the Cray X-MP, which was then still more than a year away from its first installation. The CYBER 205 processed vectors in a fashion similar to the Cray 1, but instead of using vector registers, the CDC machine draws directly from main memory and sends data through four identical general-purpose arithmetic pipelines that can add, multiply, divide, and take the square root of floating point numbers. This requires a much higher transfer rate between the pipelines and central memory than that needed by the Cray 1—about 800 million bytes per second compared to 80 million for the Cray. A *vector-stream unit* between the CPU and memory manages the flow of operands and results (Fig. 4-2).

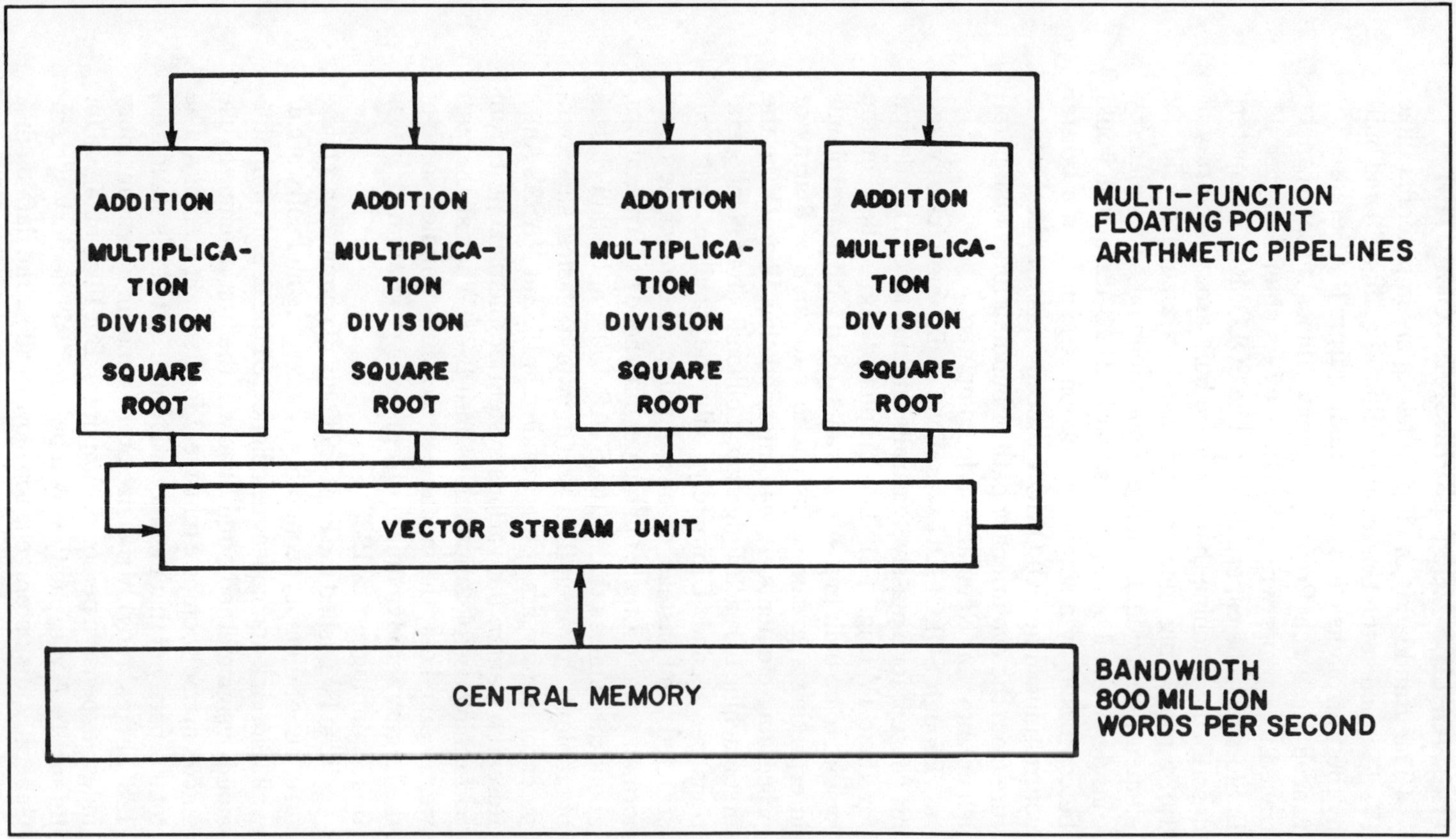

Fig. 4-2. The Cyber 205 uses four multi-function pipelines to process vectors that are drawn directly from memory and sent to the pipelines by the vector stream unit. At any given clock cycle, all four "pipes" must be performing the same kind of arithmetic operation—addition, multiplication or whatever—in parallel.

THE WORLD'S MOST EXPENSIVE COMPUTER

The granddaddy of all parallel supercomputers is Illiac IV, designed at the University of Illinois ("Illi-ac") and built by the Burroughs Corp. with funding from the Defense Advanced Research Projects Agency. Illiacs's roots can be traced to a paper written in 1962 by its chief designer, D. L. Slotnick. The paper, entitled The SOLOMON Computer, described a machine that would be built around an array of 1,024 processing elements arranged in a square grid, 32 elements on a side. Each processor would possess a memory considered small by today's standards, 512 bytes, and all would be controlled by a single instruction stream from a central control unit. The SOLOMON concept was a radical departure from the evolutionary path of building functional parallelism into von Neumann-style computers.

Though SOLOMON was never built, Slotnick revived his concept for a massively parallel architecture in the design for Illiac IV (Fig. 4-3). The original design called for the system to be built in four quadrants, each with a control unit interpreting a stream of instructions for an 8 × 8 array of processing elements. It was intended that Illiac IV be the first machine to reach 1 gigaflop, a billion floating point operations per second. Ultimately, only one quadrant was constructed, and instead of one gigaflop, the machine's performance was estimated in the neighborhood of 50 megaflops, about the same as that of the STAR 100. For certain classes of problems, however, Illiac was the world's fastest supercomputer for many years. It was installed in 1972 at NASA's Ames Research Center, but various system problems kept it from performing useful computations until 1975. When all the bugs were worked out, the machine successfully handled some of the largest aerodynamic problems ever programmed. It was finally unplugged in 1982.

Illiac IV pushed the limits not only of computer architecture, but of memory technology, packaging and software as well. Slotnick and colleagues pioneered the use of computer-aided design methods, and Illiac was the first machine to use silicon memory chips exclusively for its main memory. The total capacity of that memory was small by today's standards, 128K bytes, roughly the size of the random access memory in less-expensive personal computers. But Illiac made up for its small RAM capacity with a unique disk-memory system. Generally, disk storage is too slow to allow the data on disk

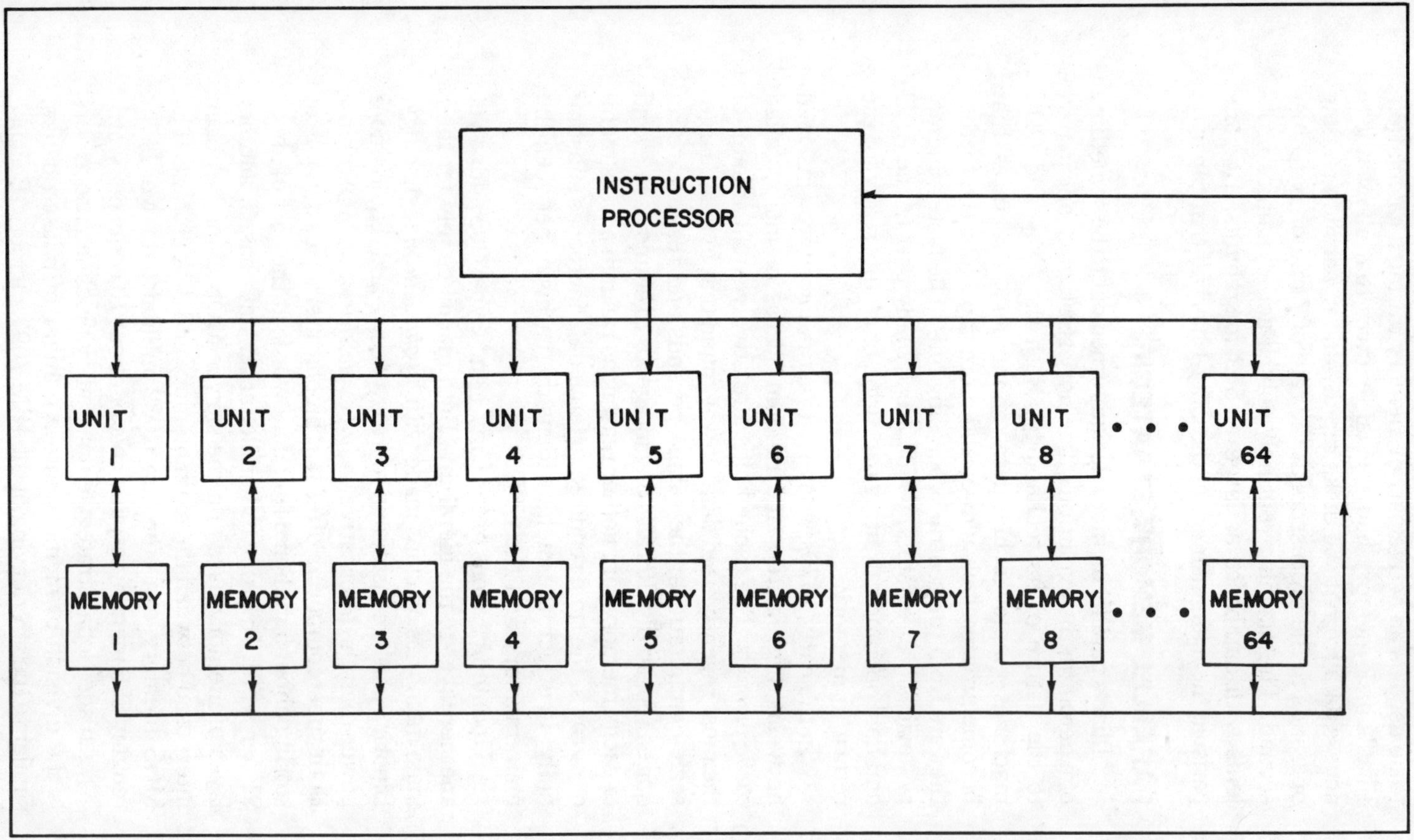

Fig. 4-3. Illiac IV was built around a square, 8 × 8 array of 64 processors that functioned in parallel under the direction of a single instruction processor. In addition, each of the processors was connected to its four nearest neighbors on the grid, allowing limited sharing of data.

to be used as an active part of memory during a calculation. Illiac's disk memory had special features that allowed it to access data from its 64 disks rapidly and in parallel, feeding operands to the processors at the rate of 7 million bytes per second. The machine routinely solved aerodynamics problems with databases as large as 512 megabytes. By comparison, the main memory of the Cray 1 has half that capacity.

PARALLEL MEMORY STRATEGIES

Illiac's parallel memory design turned out to be something of a detour in the evolution of memory strategies, due in part to the nature of its technology. Both the Cray and CDC machines employ a hierarchy of memory structures that become progressively slower and more capacious the further they are from the central processing unit. The fastest memory devices are registers, which are actually part of the CPU and hold operands awaiting execution or results ready for the return to memory.

In the early 1970s, a layer of fast memory was inserted between the registers and random access memory, called *cache memory*. The cache holds a relatively small amount of the most recently used data. It was found that in many large-scale computations, the same operands and results are required repeatedly. It's also advantageous to employ some kind of cache memory for another reason: as random access memory grows, the time required to fetch data increases substantially. In effect, the cache widens the pathway between the main memory and the CPU.

Updated versions of the Cray 1 and Cyber 205 added yet another layer to the hierarchy. Both machines rely for their main memories on chips made with *bipolar silicon* technology. Bipolar chips are faster and more expensive and require more power than the alternative, *metal oxide silicon* or MOS chips. Both supercomputers offer fast bipolar memories capable of storing about 5 million 64-bit data words at the cost of about $1 per word. In order to handle larger data bases, another layer of memory based on the slower MOS chips has been interposed between the main memory and disk storage. The MOS memory can store up to 32 million data words, or roughly 256 megabytes, at a cost of about 10 cents per word.

An additional strategy employed by pipelined processors is the division of memory into a number of phased banks, similar to the interleaving of the IBM 709's memory. Because memory access takes longer than processing, the memory banks take turns sending data to the processors. The access cycle of each memory bank is out of phase with the others, so that with each clock cycle the phase shift opens successively referenced banks, sending data streaming into the pipeline.

Magnetic coated disks have been the preferred method of long-term storage for computers for more than a decade. Their predecessors were magnetic cores, magnetic tape, and before that punch cards and punched paper tape. In disk storage, data is stored in concentric tracks of minute magnetized regions. Changes in the direction of magnetization represent binary 0's and 1's. The information is written onto the disk and retrieved from it by a recording head that is moved radially across the spinning disk to a particular track. Manufacturers are beginning to experiment with optical disk storage, in which data is read by a laser beam, but as of this writing, no satisfactory way of erasing the disk and writing in new data has been found.

MAPPING: ILLIAC'S ADVANTAGE

What gave Illiac an advantage over other machines in computations involving fluid flow was the natural *mapping* of this class of problems onto the processor array. Mapping can be defined as the distribution of calculations among the processing elements. In such problems as the flow of air over a wing or the movement of clouds in the atmosphere, space can be divided naturally into three-dimensional boxes. The calculations required to determine just what is happening within each box are performed almost entirely by a single processor, requiring relatively little sharing of data between processors. Similarly, the Cray 1 and Cyber 205 machines each have a performance advantage when compared to Illiac and to each other for certain kinds of problems that happen to fit well with their designs.

Despite its success as a special-purpose processor, many people regarded Illiac IV as a failure. Its performance was never anywhere close to the original design goal, but worse, its price tag was an astounding $40 million. The money spent on annual maintenance and operating costs alone, roughly $2 million, could have purchased all but the most expensive computers outright. Its faults were many. There was no way for the machine to detect errors caused by the random failure of components, a frequent occurrence, or electrical noise. Designers have since learned that by including redundant bits of information in each 64-bit data word, it becomes possible to detect and correct most such errors.

Yet in spite of its difficulties, Illiac IV was a success in terms of the influence it had on subsequent parallel computer designs. Scientists have a succinct and optimistic way of putting it: failure is more instructive than success. Like Babbage's Difference Engine, Illiac IV was simply an idea ahead of its time.

Chapter 5

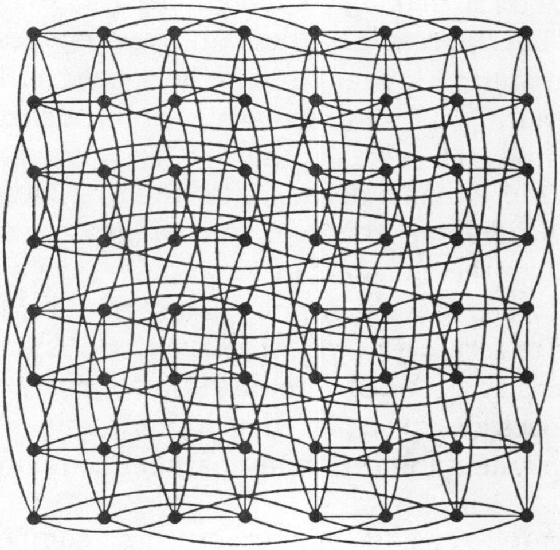

How Small Is Too Small?

Fundamental limits may permit the size of the transistors on a silicon chip to be reduced by another factor of 10—but probably not a factor of 100.

Charles Seitz
Computer Scientist
California Institute of Technology

Much of the momentum behind the computer revolution has come from the rapid evolutionary development of the basic switch that is at the heart of all digital computers. From electromagnetic relays to vacuum tubes to transistors and integrated circuits, there has been rapid progress. Since the invention of integrated circuits in 1959, progress has been measured by the number of switches that can be jammed onto a square centimeter of silicon. Random access memory chips with more than 600,000 circuit elements arrived on the marketplace in 1985, enabling the computer to store 20 pages of text in an area the size of a thumbtack (Fig. 5-1).

Until the late 1970s, the density of circuits on a chip had been doubling annually, but since then the rate of doubling has slowed to every two years. The ability to put an ever-increasing number of circuits onto a sliver of silicon has been the main factor in making computers both faster and less expensive. That approach is gradually yielding less improvement at greater cost. Many researchers believe that fundamental physical limits to increasing circuit density will be reached within the next decade.

It was more than a decade after the first integrated circuits were invented that genuine *microprocessors*, incorporating all of the elements of a computer on a silicon chip, were developed. Now the frontier of integrated circuit design has moved to *very large-scale integration,* or *VLSI.* The much greater density of VLSI circuitry allows not just one but several processors to be placed on a single chip, allowing efficient implementation of many parallel computer designs (Fig. 5-2).

Integrated circuit manufacturers compete for a multibillion-dollar market, supplying chips not only for computers but for appliances, cars, tools, and dozens of other products as well. While the initial design process is expensive, development costs are offset by production runs that are typically in the millions. The effect of progress in IC technology on the computer industry has been two-fold. At the high end of the market, it has enabled the design of more powerful machines at a constant cost, while at the extreme low end, a constant level of performance has been achieved at a lower cost.

Computer chips are usually described in terms of a scale based on the number of circuit elements—including wires, capacitors, and resistors, as well as transistors—that are housed on a chip. *Small-scale integration* is the term for chips with two to 64 individual elements. *MSI,* or *medium-scale integration,* embodies 64 to 2,000 elements; *LSI,* or *large-scale integration,* 2,000 to 64,000 elements; VLSI, 64,000 to 2,000,000 elements; and *ULSI,* or *ultra-large scale integration,* 2,000,000 to 64,000,000 elements. Memory chips capable of storing a million bits of data with about 2 million components are expected to become commercially available in the late 1980s.

THE MAKING OF A CHIP

In order to get some idea of the difficulty of achieving circuit densities in the ULSI range, it may help to understand

Fig. 5-1. A 256K random access memory chip developed at Bell Labs is dwarfed by a half dollar and is made up of more than 600,000 individual circuit elements. In the background are silicon wafers, each etched with about 100 RAM chips (courtesy of Bell Laboratories Record).

how a typical chip is made (Fig. 5-3). Assuming that a working design has already been developed, which in itself can consume 20 man-years, the manufacturing process begins with raw silicon. Quartz-bearing rocks contain a large percentage of pure silicon, as does simple beach sand, and the

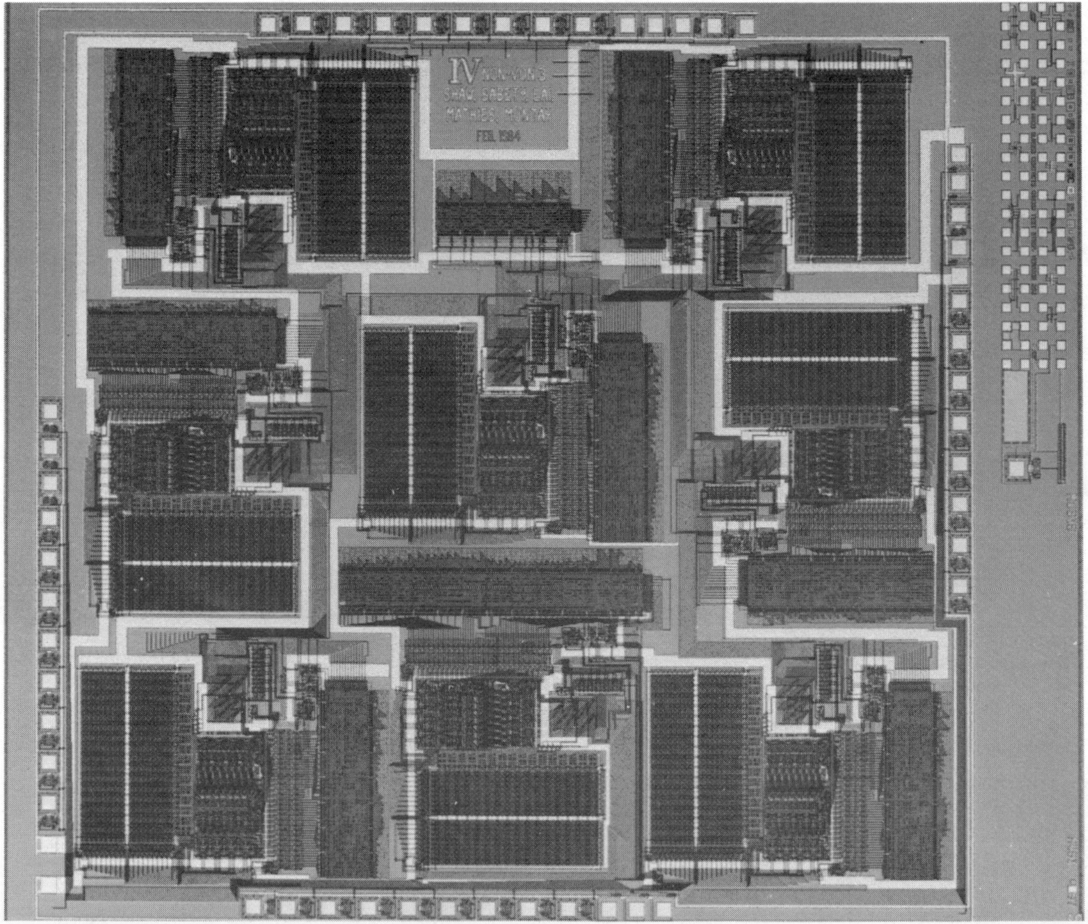

Fig. 5-2. A custom-made VLSI chip holds eight individual processors. The chip was designed by David Shaw at Columbia University for his massively parallel computer, Non-Von IV.

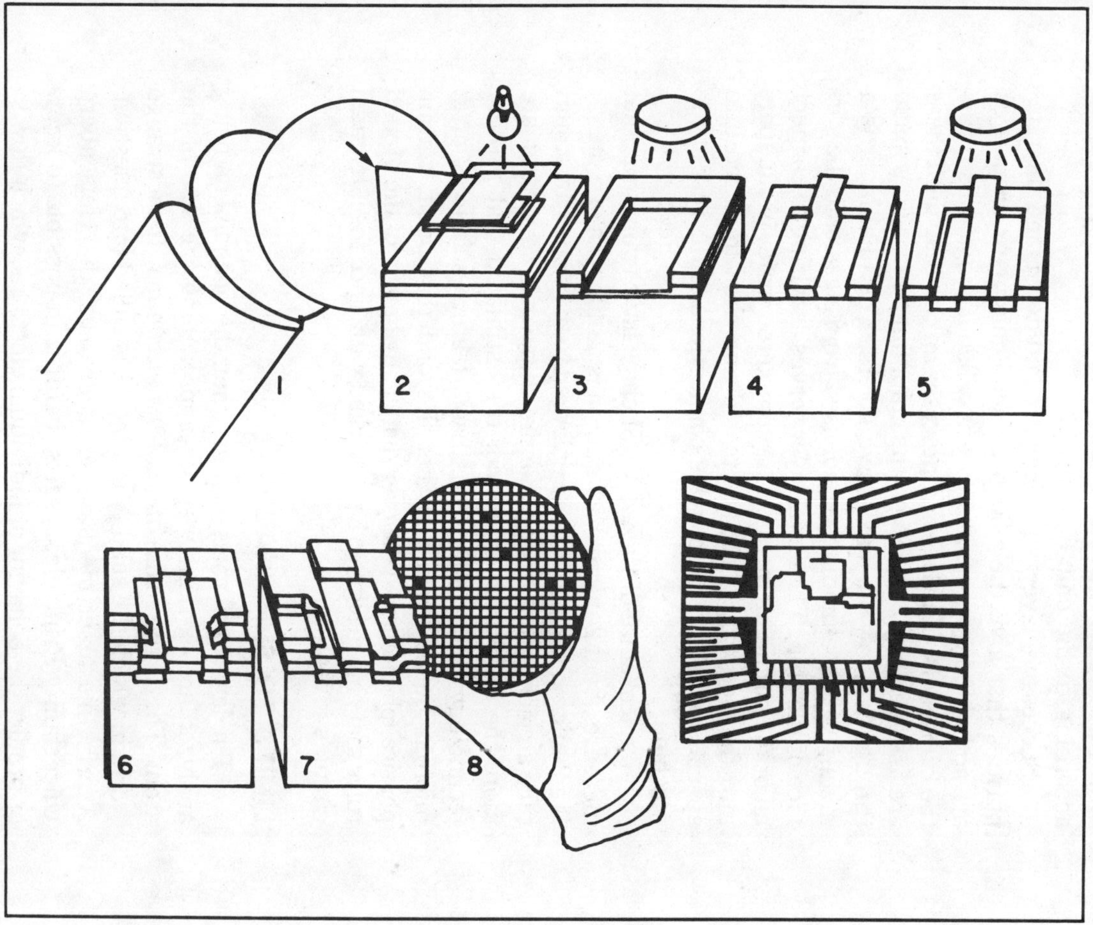

Fig. 5-3. Long crystals of purified silicon are sliced into wafers three to four inches in diameter (1). The wafer is coated with an insulating film of oxide and a light-sensitive material called photoresist. A map of the circuitry, like a stencil, is laid over the wafer. The surface is exposed to ultraviolet light (2), and the exposed photoresist hardens. Solvents are used to strip away the softer, unexposed photoresist and some of the oxide layer. Then superhot gases etch the fine details of the patterned silicon (3). Another layer of silicon is deposited on the surface, masked, and etched (4). Then chemical impurities, called *dopants*, are deposited that turn the wells on the chip into positive or negative conductors (5). These steps can be repeated to build as many as 12 layers onto the chip, with different layers connected by windows etched onto the surface (6). Finally, a metal layer is added that fills the gaps and forms wires that, in effect, turn the individual features into functioning transistors (7). Individual chips are then cut from the wafer and mounted in packages that provide the chip's connections to the outside world (8).

silicon is refined from the rocks and melted. A special process is used to grow long crystals of pure silicon. The crystals are cooled and sliced into wafers about a millimeter thick. One side of the wafer is coated with an insulator, usually silicon dioxide, and then covered with a soft light-sensitive film called photoresist. A stencil, something like a roadmap detailing the location of wires and transistors, is laid over the wafer, which is then exposed to ultraviolet light. Areas of the photoresist exposed to light harden. Unexposed photoresist and the silicon oxide beneath it are then stripped away by solvents and acid. What remains is silicon patterned according to the chip design.

Successive layers of silicon are laid down, and then impurities that give the silicon its semi-conductor properties are added in key areas, a process called *doping.* This forms the transistors. The layering process can continue until there are as many as 12 layers on the chip, linked by wires made through windows in successive layers. The final layer is a metal, usually aluminum, condensed from a gas onto the surface of the chip. The metal layer serves as wiring to connect all of the circuit elements. The completed wafer is cut apart into finished chips that are tested and then mounted into special packages that provide connections to the rest of the machine.

Typical state-of-the-art VLSI chips have transistors that measure about 2 microns. A micron is a millionth of a meter. If a 2-micron transistor were enlarged to the size of a vacuum tube an inch across, then the entire chip would cover a square more than 400 feet on a side. It's estimated that present technology could reduce this basic feature size to .1 or .2 microns but not much farther. Beyond that point, certain physical phenomena take over that change many of the ground rules that chip designers have worked with since the integrated circuit's invention.

LIMITS TO SHRINKAGE

The laws of physics change when the phenomena being analyzed are extremely small, approaching the size of the atom. This is the realm of *quantum mechanics.* It's a strange world in which the solidity of objects is called into question. A principle tenet of quantum mechanics, the Heisenberg Uncertainty Principle, asserts that it is impossible to know or predict the behavior of individual electrons, which flow to create electric current. At submicron feature sizes, electrons tend to tunnel through insulators, altering a chip's electrical properties.

Scientists working to develop chips with transistors in the submicron range have reported a roughness to the etched surfaces that they attribute to quantum fluctuations in the manufacturing process. The features being etched are so small, perhaps only 10,000 atoms across, that the statistical variation in the interaction of light and silicon makes etching smooth edges impossible. This situation can be compared to what happens when a line of paint is sprayed on a surface. In the center, the line is dark and evenly covered, but toward the edges the line breaks up into tiny dots, giving the edge a fuzziness that is only detectable on close examination. From a distance, the edge of the line seems smooth. Light interacts with matter in much the same way, but usually we're too far away to notice the fuzziness.

Several other factors that affect efforts to increase the complexity of integrated circuits are worth noting:

Chip Size. Impurities in the silicon wafer used to manufacture chips and in the manufacturing process itself mean that only a small percentage of the chips on a wafer work. A single defect will damage a chip irreparably in most cases. As the chip grows larger, the number of working chips per wafer drops dramatically. On some very large chips, the yield can be so poor that only one chip per wafer is functional. Naturally, the cost of such chips is high. Some of the earliest chips were less than a square millimeter in area. A substantial portion of future increases in chip complexity must come not just from smaller components but from larger chips. If successful techniques for manufacturing wafer-size chips can be developed, circuit complexity would take a major step forward.

Component Size. In addition to quantum fluctuations, the size of features on a chip is determined by the wavelength of the light used to expose the masked silicon. Commercial designs are pushing toward features in the 1 micron range, which is only as wide as about 3 wavelengths of the ultraviolet light used in current manufacturing processes. Engineers can't make parts smaller than their tools, so shorter wavelengths are being explored for future chip manufacturing techniques. Experiments with X-ray lasers (Fig. 5-4) and with beams of electrons that have extremely short wavelengths,

Fig. 5-4. A researcher at Brookhaven National Laboratory on Long Island adjusts the equipment that directs tightly focused high-intensity X-rays to the task of etching superfine, sub-micron features on lab prototype computer chips being developed by IBM. The source of the X-ray beam is the National Synchrotron Light Source, a high-powered particle accelerator (courtesy of IBM Corp.).

less than a billionth of a meter, have produced working chips in the laboratory with features about .1 micron in size. One expert predicts these advanced lithography techniques will come into commercial use as early as the latter part of this decade.

Electron Tunneling. This is a mysterious phenomenon that is bound up with the nature of the transistor itself. Basically, a transistor is a slice of semiconductor material with wires leading in and out. It switches from off to on when a voltage above a certain threshold is applied to one of the wires. This voltage turns the material into a conductor of electricity. When the voltage is reduced, the transistor reverts to its off stage and acts as an insulator. As the thickness of the semiconductor material is reduced, there are two results. One, it takes less voltage to turn the transistor on because the distance the current has to span is smaller, and two, *electron tunneling* occurs. When a transistor is off, this doesn't mean the voltage is zero; it only means that the voltage is less than the threshold. The barrier posed by the very thin slice of semiconductor isn't sufficient to keep some electrons from tunneling through, creating a current. If the tunneling problem is severe enough, it becomes impossible to turn the transistor off, limiting the accuracy of a computation.

Radiation. All objects give off radiation at some level. Some objects, like certain types of granite used in construction, give off substantial amounts of radiation. People living at altitudes above 5,000 feet are exposed to considerably more cosmic radiation than those at sea level. Most people are unaffected by this type of low-level radiation, but it can wreak havoc in a sensitive computer circuit. When transistors and the voltages required for switching them were comparatively large, radiation posed little problem. But transistors in the submicron range can be affected by a single gamma ray or alpha particle, which can suddenly switch a transistor from off to on. Under these circumstances, a desk, a chair, or even the computer's own housing can pose a threat. Error-correcting circuits in most machines are capable of detecting and correcting all single-bit errors, but errors of two bits or more can't be corrected with this method. As circuits continue to shrink, the number of random errors caused by radiation will increase.

Electrical Resistance. As the diameter of wires on a chip decreases, their resistance to current flow is increased. At submicron feature size, the resistance of even a few millimeters of wire grows to the point that the signal may need to be amplified along its length in much the same way that telephone signals are amplified on long-distance wires. In larger systems, the time it takes for a signal to travel the length of the machine's longest wires can throw off the timing sequence. Most supercomputers have to rely on multiple clocks distributed to different parts of the system to keep operations properly synchronized.

Heat. In order to overcome electrical resistance, it's necessary to increase the current flowing through the system. Faster chips also generally run hotter. A state-of-the-art bipolar microprocessor has switching times of less than a billionth of a second, but each chip dissipates 5 watts of energy in the form of heat. Supercomputers like the Cray 1 or Cyber 205 rely primarily on bipolar chips because of their speed, but each is forced to circulate the refrigerant Freon through the machine in order to carry off excess heat. Exotic packaging technologies developed for wafer-scale integrated circuits can dissipate up to 1,000 watts per wafer.

The nature of these physical limits is elastic. None of them inflexibly prohibits the development of smaller, more densely packed microcircuits beyond a certain point. It's more like trying to extract more miles from a gallon of gasoline. Vehicles have been developed that can travel more than 300 miles on a single gallon of gas, but achieving that kind of performance meant sacrificing general utility. No one would buy a car that gets 300 miles per gallon if they could never go faster than 5 mph. In building fuel economy into more practical cars, manufacturers have to make certain trade-offs—like mileage for horsepower. Similar compromises must be made in developing new computer chips. Greater speed can be achieved with larger switching energies, which require more efficient and expensive cooling techniques. Larger chips can be designed, but at the cost of yielding fewer chips per wafer. Chips with smaller transistors can be developed, but they may be less reliable in actual use, requiring costly error-correction circuitry or radiation shielding.

Few doubt that the potential exists for silicon-based microcircuits with features measuring less than a micron. Whether the limit will be reached at .25 micron or .1 micron or somewhere in between, no one really knows. It's conceivable that feature sizes even smaller may become practical in the 1990s. As that evolution continues, the number of functional elements on a chip will no doubt continue to increase through VLSI and into the ULSI range. Chips at that level of complexity will require design processes that are almost completely automated.

CIRCUIT DESIGN

When just a few transistors were needed to assemble a chip at the level of small-scale integration, circuit design was a fairly straightforward process. The designer would assemble components in structures that would execute specified operations. A schematic of the flow of data through the chip, like the plumbing blueprints for a house, would be laid out. Then the designer would decide where to place individual components and make sure that the design adhered to physical rules that govern layout and wiring. With SSI chips, the design was tested simply by constructing a model of it using individual components wired together on a circuit board. As the complexity of the chips increased, however, these methods were no longer adequate. The computer had to be brought in to help with the task of its own design.

There are actually two separate tasks in chip design. One is developing a design that will do what it's supposed to do. This involves the creation of a logic diagram, which is intended to represent the actual electronic functioning of the chip. The second task is *layout,* which means arranging all the pieces required to satisfy the logic diagram in the least amount of space and connecting them properly.

Logic in a computer, like numerical operations, is built around the on-off switching of transistors. Generally "on" is

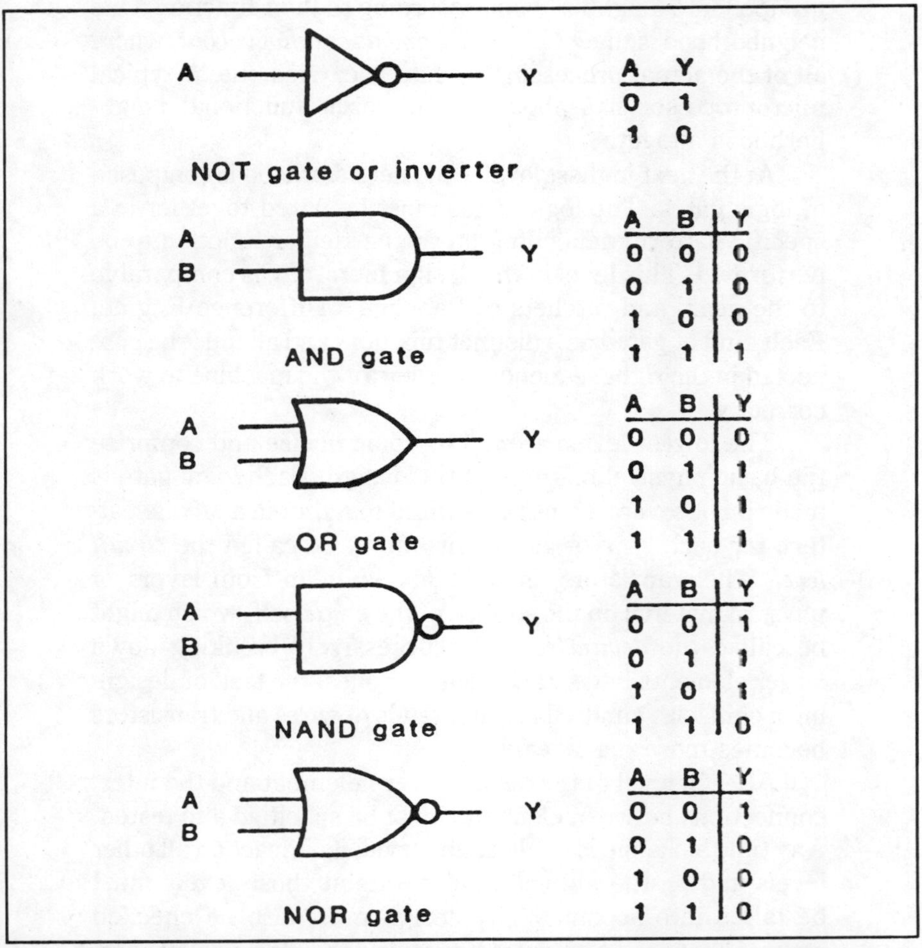

Fig. 5-5. A truth table for logic circuits shows how the switching of transistors can be used to perform logic functions, as well as calculations.

a 1 and corresponds to true; "off" is 0 and represents false. Some simple logic circuits, usually called *gates,* like the ones in Fig. 5-5 show how different operations are carried out. For an AND gate to attain a true state, for example, both of its inputs must be true, while an OR gate is true in every situation but one, when both its inputs are false. By connecting transistors in different ways, any logical circuit function can be constructed. Addition, subtraction, storing, counting, and control functions can all be achieved by specific connections among logic gates.

The design of a chip can be thought of as a hierarchy of four levels, going from the largest to the smallest elements on a chip. At the highest level, the devices on the chip are grouped into neighborhoods according to their function. One neighborhood is the ALU, or *Arithmetic and Logic Unit,* where all of the actual processing of data is carried out. A typical microprocessor has about a half dozen functional neighborhoods altogether.

At the next highest level, each neighborhood is composed of logic gates. The logic gates must be wired together in a specific pattern, depending on the particular function to be performed. This level in the design hierarchy is comparable to the gears and ratchets of Babbage's Difference Engine. Each kind of gate has a distinct function, and all must be connected in the right sequence in order for the machine to work correctly.

The lowest levels are microscopic in size and comprise the basic physical features of the design. Each logic gate is made up of several transistors wired together in a unique pattern for each type of gate. This might be called the *circuit level.* The transistors, in turn, are built up from layers of physical material on the surface of the chip itself, which might be called the *device level.* By successively breaking down larger elements into smaller, simpler ones, the task of designing a chip with hundreds of thousands of wires and transistors becomes more manageable.

At each level of the design, every element and the interconnections between elements must be specified and tested. Any time a change is made at any level, its impact on all other levels and on the individual elements at those levels must be taken into account. The design must also be checked repeatedly to see that rules governing the electrical properties and spacing of wires and transistors on the chip are not violated. Doing all of this without the aid of a computer, other than to perform the calculations related to rule-checking, is extremely time consuming. Manual chip layout proceeds at the snail-like pace of 3 to 40 transistors per day, depending on the regularity of the structure.

COMPUTER-AIDED DESIGN

Progress in the development of faster, more complex computer chips will depend in large part on the success of methods to automate more and more of the design process. Computer-aided design methods have been applied to integrated circuits almost since their invention. In the past, computers have been used primarily to simulate circuit designs and to analyze the performance of circuits and functional elements. Human designers used the machine's advice but made the actual decisions about device placement, wiring, and so on themselves. Used in this manner, the computer becomes an intelligent assistant, doing most of the dirty work for a human designer.

Current work in design automation aims at having the computer make many of the creative decisions itself, with the human designer serving more or less as a consultant helping the machine when it gets stuck. Design automation relies on a form of artificial intelligence. The machine is programmed with various rules that specify both what can't be done and what the ideal chip design would do—minimize chip area and wire lengths while satisfying all applicable design rules. A process of repeated approximation is used to refine the design. Each repetition leads to a design that matches more closely the goals set down by the programmer. The design is tested, and the results of the tests are used to further refine the design.

Total design automation, in which specifications for a chip go in and a complete set of layout masks comes out, has yet to be achieved. Most work in design automation has involved the placement and connection of individual transistors. This is the most time-consuming and error-prone aspect of the design process, and it also involves the simplest kind of decision-making.

There are two main methods of automated design in widespread use: *standard cells* and *gate arrays*. The standard cell approach relies on a library of circuit designs that perform specific functions. The designer is relieved of the need to build each circuit by specifying the location and interconnection of individual transistors. These pieces are put together like a jigsaw puzzle to form the functional elements in a particular chip design. Gate arrays are transistors that have been laid out in a regular pattern, like the cells in a memory chip, and all but the wiring layer has been added. Connections among the transistors, which will form functional elements, are made entirely by wiring.

Both automated design methods are substantially faster than manual chip design, but both also waste a significant amount of chip area. Manual design is still the only way to pack the maximum number of transistors into the smallest amount of space. When large numbers of chips are going to be produced, it may be worthwhile to pay the much higher costs of manual design. As chip complexity increases and automated design methods improve, however, the relative cost of manual design may rise beyond an economical point.

Of the two automated techniques, the standard cell method is the more flexible, because new cells can be created and added to the library. This tends to improve the system's versatility over time as the library grows. Gate arrays have the advantage of being less expensive than standard cell designs because the basic chip can be mass produced. It also takes less time to fabricate a chip based on a gate array because only the final metallization layers need to be added.

One specialized kind of gate array makes up one of the functional elements in virtually all VLSI microprocessors. It's called a *programmable logic array,* and its function within the chip is to decode instructions within the processor that determine how it performs each operation. The PLA consists of two rectangular arrays of gates called AND and OR planes. Any desired logic function can be custom-designed into the PLA by connections in the metallization layers that combine AND and OR elements and their complements, NAND (not and) and NOR. The design of PLA's is almost completely automated. Their regular structure allows the user to specify logic functions to a design program, which then creates a mask for the wiring layer that will make the desired connections. The placement of elements and routing of wires is eliminated.

It currently takes about three years for the design and testing of a new VLSI microprocessor chip using manual design methods, even with the assistance of various computer-aided design tools. Several research projects are working on reducing the design time for new integrated circuit chips by employing artificial intelligence techniques. At the Massachusetts Institute of Technology, a program called Macpitts can take a list of attributes needed in a particular chip and automatically generate a layout. As yet, however, its performance isn't close enough to that of a human designer for the program to have any commercial application.

The Semiconductor Research Corporation is sponsoring a comprehensive effort to develop design automation tools at Carnegie-Mellon University. There researchers are programming an expert system with engineering principles that will ultimately become part of an intelligent design automation system. The CMU expert system has been tested successfully against human chip designers by comparing its design for an existing microcprocessor against the actual design.

At Bell Laboratories, an automated designer called the Plex system is used strictly for the design of microprocessors. The chip architecture it uses is essentially fixed, but there is a wide range of freedom with regard to logic design and layout within those limits. Plex has proved adept at designing high-speed, single-chip microprocessors.

THE NEXT GENERATION: GALLIUM ARSENIDE

There seems to be little doubt that silicon-based chips will continue their rapid evolution well into the next decade. It's also clear, however, that the number of devices on a chip can't continue to double every two years indefinitely. Continued progress in integrated circuit design will depend not only on more sophisticated design automation systems but on new technologies, as well. There are a variety of Fifth Generation technologies under development, but only one has reached the point that its commercial introduction appears certain: gallium arsenide.

Like silicon, gallium arsenide is a semiconductor material that can act as either an insulator or a conductor. Gallium arsenide has the advantage of allowing free electrons (that is, electric current) to reach high velocities at relatively low applied voltages. The result is a faster switch—as much as 50 times faster than the best available silicon transistors. Digital circuits built with gallium arsenide are similar in construction to silicon circuits; in fact, the same layout masks can be used. The level of integration is still quite low, however, with state-of-the-art chips bearing no more than 8,000 transistors versus half a million for silicon technology. Since 1977, when the amount of federal money available for gallium arsenide research was increased significantly, the number of devices per chip has tripled each year. If this growth rate continues, gallium arsenide circuits comparable in complexity to silicon chips would be available by about 1990.

The Japanese are at the forefront of gallium arsenide circuit development. At a conference on the subject in 1983, they reported the construction of the most complex gallium arsenide chip achieved to that date. It was a memory chip capable of holding 1,024 bits of data (1K). Similar silicon chips, using a simpler basic technology, can hold 256 times as much information. Nevertheless, the Japanese chip had four times the capacity of any similar gallium arsenide memory chip then available in the United States. High-speed gallium arsenide processor and memory circuits are a key component of the Japanese National Superspeed Computer Project.

In response, DARPA (Defense Advanced Research Projects Agency) has commissioned a pilot manufacturing facility for gallium arsenide microcircuits. One reason that the technology has been slow to move into the commercial arena in this country is the high initial cost of capital equipment. Even a modest plant occupying about 5,000 square feet of space would require an ion implantation accelerator, a photolithographic machine capable of outlining 1-micron feature sizes, a plasma machine for the etching process, a vacuum deposition system for laying down successive layers of chip material, a dust-free clean room, and an automated system to carry the wafers from one manufacturing step to the next. Price tag: $7 million.

The production goal for the pilot plant is a minimum of 100 wafers per week by 1986 with a reasonably high yield of functional chips on each wafer. Both 16K RAM chips and gate arrays bearing as many as 10,000 gates per chip are expected to be produced. The Department of Defense will also provide a market for the chips, having reserved the right to buy as many as 200 wafers per week for five years after the plant reaches full production. Military applications for gallium arsenide include radar systems, satellite telecommunications, electronic signal jammers and decoys, and a unique new guided missile. The missile is dropped by parachute over the battlefield. As it floats downward, a guidance system in the missile's nose locates a target on the ground and flies unerringly to destroy it. With current technology, the missile would cost more than its target. However, a simple circuit based on gallium arsenide would make the weapon affordable.

The first mass market for gallium arsenide chips will probably come not from the computer industry but from the home entertainment field: direct satellite-to-home television broadcasting. Although presently available, the market is kept small by the high cost ($3,000 to $25,000) of the large receiving antenna required to pick up satellite signals. In order to bring that cost down, manufacturers are working on smaller antennas, 30 to 40 inches in diameter, that can receive ultrahigh-frequency signals directly from space. The amplifiers used to select the channel and boost the signal will be SSI circuits made with gallium arsenide. Eight companies in the United States have been given approval by the Federal Communications Commission for direct broadcasting services. One of those, Comsat's Satellite Television Corporation, estimates that it will be able to sell and install a 30-inch receiving antenna for a total of $100. The market for gallium arsenide circuits for this application alone, according to one researcher's estimate, is 10 million to 100 million chips at roughly $10 each.

Despite its greater switching speeds, gallium arsenide is expected only to double the processing speed of large mainframe computers. Continued refinement of manufacturing processes and the creation of powerful automated design programs will each contribute to the evolution of the silicon microchip. And at least one more order-of-magnitude reduction in the size of circuit elements can reasonably be expected, which will add proportionately to the speed and performance of future computers. Together all of the technological refinements that are planned for integrated circuits in the 1980s will probably assure the continued dominance of single-CPU systems for most applications. But the limits imposed by the laws of physics are out there somewhere in the nebulous future. It may be some time yet before the development of chip technology slows further. Already, however, in certain specialized applications and when pure number-crunching performance is needed, multiprocessor supercomputers offer the path of least resistance.

Chapter 6

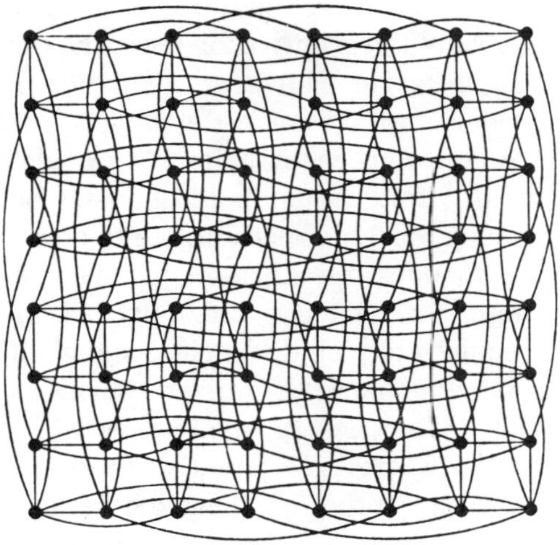

Parallelism in Profusion

The modern age von Neumann has yet to be identified. Instead of having one person pointing the way we ought to go, we have a thousand people pointing every which way.

Creve Maples, Ph.D
Lawrence Berkeley Laboratory

The early history of the computer was shaped largely by the mere fact of its existence. The von Neumann design had proven enormously successful, and the question became "What can we find for this marvelous machine to do?" The answer was far from clear. One pre-1950s pundit estimated that world demand for computers could be satisfied by 10 machines. Applications came slowly at first, mostly in physics and engineering, but insurance companies soon discovered they were useful for computing mortality tables, and other business accounting and government applications followed. The number of uses for his machine that were eventually devised probably would have astounded von Neumann himself.

As the computer evolved from generation to generation, the number of applications for it seemed to grow exponentially. With the development of the microcomputer, suddenly hundreds of new uses sprang up—game playing, word processing, education and home accounting among the most popular. Yet despite the wealth of useful tasks that the von Neumann machine performs well, there are many that it does poorly, if at all. This realization, in part, was the motivation for the development of parallel machines. Instead of searching for tasks suited to the sequential computer's design, researchers began looking for ways to build machines that could efficiently perform tasks the von Neumann machine couldn't.

In their efforts to develop parallel computers, researchers have opened a technological Pandora's box. Dozens of different designs have flooded the research journals and just sorting them out is a job for a parallel supercomputer. For though there is essentially only one way to arrange the elements of a von Neumann computer, the possibilities inherent in parallelism are virtually unlimited. They hinge on three elements: the number of processors, the size of each processor's memory, if any, and the way in which processors and memory are interconnected. All of these elements together describe a machine's architecture.

In spite of all the parallel functions employed in the Cray 1 and Cyber 205, the machine's operations are concentrated in a single central processing unit, making them essentially von Neumann computers. Cray's X-MP and the Cray 2 are true multiprocessors in the sense that they are built around either two or four independent CPUs and have banked memory units capable of feeding data to the processors in parallel. And Illiac IV, though it was under the control of a single instruction processor, was built around 64 independent, parallel processors, each attached to its own memory module.

It was with Illiac IV that the importance of the interconnections among processors became clear. Each processing unit was connected to its four nearest neighbors in a square eight units on a side. As a result, when data had to be sent to a processor across the array, it might have to pass through as many as 14 processors, in as many clock cycles, to arrive at its destination. A processor waiting for that data would have to sit idle. The bane of all parallel processing systems is communication. It's sometimes called *computing by committee*, because the same kinds of conflicts arise among processors as among people. The development of strategies to either minimize interprocessor communication or make it more efficient is at the heart of current research into parallel processing.

Parallel computers are classified according to their architecture rather than size, as von Neumann machines are. It may be easiest to begin by looking closely at a machine that occupies more-or-less middle ground in the range of designs. It was also one of the first parallel prototypes to be up and running, performing useful computations, rather than existing only as a simulation on a von Neumann machine.

THE COSMIC CUBE

The primary goal of the Cosmic Cube project at the California Institute of Technology is not to build a supercomputer but to use parallel processing as a way of making more computing power available to researchers at less cost. Charles Seitz, a professor of computer science, and Geoffrey Fox, a professor of physics, combined their talents with those of other researchers to produce a 64-processor Cube. The machine, which comprises 64 microcomputers each with the processing power of an IBM PC, is about one-tenth as powerful as the Cray 1 but cost one-hundredth as much. It sits on a bench in the basement of the computer science building and looks far too small to be as powerful as it is. The entire machine occupies about six cubic feet of space. Its performance exceeds that of the VAX 11/780, one of the most commonly used computers for science applications, by a factor of 10.

The first task assigned to the Cosmic Cube (Fig. 6-1) was a problem in physics involving the predictions of the theory of quantum chromodynamics, which seeks to explain the structure of subatomic particles such as protons. Without getting into too much detail, the machine was programmed to calculate the short- and long-range forces between the parts of a proton, called *quarks,* and the glue-like field that holds them together. Even with the machine grinding through more than a billion arithmetic operations per hour, the entire computation required 2,500 hours of continuous running time. To see the difference that the speed of a next-generation supercomputer would make with this kind of problem, a machine capable of 10 gigaflops would require less than six minutes to complete the same calculation.

Since then, researchers and graduate students at Caltech have come up with a variety of other applications for the

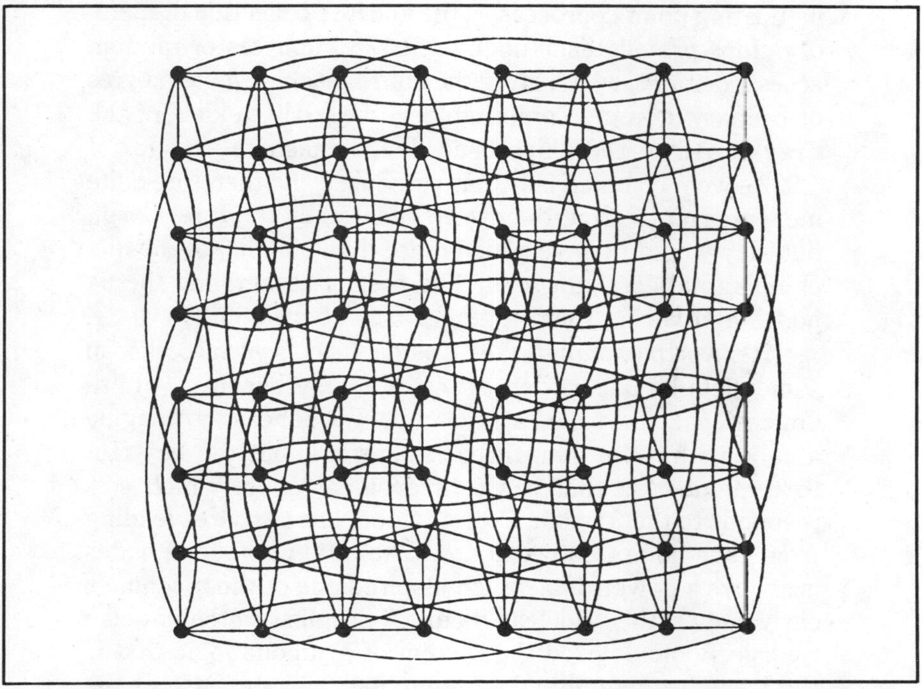

Fig. 6-1. The Cosmic Cube's architecture is based on a 6-dimensional hypercube, which has six wires leading from each node to its nearest binary neighbors.

Cosmic Cube, modeling everything from the origins of the universe to the motion of grains of sand in a windswept dune. The common theme running through all of these calculations is their three-dimensionality. In each of them, the world is broken down into smaller, more manageable chunks. The size of that world can range from a millionth of a millionth of a centimeter, as in the quantum chromodynamics problem, to the vastness of the universe itself. Space is mapped onto a grid of cubes that can each be handled discretely by a *node*, or processing unit, of the Cosmic Cube. Not all problems lend themselves to this kind of treatment, but in the early stages of the machine's development, it was decided that the Cosmic Cube would be built for the vast array of science and engineering problems that would readily lend themselves to treatment in three or more dimensions, rather than attempting to build a general-purpose, parallel computer.

The nodes are almost identical to the main circuit boards on a personal computer, and this is the secret to the Cosmic Cube's economy. Each processing unit is built around two chips, the Intel 8086, a single-chip instruction processor, and its floating point coprocessor, the 8087. A collection of memory chips provide each node with 128 kilobytes of random access memory, which gives the entire machine 8 megabytes of primary storage, comparable to the early models of the Cray 1. All of the chips used in the machine—a total of 4,992—were commercially mass-produced and therefore quite inexpensive. (In fact, they were donated by the Intel Corp., but they wouldn't have added more than $50,000 to the machine's total cost, anyway.) The cost of assembling the 64 nodes and wiring them together was about $80,000.

It's worth examining the Cosmic Cube's architecture in some detail. The nodes are wired together in a multidimensional cube called a hypercube. It's not easy to imagine a cube with more than three dimensions, but the key fact to remember is that a six-dimensional cube, which corresponds to the 64-node Cosmic Cube, has six wires leading from each node to other nodes. The total number of nodes is always a power of 2, which inspired one of the machine's early names, the "Boolean n-cube." (English mathematician George Boole devised the system of symbolic logic that is the basis for computer logic functions.) In the case of the Cosmic Cube, 64 is equal to 2^6 and the number of connections between nodes matches the exponent. A 128-node machine is 2^7 nodes and would have seven wires per node. It's easy to see that, as the number of nodes grows, the number of wires increases in lockstep. A 1,024-node machine would require more than 10,000 wires interconnecting the nodes, placing a practical upper limit on cube construction.

The scheme used in wiring the nodes together gave the Cosmic Cube another of its nicknames, the "nearest-neighbor processor." In this case, a neighbor is not the node that is physically closest in the machine, but a binary neighbor. Nodes are numbered from 0 to 63. In binary notation, 63 is expressed as 111111. Number 63's nearest neighbors are those processors with identifying numbers differing by a single binary digit: 111110, 111101, 111011, 110111, 101111, and 011111. Translated into decimal notation, No. 63's neighbors are 62, 61, 59, 55, 47, and 31.

Communication in the Cosmic Cube takes the form of messages, which are packets of data passed from one node to another. Each message carries an address, which is simply the binary representation of the node's number. The messages are delivered like letters in a mail system. If a node is still in mid-calculation and not yet ready to receive messages, they are stored in a queue until the node is ready for them. In other systems, communication takes place through a switching network, and a multi-unit memory is shared by all of the processors. The communications channels are temporary, like those of a traditional telephone system. The line stays open only as long as it's needed and is then broken off. A machine that operates in this latter fashion is capable of reconfiguring the connections among processors and memory in a way that is best suited to a particular algorithm.

With most parallel prototypes, one goal has been to disguise the parallelism from the user and make the machine appear to function in a sequential manner. The designers of the Cosmic Cube, for scientific reasons, chose the opposite course. While the machine uses unmodified sequential programming languages, the parallelism of each calculation must be explicitly stated by the programmer. In other words, the problem must be mapped onto the nodes directly, a somewhat tedious task but one that allows the greatest control and efficiency.

For example, John Salmon, a graduate student at Caltech, is trying to model the evolution of the early universe by scattering "galaxies" randomly in a three-dimensional space, calculating the gravitational force on each galaxy and "evolving" the model over time. The goal is to find a set of initial conditions that cause the galaxies to clump together in a way that resembles the universe as we see it today. The three-dimensional space is mapped onto a 64 × 64 × 64 cubic grid, and each node of the Cosmic Cube is assigned to compute the forces at 4,096 grid points. Salmon's program is about 1,500 lines long. A similar program written for a sequential machine would be 750 to 1,000 lines long.

The efficiency of a parallel machine is directly related to the cost of communication among its processing elements. A 64-node machine working on a problem that required no interprocessor communication would operate 64 times faster than a single node performing the same calculations serially. In a problem such as the model universe above, the forces on each galaxy are affected by every other galaxy, which requires that nodes share data on each of the 15,000 galaxies in the model. The cost of this communication among nodes thus reduces the speedup to 77 percent of 64 times the speed of a single node. In other words, 23 percent of the total calculation time is spent communicating or waiting for data from other nodes.

Processing in the Cosmic Cube takes place in several stages: the nodes are initially issued data and instructions; calculations are carried out independently until new data is required from another node; requests for data are sent by each node to the others, and each responds to requests from other nodes; independent calculation resumes; and the cycle continues until all calculations are completed or the user halts the machine. If a node finishes its calculations before the others, it must wait until the nodes it needs to communicate with are finished, too. For this reason, mapping the problem evenly across all the nodes is vital to achieve maximum efficiency.

The communication among nodes in the Cosmic Cube takes place along lines established directly between nodes. If a message must pass between a pair of nodes that are not physically connected by wires, then intermediate nodes pass the message along to its destination. This kind of direct connection has been wired in a variety of geometric forms in various parallel architectures. Rings, trees, twisted cubes, toroidal meshes, and a variety of other forms have been tried in addition to the hypercube. The goal of all this experimentation has been to find the shortest overall distance between processors, on the one hand, and to minimize long-distance communications, on the other.

NETWORK-CONNECTED ARCHITECTURES

There are almost as many different kinds of switching networks as there are direct-connected architectures. The simplest is a straight cross-bar switch. With processors on one side and memory units on the other, each processor has a wire connecting it with each of the memory units. Some connections are quite short and others can be extremely long. In addition, since each processor must have a wire connecting it with each memory unit, the number of wires required grows exponentially: two processors, four wires; eight processors, 64 wires; 100 processors, 10,000 wires; and so on.

A parallel supercomputer under construction at Lawrence Livermore labs uses a cross-bar switch that will ultimately connect 16 processors comparable in size and performance to the Cray 1. The S-1, which is being built for the U.S. Navy, will first take shape as a six-processor prototype. One of the major problems confronting Livermore's researchers is how to accommodate the mere physical presence of 16 machines 5 feet wide and 15 feet long. In its full configuration, the S-1 will be a top contender for the most powerful scientific computer in existence.

For larger numbers of processors, a more economical switching system is the *omega network,* a key element of the Ultracomputer, which is under development at the Courant Institute of Mathematical Sciences at New York University. The Ultracomputer (Fig. 6-2) is designed to achieve parallel efficiency equal to that of the Cosmic Cube, but processors and memory are organized in an architecture radically different from that of the Cube.

Instead of trying to overcome the von Neumann bottleneck by joining memory and processing elements together in nodes, the Ultracomputer makes use of the omega net-

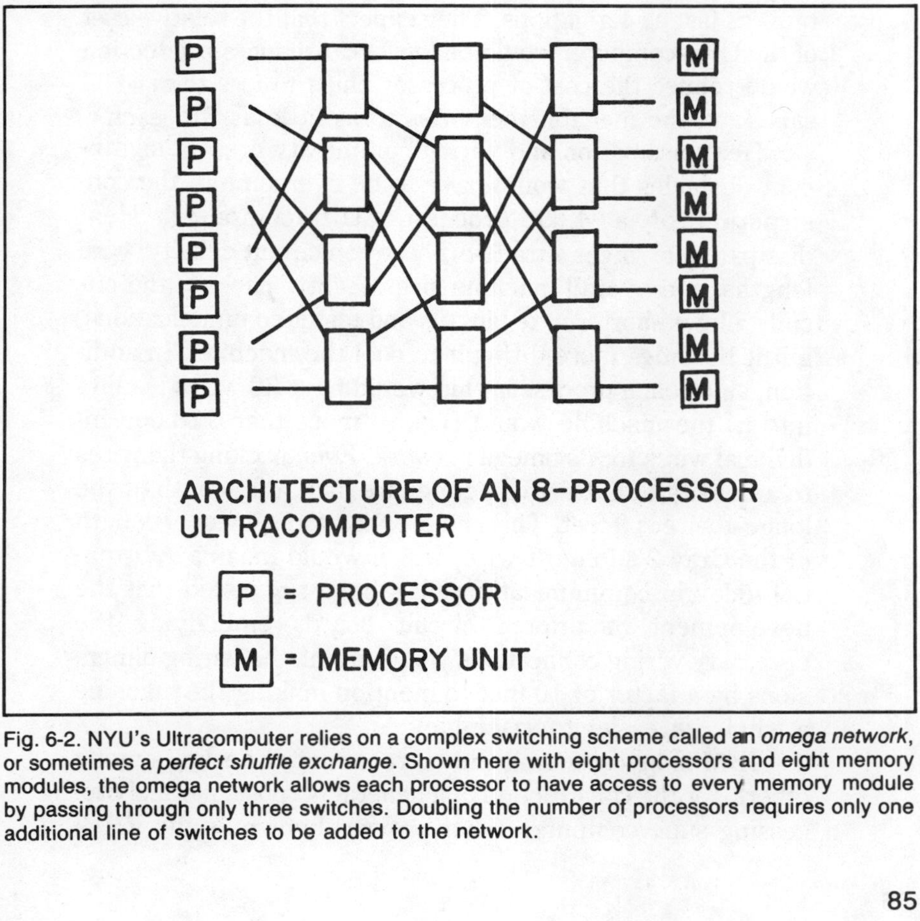

Fig. 6-2. NYU's Ultracomputer relies on a complex switching scheme called an *omega network*, or sometimes a *perfect shuffle exchange*. Shown here with eight processors and eight memory modules, the omega network allows each processor to have access to every memory module by passing through only three switches. Doubling the number of processors requires only one additional line of switches to be added to the network.

work, which dramatically increases the number of pathways between the processing elements and memory. Each switch in an omega network is connected to four others, two on one side and two on the other. A 1,024-processor Ultracomputer would have an omega network comprising 10 rows of switches, allowing any processor to reach any memory unit in 10 machine cycles. The Ultracomputer is thus said to have a *shared-memory architecture.* The difficulty with shared-memory machines is in minimizing the conflict between processors when two or more are trying to gain access to the same data.

The original inspiration for the Ultracomputer came from NYU researcher Jacob T. Schwartz, but the development of a prototype machine has been led by Allan Gottlieb and B.D. Lubachevsky. The Ultracomputer's designers foresee the construction in the next decade of supercomputers based on their work and using 4,096 state-of-the-art, 32-bit microprocessor chips and an equal number of 1-megabit memory chips as the basic units. Such a machine would be capable of processing rates as fast as 4 gigaflops. They expect that the relative cost of the Ultracomputer would be low because mass production would reduce the cost of processor chips to less than $100 each, and the megabit memories to as little as $10 each.

Heat dissipation and wiring complexity present significant obstacles that would have to be overcome in the construction of a 4,096-processor Ultracomputer. Heat dissipation involves a trade-off between circuit density, wire lengths, and overall machine size. Tightly packing the circuits allows shorter wire lengths and faster communications, but it becomes more difficult to cool the machine. In addition, since each processor chip would have 32 wires leading into it, the machine would require more than 130,000 individual wires for its omega network. Even packing the wires to a density of 500 wires per square inch, the length of the longest wire is 9 feet. This is more than four times the length of the Cray 2's longest wire, which would mean a substantial delay in communications. It's been suggested that the development of printed circuit boards embodying the necessary wiring connections would shrink the wiring dimensions by a factor of 10 (not to mention making the machine a whole lot easier to assemble).

IBM is investigating the Ultracomputer design, among others, for the construction of a general purpose, parallel processing supercomputer. That project, known as the RP-3, involves the construction of a 512-processor machine connected to an equal number of shared memory elements via a network similar to that of the NYU machine. The main distinction is that the RP-3 makes the use of a closely guarded switch design that allows memory elements to be divided into local and global sectors based on the needs of the computation. Accessing local memory is considerably faster than having to traverse the network to reach the shared memory. If a machine can adjust the amount of local memory storage it has available to each processor, a significant increase in overall processing speed is possible. Such a switch would also minimize memory conflicts among processors and reduce traffic on the network while maximizing the total available global memory.

FINE-GRAINED ARCHITECTURES

Both the Cosmic Cube and the Ultracomputer are based on processor-memory combinations similar in size, power, and capacity to that of a personal computer. One common way of classifying parallel machines is by *grain size*, which is simply the relative size of its individual computing elements. The Caltech and NYU machines are both near the middle of the range. Considerably finer-grained computers are most often called *database machines,* because they're most useful as intelligent databases. Large-grained machines, like the Navy's S-1, generally comprise a relatively small number of powerful von Neumann-type computers wired to function in a loosely parallel manner.

Grain size, like communication cost, is a key factor in the design of parallel machines. The smaller the size of the basic processing unit, the more limited are its computational capabilities. But number crunching isn't the goal of such specialized, fine-grained machines as the Connection Machine. Based on the work of D. Hillis at the Massachusetts Institute of Technology's Artificial Intelligence Laboratory, the Connection Machine is being developed commercially by Thinking Machines Corp. of Massachusetts. The purpose of the Connection Machine is the manipulation of data for artificial intelligence applications.

Knowledge is represented in the machine as a collection of objects and their attributes together with a set of rules describing the way they relate to one another. A given object, a zucchini, might have relational connections to sets that include all other squashes, things that are green, and ingredients needed to make ratatouille.

A knowledge base of this type can be represented in a sequential machine, but as the amount of information it contains grows, the speed of operations—matching, sorting, searching, and deduction—slows down dramatically. In effect, the Connection Machine moves processing power into the memory. Machine designs with as many as 100,000 processing elements are being developed. Each processor would be small enough so that 32 or 64 of them would fit on a single chip along with sufficient random-access memory to store an object and its relational connections. Since many of the operations performed on the knowledge base can be performed in parallel, both storage capacity and overall processing speed increase in proportion to the size of the machine.

A similar effort is under way at Columbia University, where David Shaw is working to design a "smart memory" with a somewhat larger grain-size called Non-Von (Fig. 6-3). Shaw's machine is organized in a binary tree structure, which is an imposing name for a simple network that has two branches at every node. In this kind of tree, the root is at the top and the leaves are on the bottom. The root, which is a traditional serial computer, communicates with each of the top two processing elements, and each of those to two others, and so on, with the total number of processors doubling in each successive layer. After only 20 branching layers, the number of leaves increases to more than a million.

A machine such as Non-Von 3, in which a single processor controls the operation of an array of processors, each with its own small memory, is said to have a *single-instruction, multi-data stream* architecture. A pipelined computer, like the Cray 1, could also be called an SIMD machine, because each pipeline acts independently of the others but under the direction of a single instruction processor. In contrast, the Cosmic Cube, the Ultracomputer, and the Cray X-MP each operate with multiple instruction streams. The primary advantage of SIMD architectures is ease of progamming, while the main disadvantage is a familiar one—the von Neumann bottleneck. MIMD architectures get around the bottleneck, but the task of getting maximum efficiency from independently-controlled processors presents a significant programming challenge.

The binary tree suffers limitations like those of a serial

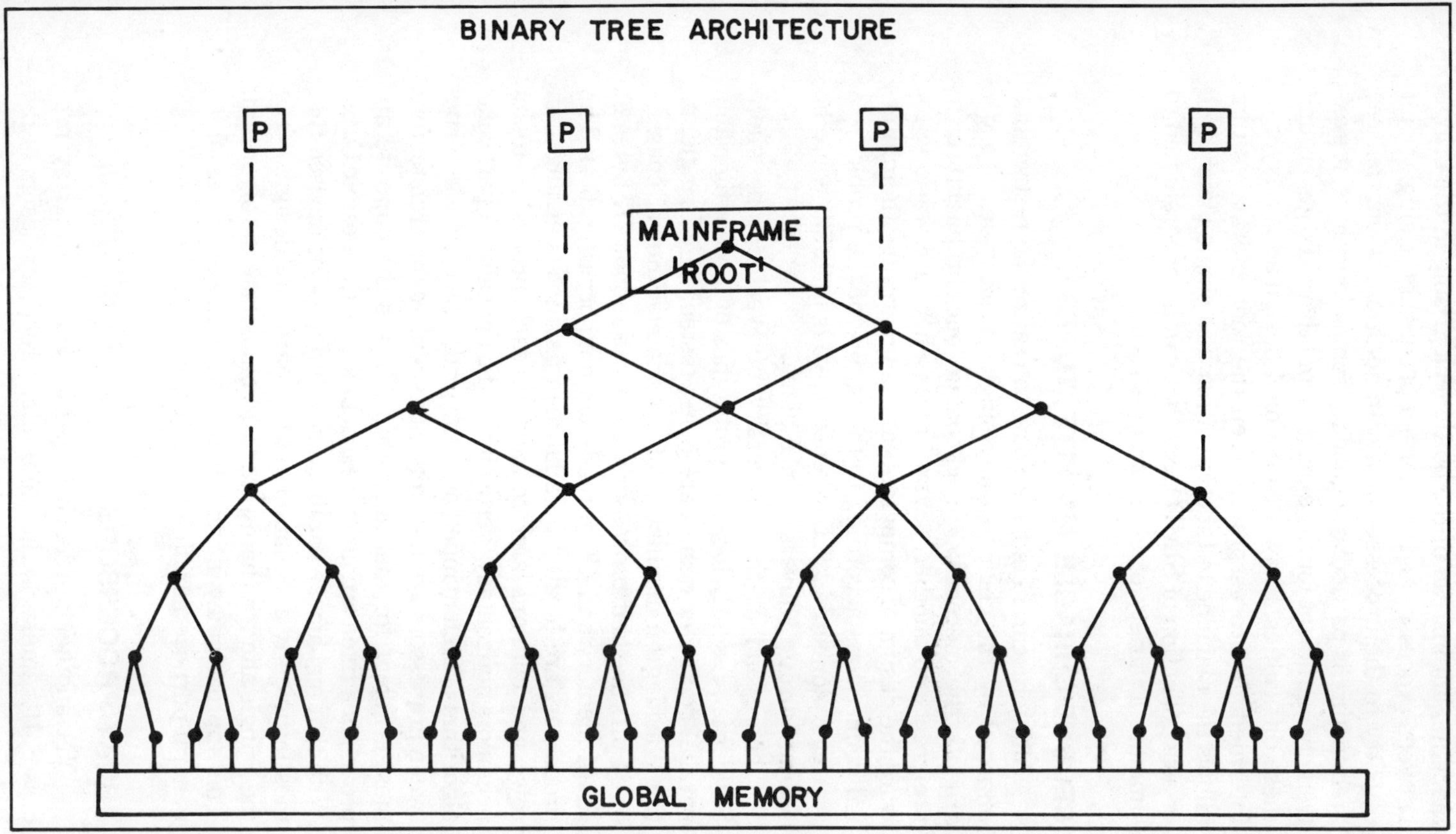

Fig. 6-3. David Shaw's Non-Von design is based on a binary tree architecture. Operands and instructions are sent to the processors from the root, a mainframe computer. Congestion caused by the narrowing at the top of the tree inspired Shaw to add an intermediate layer of processors that would facilitate communication and allow the machine to simulate a variety of other architectures.

machine, but instead of the bottleneck arising at the bridge between processor and memory, it occurs at the single point of entry to the processor array. In addition, while the tree architecture is particularly good for some algorithms, it's extremely inefficient for the execution of others. To get around these difficulties, Shaw's Non-Von 4 design adds a layer of intermediate processors between the root and leaves that allows the machine to function either as a single binary tree or as a collection of SIMD trees that can be programmed to simulate a variety of other architectures.

RECONFIGURABLE ARCHITECTURES

Many researchers have come to realize the restrictions imposed by the choice of any single architecture. To get around the necessity of choosing one architecture in preference to another, several researchers are working toward the design of computers that can rearrange their internal connections according to the nature of the problem—a strategy pioneered by Lawrence Snyder in 1982, while he was at Purdue University in Indiana.

There and at the University of Washington, where Snyder is presently located, prototypes of a reconfigurable parallel computer design are being tested. The Pringle, as the Washington machine is affectionately known, consists of 64 off-the-shelf processors, each with about 2K bytes of RAM memory and 4K of read-only memory (Fig. 6-4). The processors are located on a lattice of switches arranged in rows and columns and connecting each processor to its neighbors horizontally, vertically, and diagonally. A particular algorithm is then mapped onto the grid. The connections between processors are then made to simulate the architecture most efficient for that algorithm. This is the opposite approach of a fixed architecture machine like the Cosmic Cube. With that machine, a parallel algorithm must be devised that most efficiently accommodates the hardware design, while the Pringle alters its hardware to accommodate the algorithm. This approach may ultimately prove the most successful for general-purpose parallel computers.

ARRAY PROCESSORS

Yet another approach to parallelism is the array processor. It's similar to the multi-microprocessor design of the

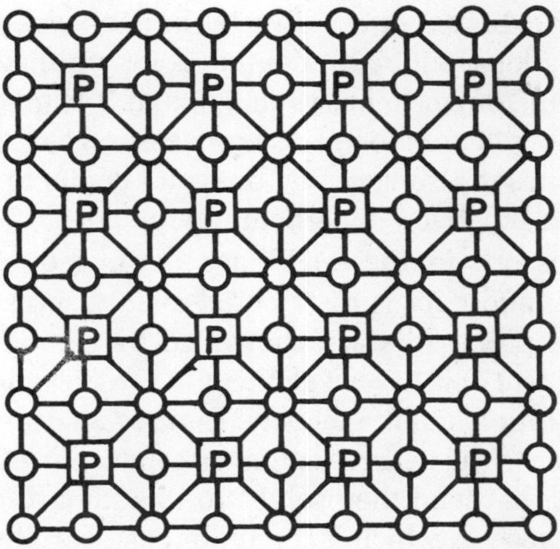

Fig. 6-4. The design of the Pringle prototype at the University of Washington allows it to reconfigure itself during computation to best fit the algorithms to be executed. It can simulate rings, hypercubes, toroidal meshes, binary trees, and square arrays, among others.

Cosmic Cube or Ultracomputer, but the individual processing elements are generally much smaller and simpler, and usually without any local memory of their own. Such machines also tend to be limited to certain classes of problems. Array processors were the first parallel machines. Taking their inspiration in part from Slotnick's proposed design for the SOLOMON computer, several arrays were built in the late 1960s and early 1970s.

One of the newest array processors is the Massively Parallel Processor system under development for NASA by the Goodyear Aerospace Corporation. The MPP, currently the largest array processor, is designed around 16,384 processing elements arranged in a 128 × 128 array. Each processor has 256 bits of local memory and performs arithmetic 1 bit at a time, rather than the usual 8-, 16-, or 32-bit parallel operation common to larger processors. Estimates of the MPP's performance are, more than in most machines, dependent on the complexity of the operations each processor must perform. For example, it can do 8-bit integer addition at a rate of 6.5 gigaflops, but 32-bit floating point multiplication slows the machine down to between 291 and 373 megaflops, still fast but not phenomenal. Each processor's cycle time of 100 nanoseconds is also very fast but can't compete with that of the vector pipelined supercomputers.

Processors in the MPP are organized in rows and highways, and data is distributed evenly across the array. All of the processors are controlled by commands from a single control unit. Every element in the array performs the same operation simultaneously. Limited sharing of data can take place via the nearest-neighbor connection of processors. Problems that lend themselves to this kind of communication are those in which a three-dimensional physical space can be mapped directly onto the array, similar to but far less versatile than the approach used with the Cosmic Cube.

A primary advantage of using smaller, simpler processors is the possibility of packaging several together on a single VLSI chip. The MPP's design is being modified to permit the use of newly fabricated chips holding eight processing elements apiece. About 8,000 transistors were used to implement the chip design. This level of integration is considerably less than that of the newest 32-bit microprocessors, which pack 450,000 transistors on a chip.

DATAFLOW ARCHITECTURES

A radically different computing strategy pioneered by Jack Dennis at the Massachusetts Institute of Technology lets the data control the computation. Dataflow machines (Fig. 6-5) are built around an array of processors that act independently in executing only those instructions stored in each one's local memory—but the trigger that activates a particular computation is not the next step in an instruction sequence but the arrival of data from other processors. In conventional programming, each of the steps to be executed is numbered and the order of operations is inviolate. If the data for one part of the program is unavailable, the processor can't skip to the next step. It sits idle. The goal of dataflow programming is to maintain a constant flow of operands, known as *tokens*, to all of the processors.

Dennis' machine is known as a *static dataflow architecture*. The instructions for each processor must be distributed

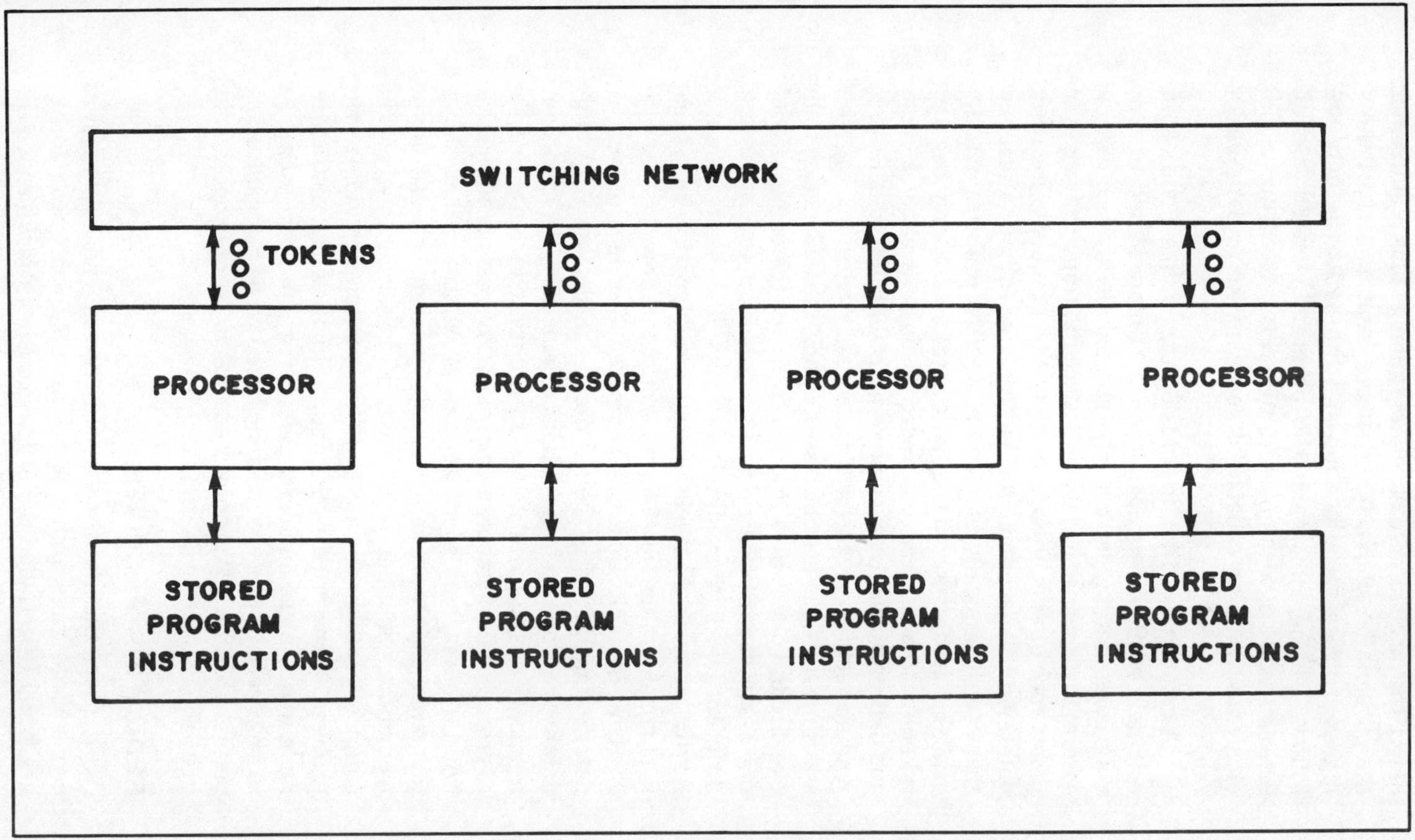

Fig. 6-5. Dataflow architecture passes data in the form of tokens to processors, which perform the calculations according to a set of stored instructions as the tokens become available. Processors can also create tokens to pass to other units for further execution.

before the machine actually starts running. This requires that the problem be analyzed and mapped out on a chart showing each processor's location and the paths the data will follow. During execution, the program is fixed. Dennis estimates that his design using an array of 1,000 processing elements would be capable of performance in the gigaflop range.

A colleague of Dennis at MIT, Arvind, has modified the original dataflow concept into a form more suited to symbolic computation, particularly artificial intelligence. Arvind asserts that most artificial intelligence programs defy analysis in advance of execution, a necessary prerequisite for static dataflow. It's necessary for AI problems to have a machine that can dynamically map and remap the problem onto the available processors. In the static architecture, only one data token could pass between processors in a given clock cycle, and only one instruction could be activated and executed. Arvind's machine gives each token an identifying tag that specifies the node it's addressed to and the instruction to be executed. Tokens awaiting execution of the same instruction are placed in a queue, but a processor can execute several different instructions simultaneously. The disadvantage to Arvind's approach, at least for numerical processing, is that it is considerably slower than static dataflow.

One obstacle that has hampered the development of dataflow machines is their difficulty in dealing with large databases. The larger the database, generally, the more communication is required as tokens are routed from processor to processor throughout the machine. The cost of communication in this fashion soon becomes prohibitive. Artificial intelligence databases are necessarily large because of the tremendous amount of knowledge required in even the simplest real-world problem. One possible solution to the problem, being tried by Arvind, is to allow the data to remain in one place and send the instructions from processor to processor. A protype machine based on 64 Symbolics Corporation 3600 LISP processors is due to become operational in 1985.

REDUCTION MACHINES

Perhaps the most exotic architectural concept is that of Gyula Mago, a researcher at the University of North Carolina in Chapel Hill. Called the *Mago Reduction Machine*, MRED for short, it continually rewrites both the program and the data, incorporating the results of each computation until no further operations can be carried out. Its structure is a tree machine, with computation beginning in the leaves and proceeding steadily toward the root. Resource controllers at the root of the tree cooperate to control the leaves, sending them data and control information and receiving the results of their processing. This exchange takes place in a wavelike manner at various points throughout the computation cycle (Fig. 6-6).

Both dataflow and reduction architectures are being studied by the Japanese for use in their Fifth Generation machines. The appeal of these architectures is their ability to uncover subtle forms of parallelism in complex algorithms. Problems are decomposed into smaller, more numerous subparts than is required for other approaches, and this process often points up inherent parallelism not apparent in larger constructs. But the difficulties associated with communication and control in large numbers of processors makes the

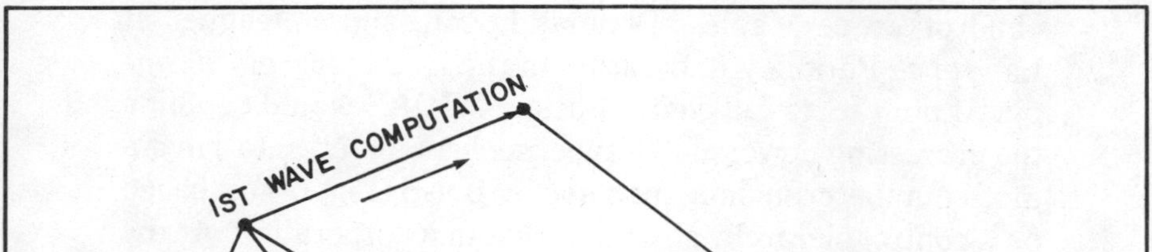

Fig. 6-6. A reduction machine is based on a binary tree architecture, but processing begins with operands and instructions loaded side by side into individual leaves of the tree Processing proceeds in waves up the tree to the root and then back down to the leaves.

future of dataflow and reduction machines as uncertain as all the others.

LARGE-GRAIN MULTIPROCESSORS

In the meantime, combining the processing power of large machines into one superpowerful number-cruncher still seems to be the most effective, if not the most efficient, approach to supercomputer design. All of the commercially available parallel machines, aside from the single-bit array processors, make use of this strategy. Both of Cray's multiprocessors have four processors. Denelcor's HEP has a maximum configuration of 16 processors. Control Data's Cyberplus system, while it may be expandable eventually to 64 processors, is currently available only in a 16 processor configuration. Bolt, Beranek, and Newman's Butterfly machine uses 10 processors connected by an unusual switching network they call the Butterfly. Expansion to 128 processors is planned, according to BBN.

One of the more interesting prototypes carries this strategy to an extreme. The MIDAS machine is the brainchild of Creve Maples, Douglas Logan, and colleagues at Lawrence Berkeley Laboratory of the University of California. If built to its full configuration, MIDAS would combine the processing power of 270 supermini-computers into a mammoth numbercrunching machine. MIDAS (Fig. 6-7) is based on a control hierarchy similar to that of a corporation. At the top is the boss, a primary computer that oversees the operation of the entire system and delegates tasks to subordinates. Machines at the secondary level, analogous to middle management, supervise a staff of eight to 32 third-level processors, and can also handle individual problems, as necessary. The processors at the third level, each one comparable to a CDC 6600, are organized into multiprocessor arrays. This is where most of the dirty work is done. Data and instructions are passed from the primary computer to the secondary, which then distributes the load among processors in the array. The secondary has complete control over the third-level processors and can run, halt, resume, or single-step each one independently or collectively. It can also monitor and modify the contents of each processor's memory.

The MIDAS machine's memory, like its processors, is also organized in a hierarchical fashion to achieve the greatest possible combination of speed and flexibility. Each CPU in

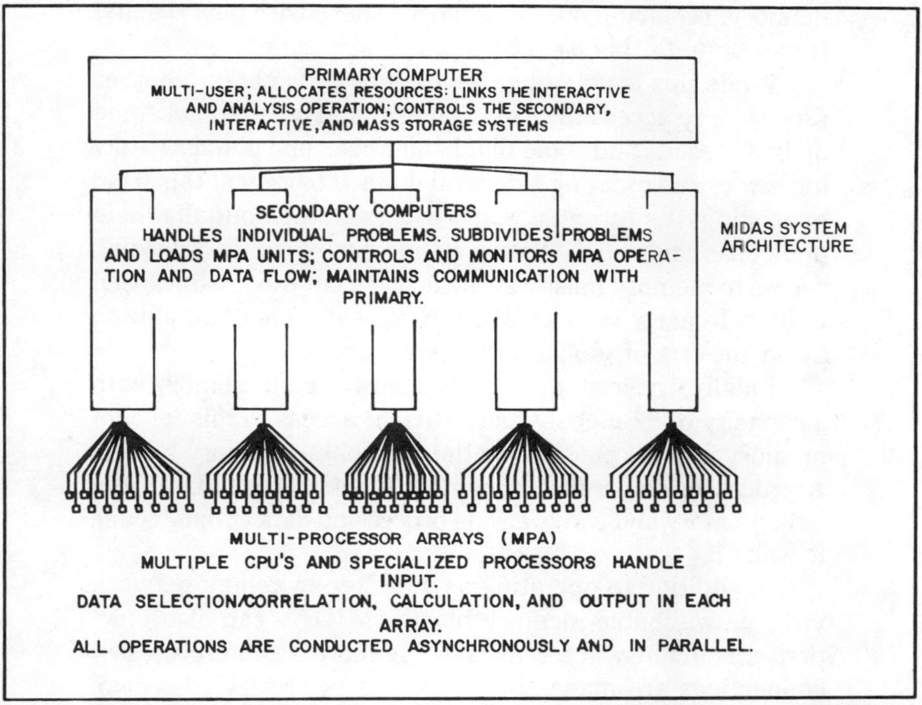

Fig. 6-7. The MIDAS machine at Lawrence Berkeley Laboratory uses a hierarchy of machines to control and carry out processing. The top level is a large mainframe computer that distributes work to the secondary processors and interacts with users. Second-level machines do some calculation and farm the rest out to processor arrays at the third level.

the array has its own local memory wired directly to it and inaccessible to all but the secondary. Then, between local and global memory, there is an intermediate level called *bank-switched memory*. The switched memory is divided into 16 blocks, each with a capacity of 256K bytes, that can be attached to any of the processors at any time. Once a processor-memory connection occurs, the block becomes, in effect, a part of that unit's local memory. Communication between processors can thus be accomplished by switching a memory block from one unit to another in the array, which takes about 50 nanoseconds—meaning that the cost of communication at this level is small.

Beyond the switchable memory blocks is global memory. The addition of a large-capacity memory accessible to all of the processors in the cluster adds to MIDAS's flexibility, but the cost of using it gets higher the more it's used. To understand why this is so, imagine that a single processor is updating a long string of floating point operations in global memory, replacing operands stored there with new results. It can only do this 64 bits, a word, at a time.

While this is going on, it would be possible for another processor to access the same data set and it would get some updated results and some that hadn't been updated, introducing errors and creating a general mess. To prevent this from happening, it's essential that a processor lock out all others until it has completed all memory updates. Processors needing access to memory must wait, which can cut processing speed in half. In early tests of MIDAS, researchers were able to avoid the use of global memory entirely.

Finally, the system also has a slower bulk memory with a capacity of 32 megabytes. Efficient access to this level of memory is made possible by the switchable memory blocks. A processor dispatches a memory block to fetch data from bulk memory and can continue processing data at hand while it waits.

In addition to operating as a packet-switching network via the switchable memory blocks, MIDAS can also function as a circuit-switched machine. In this case, interprocessor connections are made and broken as necessary to accommodate exchanges of information. The switched memories play a static role and serve simply as communication pipelines. So far, only a single cluster, consisting of one secondary and eight third-level processors, has been built. On several of the calculations used to test the cluster's performance, it showed an efficiency of 100 percent. In other words, processor contention was avoided entirely and the speed of the machine overall was a multiple of the number of processors, eight in this case, times the speed of a single processor. Calculation rates in the neighborhood of 5 megaflops were achieved on most problems. The algorithms that showed the poorest results, known as *tree search problems*, are common to artificial intelligence and certain kinds of pattern-matching systems for vision and speech processing. These showed a speedup for eight processors of only 66 percent, which is still quite good.

Future plans for MIDAS include the installation of newer, faster CPU's in the multiprocessor arrays and a doubling or tripling of the number of processors in each array. When the full three-level cluster is installed, the researchers estimate that it could readily accommodate five to 10 independent clusters, bringing the total number of processors in the larger configuration to 270. Though no estimate of the speed of such a system is offered by the researchers, speeds in the neighborhood of 5 to 10 gigaflops seem conservative, based on test results reported so far.

Needless to say, such a machine is going to be expensive. The price tag for 270 high-speed uniprocessors could range anywhere from $27 million to $270 million. Whether a similar design could be scaled down sufficiently to be affordable for university and corporate buyers is an open question. In the meantime, work will continue toward finding the right combination of processor size, number, and interconnection schemes for the implementation of parallelism in VLSI chip technology. The success of this line of research could well lead to another quantum leap in performance at constant or lower cost.

Chapter 7

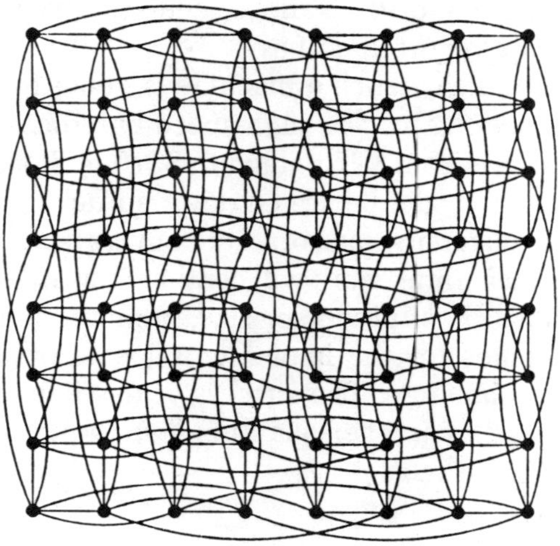

Crunching by Number

Science has passed a watershed in using computers for research. Computers are no longer just tools for measurement and analysis, but large computers in particular have become the means for making new discoveries.

Report on Large Scale Computing in Science and Engineering
National Science Foundation, 1982

The development of parallel supercomputers that can perform calculations in the gigaflop range, while an evolutionary development in itself, holds the prospect of revolutionary advances in the sciences and the opening of entirely new fields of inquiry. By making greater computing power available at a lower cost, the next generation of machines will allow researchers to approach questions they've long known how to ask but didn't have the means to answer.

One of the principal limits to scientific and engineering research in a variety of fields is the economics of high performance computing, known in computer jargon as *number crunching*. Because of the high cost of supercomputers and their relative scarcity, the time available inexpensively on these machines at government laboratories must be carefully rationed. Most is allocated to researchers doing work for the military. Commercial time-sharing is financially out of reach for most institutions, costing from $5,000 to $10,000 per hour. The alternative for most scientists is a subclass of machines that are sometimes called supermini-computers, such as Digital Equipment Corporation's VAX 11/780, which is less expensive and more widely available. But calculations that would require a dozen hours on a Cray may take hundreds or even thousands of hours on a smaller machine, making the solution of extremely large, computationally intense problems uneconomical.

There's an important distinction between computationally intense problems and those associated with artificial intelligence research, which also include vision and speech processing. The methods needed to solve the problem of vision, for example, are not well understood. But there is a large class of problems in the physical sciences for which the method of solution is well known, but the processing power needed to execute the solution is not readily available.

CONTINUOUS FIELD SIMULATIONS

In most cases, the intensity of computation is due to the sheer number of calculations a problem requires, rather than the complexity of individual calculations. Many computationally intense problems involve the simulation of worlds with so many interacting elements that a complete description of their behavior, resulting in an exact solution, is virtually impossible. Such problems require numerical techniques based on approximation. In this approach there is no formula that will produce a right answer. With each calculation, the answer becomes more and more accurate, but it's like starting with two points a mile apart and repeatedly halving the distance between them. The two points get closer and closer until the distance between them becomes infinitesimally small, but the points never actually converge.

These problems are known to scientists as *continuous field simulations,* and they include the modeling of phenomena in such diverse fields as aerodynamics, seismology, and meteorology, and atomic, nuclear, and plasma physics. In solving these problems, scientists make use of a conceptual simplification that divides a physical space up into three-dimensional chunks. Since every region of space contains an infinite number of points, a precise description of each area would require an infinite amount of data. Therefore, a finite number of points are distributed throughout the region and each one's location is pinpointed by a set of coordinates. Objects are located on this three-dimensional grid much the same way towns and streets are by a map's two-dimensional coordinates. Computations involve only the grid points and ignore the actual positioning of objects in space. Naturally, the greater the density of grid points, the more accurate the approximation of real values becomes.

Three-dimensional grids with as many as a million points have been needed to simulate the flow of turbulent air over objects as geometrically simple as an airplane wing. Tens of millions of points may be needed to obtain sufficiently accurate approximations of air flow around complex geometries, like that of an entire fighter plane. Similar levels of complexity are involved in computing the density, velocity and temperature of a moving gas or the mechanical stress in a solid.

Many of these problems involve the dynamics of fluid flow. In each case the problem requires that an initial set of values is supplied for each point on the grid. Then, typically, the entire system is stepped from instant to instant as the computer calculates its evolution over time. Numerical quantities describing the present state of the grid must be stored in the computer memory and updated periodically according to a system of algebraic equations describing the forces acting on each point. The number of such quantities in a representative simulation of aerodynamic flow ranges from 5 to 30. At each repetition of the basic calculation step, the computer may be required to perform anywhere from 10 to 500 operations per data item in order to arrive at a new value for each grid point. Some calculations in nuclear physics and aerodynamics can eat up more than 48 hours of time on a supercomputer, which grinds through as many as 3.5 trillion arithmetic operations in that time period.

AND NOW THE WEATHER

Another problem in fluid dynamics that has bedeviled researchers for decades is long-range weather forecasting. It was in seeking a solution to this problem that one of the first printed references to computation in parallel was published. In 1922, British mathematician L.S. Richardson, having computed an entire weather forecast by hand, proposed an operational forecasting factory: a hall staffed with 64,000 human "computers." Each individual would deal with a column of atmosphere above a particular location on the earth's surface. The ensemble would be controlled by a director who coordinated the activity and kept the "computers" synchronized.

Computing power is the essence of weather forecasting. The reason is that the amount of data needed to accurately predict weather patterns a week or more in advance is substantial—in the neighborhood of 80 million bits. Roughly 500 billion arithmetic operations are needed to transform that raw data into a useful picture of the atmosphere's behavior over the entire globe. To make even a seven-day forecast for Western Europe, for example, data on present weather conditions must be gathered from points as distant as Buenos Aires, Indonesia, Afghanistan, Honolulu, and the North Pole. Information is collected from more than 9,000 surface weather stations, 750 instrument-laden weather balloons, ships at sea, and commercial planes in flight. Once this vast ocean of data has been gathered, it is translated into a picture of the atmosphere at a given time, which becomes the starting point for forecast calculations.

A three-dimensional grid is then mapped out across this global model, similar to Richardson's columns of air. The European Center for Medium Range Weather Forecasts uses a grid with points spaced 200 kilometers apart each way on the horizontal plane and with 15 vertical layers—a total of 273,630 points. Then a Cray 1 supercomputer grinds through the calculations, involving as many as 200 different observational factors from each grid point, to produce a numerical picture of weather.

The greater the number of points in an atmospheric model, the finer its accuracy and the more calculation it requires. Similarly, looking farther into the future also requires more calculation. But some researchers suspect that a barrier to long-range forecasting will be reached at 10 to 12 days and 70 percent accuracy. Errors in description of small-scale phenomena, not calculation, combine to cause large-scale errors over time.

COMPUTER MODELING

Supercomputers are also being used to model and make

visible physical phenomena that are unobservable directly (Figs. 7-1 and 7-2), like the collision of two atomic nuclei. Researchers at Lawrence Livermore Laboratory used a Cray 1 to calculate what happens when a krypton nucleus and a lanthanum nucleus collide under varying circumstances—then turned their results into a motion-picture display that shows the event happening in slow-motion as if it had been filmed. The model was based on a system of 146 equations, describing the wave behavior of subatomic particles known as quantum mechanics. Each equation is related to all the others in such a way that they cannot be solved one by one. They must be solved in ensemble, or simultaneously. It took nearly a year to figure out how to program the computer to solve the problem, but the Cray took only an hour to actually perform the necessary computations. The event itself, however, takes about 10^{-21} seconds, a space of time so short that light itself could travel only a billionth of an inch.

There are a number of other modeling tasks that require

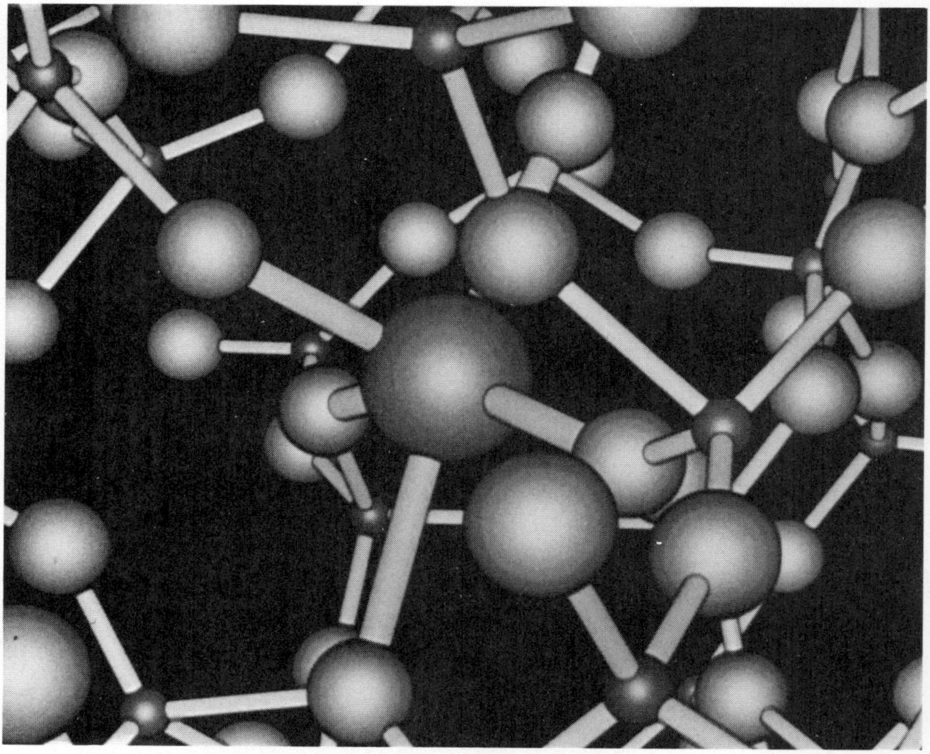

Fig. 7-1. A supercomputer simulation of the atomic structure of neodymium laser glass (courtesy Lawrence Livermore National Laboratory).

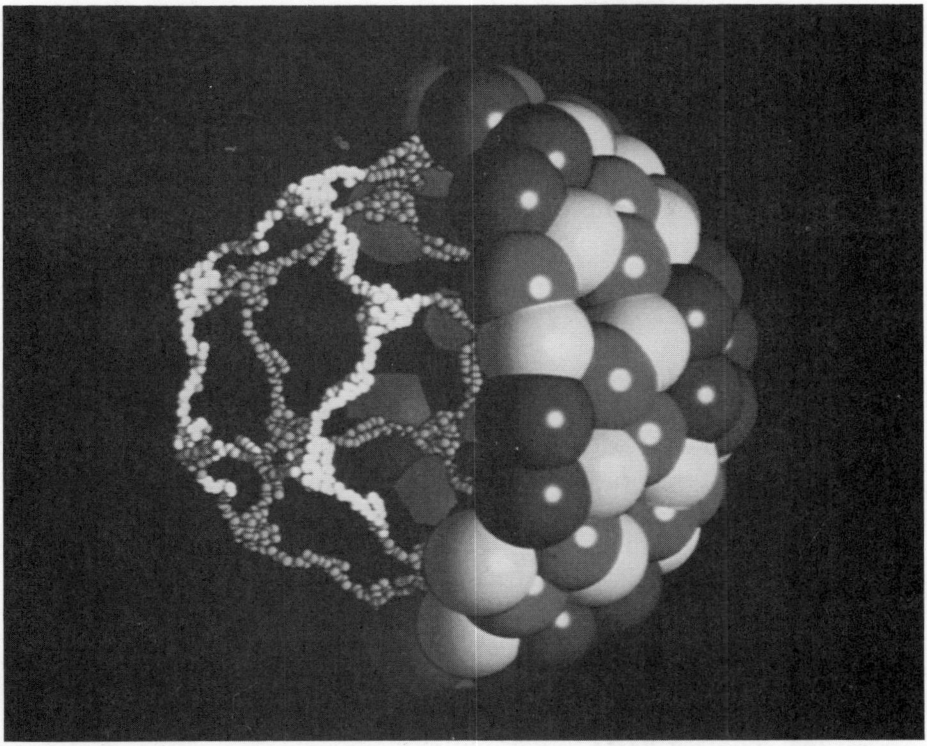
Fig. 7-2. Model showing 90 of 180 amino acid subunits in the protein coat of the tomato bushy stunt virus (courtesy Lawrence Livermore National Laboratory).

the number crunching power of a supercomputer:

—Oil companies use a multitude of seismic data to determine the width, breadth and depth of underground pools of oil. Water must be pumped into the reservoir as oil is taken out, and if this is not done precisely, millions of gallons of oil can be irretrievably lost. A similar application involves the use of sonar data for the development of three-dimensional models of the ocean floor.

—Supercomputers are used in simulated testing of nuclear reactor vessels under a variety of load conditions and physical stresses like earthquakes. Studies of the behavior of superheated plasma at the core of a fusion reactor are also done by computer, in part because direct observation of a fusion reaction isn't possible. And more than 40 years after ENIAC checked the calculations used to design the first hydrogen bomb, the world's fastest computers are still being used, under tight security at Lawrence Livermore and Los Alamos National Laboratories, to evaluate the design and explosive power of thermonuclear warheads.

—"Event simulation" is a growing area of research that could not exist without the computer. These models are designed, essentially, to answer "what if" questions. One such program, designed at Lawrence Livermore on a Cray 1, simulates what would happen in the event of a radiation leak into the atmosphere. Using data on weather conditions at the time of the leak, population statistics and geographical features, the system would provide information to emergency teams on the size of the area to be evacuated downwind of the source.

—A similar program was developed in the aftermath of history's largest oil spill, the Ixtoc I blowout of June 1979 in the Gulf of Mexico. With data on the amount of time since the spill, temperature and the oil slick's surface area, the model can provide clean-up crews with information on the location and probable impact of the oil on coastal areas.

—The Japanese plan to use their newly developed supercomputers, the Hitachi M280H and Fujitsu M380, to analyze images from the Earth Resources Satellite, perform structural and thermal analysis of satellites, study power flow and stability in the nationwide electric power grid, and to design and simulate VLSI integrated circuits.

—Detailed engineering simulations also become feasible. A computer model used to predict the structural strength, aerodynamic qualities and energy consumption of a building prior to construction could reduce its cost by allowing economies to be tested and built in. A model of this kind could help to avert disasters large and small, such as the fatal collapse of a pedestrian walkway at a Midwestern hotel or the tendency of windows to pop out of the Hancock Tower in Boston.

—A program under development at Lawrence Berkeley Labs would allow scientists to predict the physical properties, such as ductility, malleability, and conductivity, of alloys that have never actually been created. Such a program would allow engineers to custom-make alloys with characteristics suited to a particular application.

—In manufacturing, advanced computer graphics already allow engineers and product designers to turn their blueprints into three-dimensional perspective drawings that can be rotated and examined from any direction. Instead of building expensive prototypes, a model with all the characteristics of a prototype is constructed in the computer's memory and put through simulated tests.

Many of the applications mentioned so far are not particularly new. What's most exciting about the potential of massive parallelism is the prospect of making superpowerful computers available in fields where they were previously too expensive. Economics, sociology, and urban planning all rely on computer modeling of human behavior, which by its very nature requires complex statistical analyses. New computer graphics techniques, which also require substantial computing power, have given artists and filmmakers an entirely new medium in which to work. And medical imaging techniques that require the use of high-powered computers have all but eliminated the need for exploratory surgery.

Sophisticated modeling of physical phenomena could have tremendous economic impact. A project under way at Lawrence Berkeley Laboratory is modeling the combustion of fuel in an automobile engine. Approximately 30 percent of the fuel is not burned during combustion and is exhausted as hydrocarbon vapor. By varying the shape of the cylinder and the conditions of combustion in the model, it may be possible to cut the amount of wasted fuel in half. Not only would such an achievement dramatically reduce hydrocarbon exhaust emissions, resulting in less pollution of the atmosphere, it would also reduce gasoline consumption by approximately 15 billion gallons per year in this country alone.

Another possibility is an automated freeway system. Given the invention of an appropriate car-computer communications link and guidance system, it would be readily possible for a parallel supercomputer to guide each car to its destination. The world of such a system would be the horizontal grid of freeways, perhaps 1,000 miles altogether. As a car rolls up the on-ramp, the driver punches a destination code into the guidance terminal and sits back while the main computer takes over. Each processor might be responsible for the position and speed of all the cars in a mile of freeway. Because human reaction times need not be considered, the cars could be spaced much more closely and could travel at considerably higher speeds. As a car reached the boundary of one processor's area, the data on speed, position and destination would be passed to that processor's neighbor in the grid, and so on until the destination was reached. The calculations required of an automated freeway system would be extremely simple. It's only the number of calculations that causes complexity.

STATISTICS BY BRUTE FORCE

Supercomputers are also making entirely new methods of statistical analysis available to researchers. These methods offer freedom from two limiting factors that have dominated statistical theory from its beginnings: the assumption that the data conform to an established curve and the need to use such mathematical simplifications as the mean and the standard deviation. Computer-intensive methods are particularly valuable in the analysis of a very small number of observed events. One approach, called the *bootstrap*, is a computational spendthrift that can easily perform a million arithmetic operations in the analysis of a dozen data points. The technique involves the exact duplication of the available data a billion or more times, and then artificial samples are selected at random from this newly created mountain of data. In effect, the amount of data available for analysis is increased to the point that a statistically accurate result can be obtained from a small initial sample.

One practical application of the bootstrap involved the development of a map showing the distribution of acid rain in the Eastern United States. Measurements of the acidity of rainfall from September 1978 to August 1980 were taken at nine widely separated weather stations east of the Mississippi River. The data was used to develop a map that showed definite corridors of high acidity. Extrapolating from nine isolated points across the eastern half of the country would have been impossible without the bootstrap.

Another unorthodox technique for computer-intensive statistical analysis makes use of the computer's graphics capabilities. Instead of using traditional numerical analyses, a small group of scientists working at the Stanford Linear Accelerator and at Harvard University are looking directly at the data. Using a powerful computer designed specifically for graphics, data representing up to 14 dimensions can be displayed on a screen and rotated in any direction. In essence, the scientists scan the images looking for patterns (nonrandom clusters of data points).

A pair of Harvard researchers using a computer graphics display to study the consumption of fuel by automobiles made in various years noticed an unusual pattern in the data. On closer examination, they discovered that the definition of horsepower had been changed during the years that the data was gathered. The change had been overlooked by previous analysts.

The Stanford group designed its own hardware for statistical displays based on pioneering work by John Tukey and Mary Ann Fisherkeller, who developed the first such machine in 1972. The Stanford workstation has as much power as most university computing centers at a cost of about $40,000. Hard-wired into the system is an algorithm that mathematically analyzes the tendency of data points to cluster. Points of particular interest can be highlighted on the screen in one of 256 colors. Work is continuing on an algorithm that will allow the computer to aid users in finding the best (least random) patterns. The combination of massive computing power and low cost will, one researcher predicts, lead to a totally new style of data analysis.

Inexpensive computing power is the motive force behind the development of a variety of special-purpose, parallel processors. At the Fermi National Accelerator Lab, for example, a machine designed purely for computations involving high-energy physics has been built that significantly outperforms a supercomputer in doing the one task that it does best. Essentially the ECL-Camac computer, as it's called, is an ultrahigh-speed dataflow machine designed to analyze the outcome of particle collisions in the accelerator. As the collision occurs, the computer performs a set of complex computations to identify particular particles of interest and records huge quantities of data relating to the behavior of those particles—all in a few microseconds.

Some of the early steps in vision processing involve calculations numbering in the tens of billions. In a single high-resolution image, the computer records brightness values for a million different points. Before object recognition algorithms can begin to work, using artificial intelligence, the brightness values must be filtered through a mathematical sieve that smoothes the picture and emphasizes significant features. A conventional supercomputer may require four or five seconds to perform the necessary calculations, but a new device built at MIT's Artificial Intelligence Laboratory cuts that time to about 1 second. The *vision convolver* performs at the rate of a billion arithmetic operations per second, bringing real-time image interpretation within reach for the first time.

A subsidiary of the TRW Corp., ESL Inc., is developing a high-speed computer that will be used specifically for signal processing, which can also include sonar and image analysis. When it's completed, the DDSP (Data-Driven Signal Processor) will use 32 processors and perform at a rate of about 71 megaflops. It also makes use of the data-flow concept. One of the machine's primary applications will be the analysis of sonar data from the United States long-range underwater surveillance network, the Sound Surveillance System, or Sosus. Long chains of hydrophones, each tuned to a certain frequency range, are located on the edges of the continental shelves of the United States and elsewhere. Human sonar operators quickly become fatigued in straining to hear patterns in the sounds gathered by Sosus. The DDSP will help free these operators from information overload and may eventually be refined to the point that individual classes of ships can be identified by their sonar patterns.

IBM has also gotten into the game with a 256-processor machine that is used exclusively for the simulation of computer logic operations. The Yorktown Simulation Engine is programmed to mimic the performance of complex circuits in order to enable chip designers to find any flaws that may exist in the chip's logic. When completed, the YSE will be able to simulate up to 2 million logic gates and operate at a rate of more than 3 billion gate simulations per second (Fig. 7-3).

As computing power becomes less expensive and more widely available, there will no doubt be a vast number of other applications that have not yet even been considered. The history of the computer is characterized by the repeated discovery of novel uses for the available technology. When the microprocessor chip was first developed by the Intel Corp., the computer industry virtually ignored it. Not until Hewlett-Packard pioneered its use in hand-held calculators did the microchip find its place in the market. And since that time, the variety of uses that have been found for the microchip has truly exploded: everything from "talking" automobiles to "intelligent" toys and kitchen appliances that do everything but set the table. A new generation of paral-

Fig. 7-3. The Yorktown Simulation Engine is a parallel processor consisting of up to 256 logic boards, some of which can be seen at left. Each board can simulate the switching action of about 8,000 gates (courtesy IBM Corp.).

lel computers, together with advances in robotics and computer graphics, will have impacts as unforeseeable today as electronic bathroom scales were in the early 1970s. It seems certain, however, that these new technologies could, in a fundamental way, dramatically reshape the human environment.

Chapter 8

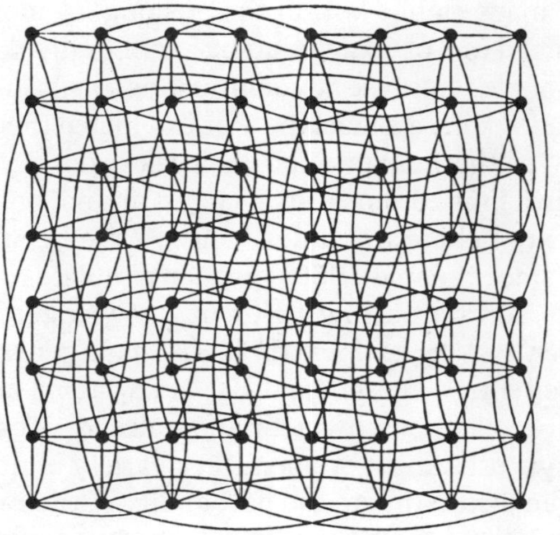

Artificial Intelligence: The Golden Promise

This is the age of euphoria for AI. It's like being at Kitty Hawk when the Wright brothers' plane took off.

Patrick Winston
Massachusetts Institute of Technology
in *Business Week*

Artificial intelligence is the buzzword of the 1980s. Money is pouring into the field as projects sponsored by government, corporations, and universities spring up across the country and around the world. After decades languishing in the wings, seen merely as the arcane pursuit of idealistic eggheads, AI has suddenly entered the limelight. Machine intelligence is making headlines in newspapers and magazines, and attracting the interest of the venture capital crowd. It's the subject of congressional hearings and television news segments. This is truly the age of euphoria for AI—and the hangover is sure to follow.

Expectations for AI have been raised beyond all reason. A promotional brochure for an investment newsletter mailed in early 1985 breathlessly announced the "discovery" of a computer "that actually thinks for itself . . . like a human being—only faster" and that the existence of such a machine would be made public within the ensuing 24 months. This is the worst kind of exaggeration, admittedly from an unreliable source, because it could just as easily be 24 years or 24 decades before a machine that can match the power and versatility of the human mind is developed.

Yet, in a limited sense, such claims are not only accurate but 20 years behind the times. There have been programs available since the mid-1960s that can simulate the thinking process in certain narrow fields of knowledge. These are called *expert systems*, and it is these that have generated much of the excitement and hoopla. Expert systems are nothing more than collections of facts and rules that can provide educated guesses about problems in a variety of fields. Many of them can also estimate the probability of their conclusion being correct and show their line of reasoning. The creation of these systems is called *knowledge engineering* and represents the applications end of artificial intelligence. Basic research in AI is concerned not with expert systems, but with the study of human thought processes, which has come to be known as *cognitive science*.

INTELLIGENCE OR ACTING INTELLIGENTLY

Ultimately, artificial intelligence is concerned with such questions as how human beings acquire knowledge and how that knowledge is applied to the vast variety of situations encountered in daily living. There have been endless debates within the discipline regarding the exact nature of intelligence, but the argument is regarded by many in the field as sterile and unproductive. The functional definition of intelligence—a machine's behavior is intelligent if it acts intelligently—is tautological in a philosophical sense but has allowed room for fruitful experimentation. The fact of the matter is that the best AI programs do not mimic human thought processes at all. They often reach the same conclusions, but by an entirely different route.

Marvin Minsky of MIT has long been a leader of the "intelligent machines act intelligently" school. One of the key assertions in Minsky's approach to AI is that many of the vague terms used to describe human mental processes, such as "intuition," serve merely to obscure logical, and reproducible, mechanisms. He has even gone so far in his mechanistic view of intelligence as to call the brain merely a "meat machine." One of his more famous sayings is that to understand a piece of intelligent behavior it's necessary to look for three algorithms. The number "three" is arbitrary, but the underlying principle is serious: A small number of simple processes can, in combination, create an impression of unfathomable complexity.

An example of this phenomenon is the rippling of water in a pond. After one stone has been tossed in, it's easy to deduce from the concentric rings of wavelets that they were caused by a single stone. Two stones produce a similarly intelligible pattern. Three stones, however, generate a pattern so complex that sophisticated analysis is required to deduce the number of stones that had created it. That appearance of complexity, then, results from the synergy of a few simple phenomena.

Some writers have described the development of AI as the second computer revolution, most notably Feigenbaum and McCorduck. That view amounts to a prediction, because the impact of machine intelligence so far has been revolutionary only in the eager eyes of the news media. The Japanese Fifth Generation Project—and the opinion of some American researchers that it constitutes a serious threat—has lent credibility to what would have been viewed as wild speculation as recently as 1980.

By setting a definite date for the achievement of their goals, 1992, the Japanese have raised the expectation that intelligent machines with astounding capabilities are just around the corner in the next decade. The oft-repeated caveat, that success in reaching only 10 percent of their project's aims would please the Japanese, has gotten lost amidst the ballyhoo. As a result, many researchers are awaiting with clenched teeth the disappointment and anti-AI backlash that they feel is sure to come.

AI researchers first felt the sting of public criticism in the mid-1960s. The idea that the electronic brain would equal and exceed the capabilities of its human counterpart has been advanced repeatedly since the computer was invented. But progress in the field has historically been slow. In the early days of AI, immediately following World War II, intelligence was seen as a natural and eventual consequence of the computer's growing power. The physiology of the brain was poorly understood, and it seemed logical to equate individual neurons in the brain with circuits in the computer. Because neurons outnumbered circuits 100 billion to one, it was assumed that as faster and more complex computers were built, intelligence, thought and "consciousness" would surely follow.

But even in the late 1940s and 1950s, researchers were aware of important distinctions between brain physiology and electronic computing. It was clear, for example, that the neuron's mode of communication was not digital. Rather than functioning as a simple on-off switch, a sensory neuron fired more rapidly as the intensity of a stimulus increased. This seemed to suggest that the brain was an analog, rather than digital, computer.

The still-common notion that the brain achieves its processing power through a kind of parallelism akin to multiprocessing has given way to new discoveries. Researchers have found that a considerable amount of communication within the brain takes place by means of chemical substances called *neurotransmitters*. About 50 different compounds have been discovered so far, the best known of which is probably the brain's natural opiate, beta endorphin.

In spite of its difficulty, man-made intelligence has inspired computer researchers from the beginning. Von Neumann himself was explicit in comparing his theoretical "cellular automata" to the brain. Alan Turing, the British mathematician who was instrumental in the development of Colossus, was convinced that machine intelligence would be indistinguishable from human intelligence by the year 2000. In 1936, he devised a test that would reveal whether or not a machine was intelligent. He envisioned a room with two teletype machines, one connected to a human being, the other to a computer. An interrogator would type questions on each of the teletype machines and try to judge by the response which one was human. If he guessed wrong or couldn't tell, the machine would be proved intelligent.

Almost as soon as computers were equipped with enough memory to handle AI programs, researchers were writing them. The term "artificial intelligence" wasn't coined, however, until 1956, when it was used to describe a summer workshop at Dartmouth College organized by John McCarthy, who has since become the director of the Artificial Intelligence Laboratory at Stanford University. Initial attempts to create machine intelligence focused on duplicating the problem-solving strategies of the mind. In the absence of any satisfactory theory, early researchers concentrated on building and testing models of the thinking process. Theirs was a computational interpretation of the mind, shaped by the mechanistic, step-by-step logic of the computer.

THE FIRST AGE OF EUPHORIA

Enthusiasm for the potential of AI ran high in the discipline's early years. Claims made on behalf of intelligent machines were perhaps even more grandiose than they are today. Another pioneer in the field, Herbert Simon, was moved in 1957 to predict that within 10 years a computer would defeat the world's chess champion, compose music of serious aesthetic value, discover and prove a significant mathematical theorem, and emerge as the predominant paradigm for the explanation of psychological phenomena. The fact that none of these came true, and still haven't, didn't prevent Simon from becoming, with Alan Newell, co-director of the artificial intelligence lab at Carnegie Mellon.

An early skeptic, Hubert Dreyfus, wrote a report published by the Rand Corp. in 1965 entitled "AI and Alchemy," in which he asserted that the two were scientifically equivalent. Dreyfus was one of the first who argued that certain activities, such as playing chess, required "real" human intelligence and that mere mimickry was the science of charlatans. He wrote that citing chess-playing programs as a step toward artificial intelligence was like saying that an ape climbing a tree was taking a step toward the moon.

In response, researchers at MIT challenged Dreyfus to a game of chess to avenge the honor of AI. Dreyfus would play against a program called MacHack, developed by Richard Greenblatt. It was a close match, but Dreyfus lost, much to the delight of the AI community. Dreyfus himself was unmoved, however, declaring that his loss as a "rank amateur" hardly proved the intelligence of the machine. In fact, he went on to write a book that catalogued many of the more embarrassing failures of AI, which he called, "What Computers Can't Do."

While early theories on machine intelligence formed the basis for some good science fiction, in practical terms they proved somewhat naive. One of the brightest hopes in the late 1950s was a program that would embody the full range of human problem-solving abilities. Perhaps the most influential effort along these lines was the General Problem Solver, devised in 1957 by Newell, Simon, and J. Clifford Shaw of the Rand Corp. It was based on the idea that humans make decisions based on an analysis of means and ends. A set of initial conditions is the program's point of departure, and each step it takes must move it closer to the set of end conditions that comprise its goal. In all but the simplest cases, however, the program was overwhelmed by the number of possible solutions that had to be considered.

Scientists call this the *combinatoric explosion*. It means that, as a problem grows more complex, the number of possible paths to solution increases at an explosive rate. A classic illustration of the combinatoric explosion is known as the traveling salesman problem. Starting simply, suppose the salesman is trying to find the shortest route that passes through three towns on his itinerary without hitting the same town twice. If he starts in Town A, he can either go to B first or to C first, then on to the other. If a fourth town is added to his itinerary, the number of possible routes increases to six: ABCD, ABDC, ACBD, ACDB, ADBC, and ADCB. Adding a fifth town increases the number of possibilities to 24; a sixth town, 120; a seventh, 840; an eighth, 6,720; a ninth, 53,760; and so on. A completely general program would essentially have to examine every possible route, totaling the distance between towns, until it found the shortest. The salesman, meanwhile, might look at a map and, without even thinking about it, discard all but a few of the most likely routes.

This ability the brain has for intuitively selecting the best candidate solutions from an enormous field of possibilities has baffled researchers. For the most part, it's nonverbal and does not appear to involve any kind of formal logic. Another familiar example is the game of chess. Human beings have a remarkable ability to pare down the number of moves to be considered to a manageable few, and as a result, can plan ahead more moves than even the most sophisticated computer chess programs running on the most powerful of supercomputers. Any chess-playing program soon has to face the fact that there are 10^{120} sequences of legal moves to be considered. A billion of the fastest computers ever built could spend the lifetime of the universe calculating and still not have considered even half the possibilities. Even a simpler game like checkers has 10^{40} possible move sequences.

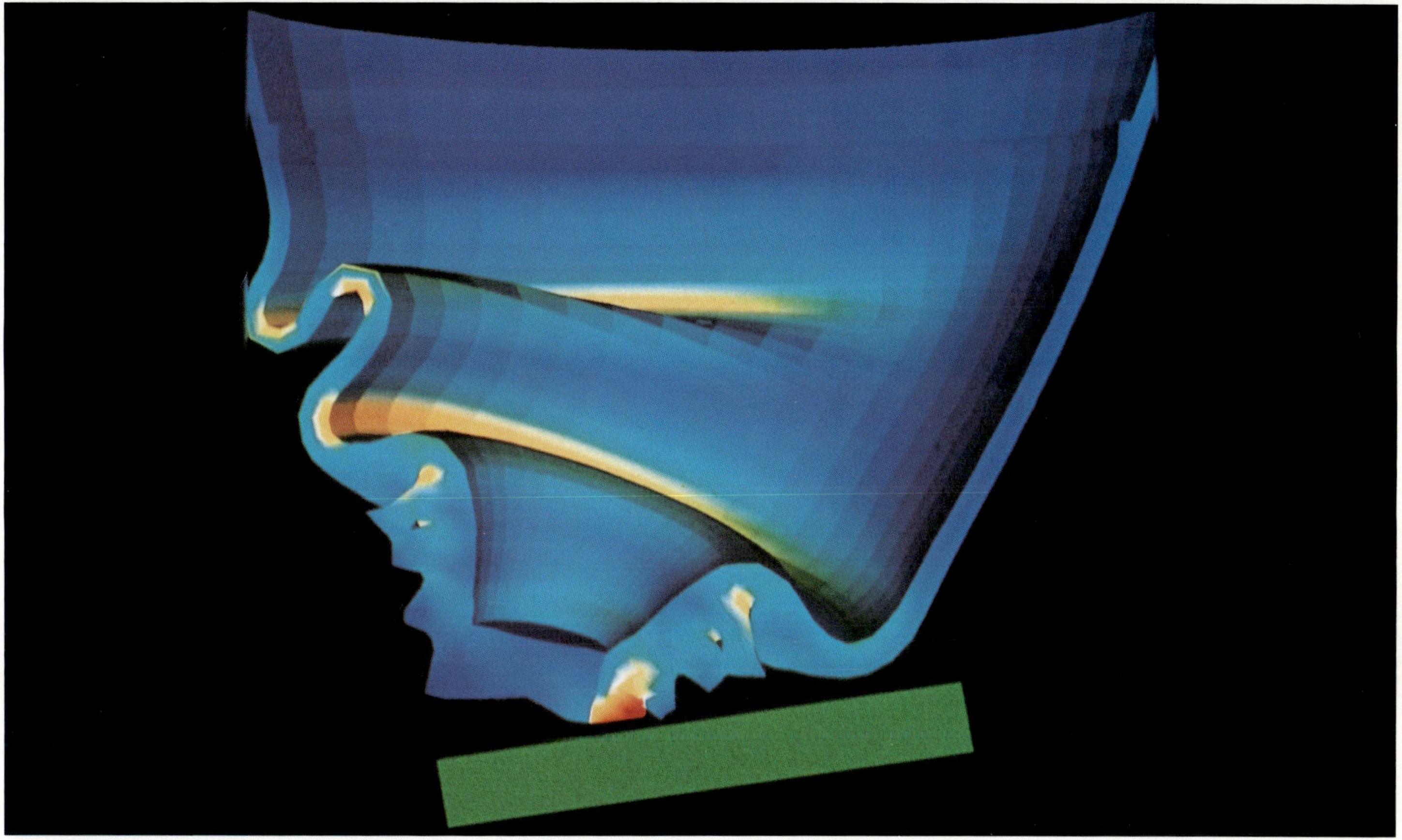

Produced by a supercomputer, this is a model of the calculated deformation of a steel nose cone upon impact, showing effective plastic strain within the steel (courtesy of Lawrence Livermore National Laboratory).

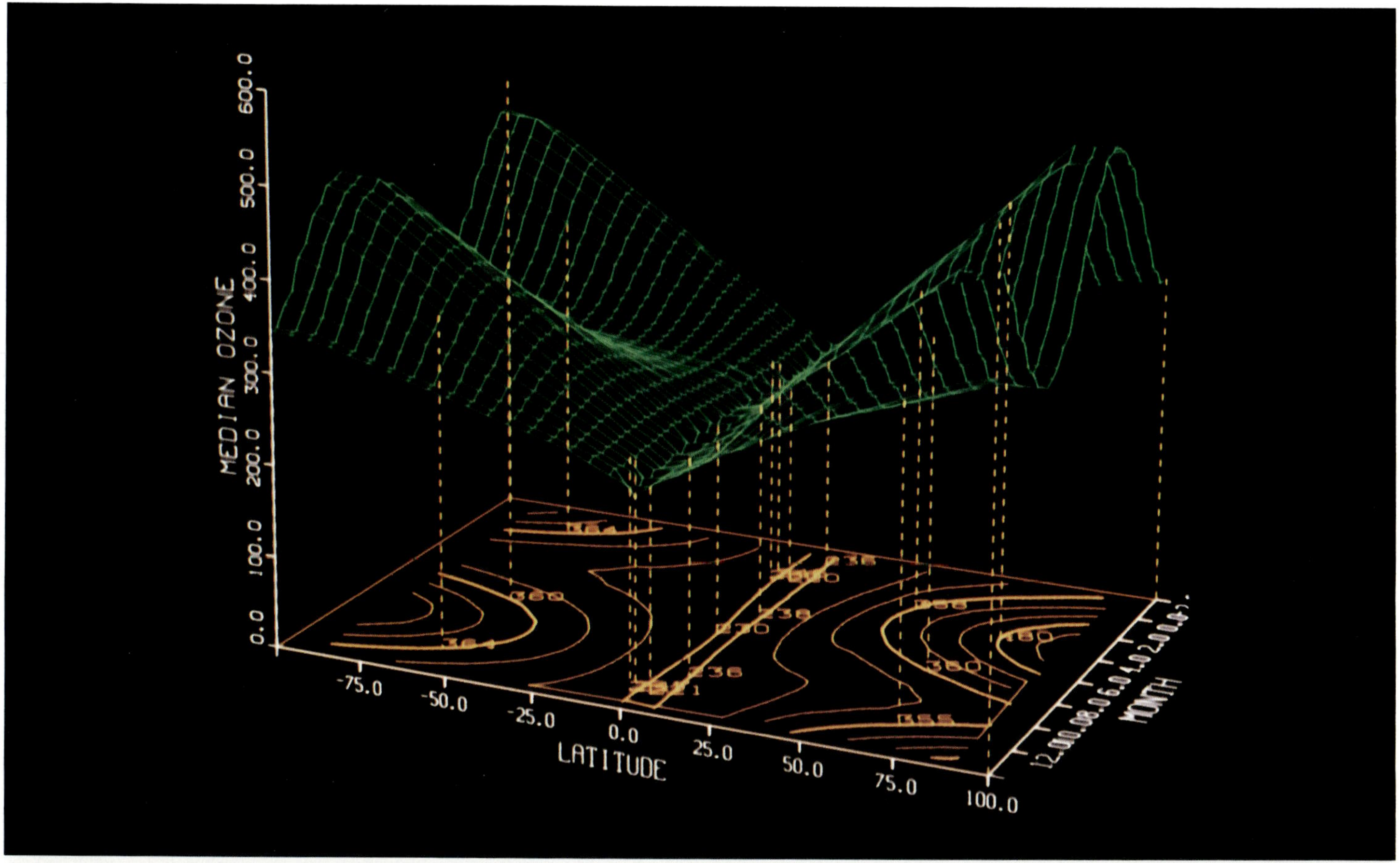

A simplified ozone model showing seasonality and increase in ozone from the equator (courtesy of Lawrence Livermore National Laboratory).

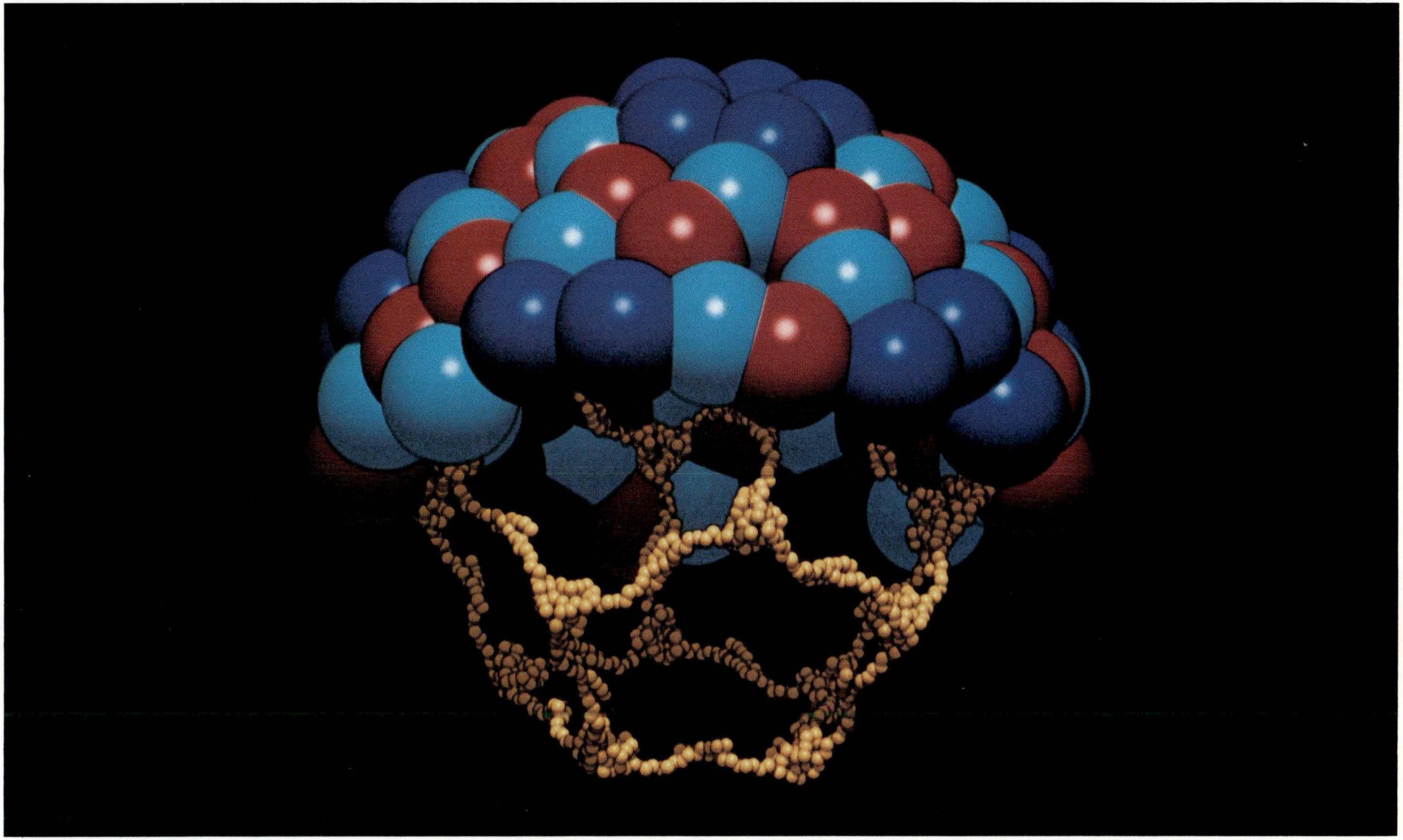

A model of a hemisphere of 90 of the 180 amino acid subunits in the protein coat of the tomato bushy stunt virus (courtesy of Lawrence Livermore National Laboratory).

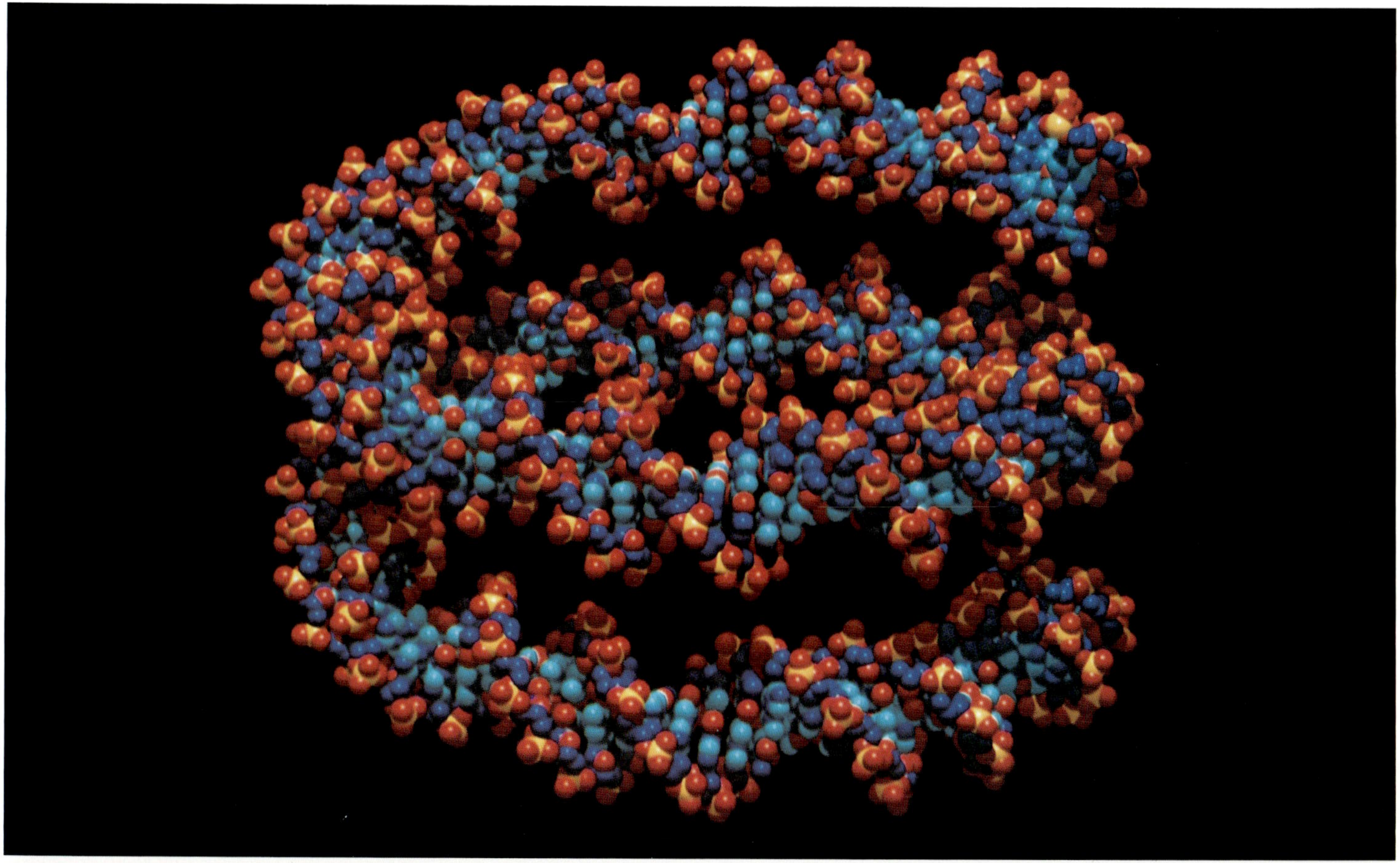

A model of a DNA supercoil having 171 base pairs—some 7000 atoms (courtesy of Lawrence Livermore National Laboratory).

CHESS BIT BY BIT

Game-playing has nevertheless been one of the most successful fields of AI endeavor. A program written by Hans Berliner of Carnegie-Mellon University, called Mighty Bee, defeated the world backgammon champion in 1979. In chess, however, humans still reign supreme. Some programs play well enough to be rated "master," but that's still a notch below the pinnacle, "grandmaster."

All of the chess-playing programs have two modes of operation. The early part of the game generally follows a set of standard moves stored in the machine's memory. There is no actual calculation or thinking involved at this stage, and the programs are said to be operating "on book." As the game progresses, however, situations develop that no longer fit with the stored move sequences. It's then that the thinking begins and rules of thumb called *heuristics* come into play.

The range of possible moves is often compared to a tree. There are usually about 35 legal moves branching out from any initial position. Each one of those moves then provokes one of about 35 countermoves, each of which leads to 35 counter-countermoves. The number of possibilities soon multiplies beyond the point that an exhaustive search of all moves is possible. Looking only three moves deep for each player would require a computer unguided by heuristics to examine more than 1.8 billion moves.

The chess program must have a method for evaluating each possible move. Most use a scoring system based on the value of each piece and the threat that any piece will be captured on the next move. The end score for each move sequence is then compared with each of the others, and the move with the highest score is chosen. In order to prune the search tree, heuristics are applied that select the most promising move sequences early in the search, discarding the less likely ones. A typical heuristic might tell the machine to examine only the five most promising moves. There is no guarantee, without searching every possible option, that the best move sequence is found. It is merely a way of limiting the search and defusing the combinatoric explosion.

One of the most powerful chess programs, Belle, is actually a supercomputer custom built at Bell Labs with chess heuristics hard-wired directly into its circuits. Belle looks at about 160,000 positions per second. In searching four moves deep, Belle evaluates a pruned tree of approximately 30 million possibilities in the three minutes allowed for deciding on a move. Belle's tournament rating is 2,160—a rating of 2,000 to 2,199 qualifies a player as an expert.

Many of the chess programs regularly beat their human programmers, some of whom admit to knowing very little about chess. It turns out that chess knowledge is less important than programming knowledge, because the computer's approach to the game is far different from that of a human being. A good human player generally examines no more than about 100 board positions before choosing a move. The human player relies on strategy. He selects a particular goal, such as the capture of the opposing queen, and then looks for ways to achieve that goal. Because only the most promising lines of attack are considered, the number of positions to be evaluated is small, allowing examination of moves in greater depth. Even with an effective set of heuristics, the best computer chess programs still rely primarily on a calculational blitz.

This difference in approach leads to some characteristic distinctions between human and computer chess that emerge when man meets machine in tournament play. The computer's ignorance of all events that may occur beyond its depth of search allows a human player to disguise an attack behind a layer of pawns. The machine perceives no immediate threat and therefore makes no defense. Another weakness that human opponents sometimes exploit is the tendency for the computer to sacrifice an eventual large gain in favor of smaller immediate advantages. There are also rare occasions when the program will do something that seems completely irrational. For example, if it can't find a move that satisfies its heuristics, it will waste a move shifting the king left or right in the back row.

Perhaps the most interesting distinction between human and computer chess is a strategy that some human players use to defeat the machines—they lie. A human player will deliberately play poorly, making moves that don't fit with the program's expectations for countermoves. The human will go on blithely sacrificing pieces here and there, the computer guilelessly accepting this charity as mere human folly. All the while, a crushing blow is being readied for the hapless machine.

That humans will sometimes lie, cheat, and commit all manner of sins to achieve their aims pinpoints an essential question that has divided the AI community. Should artificial intelligence strive to duplicate the mechanisms of human intelligence, or is it sufficient merely to develop programs that produce intelligent behavior? Current chess programs do a reasonably good job of the latter, but they fail miserably at the former. One of the newer programs under development, Chunker, takes a more human-like approach. Pieces are grouped together in logically related chunks, each of which is endowed with certain properties that are stored in the machine's memory. The program's developer, Carnegie-Mellon's Berliner, has used it to analyze the chess end game in which both players have a king and three pawns each. Positions that for 300 years have been thought to end in a draw can actually be turned to a forced win, the machine found. But to do so, one must apply a set of rules too complex to be remembered by a human player, although well within the capacity of a computer.

COMPUTERS AND COMMON SENSE

For the most part, getting machines to function in ways that resemble intelligence is a lot easier than programming them to think in human terms. Expert systems are an example of simulated intelligence that have proven successful enough to be marketed commercially. The difficulty in developing intelligent machines is in determining the nature of intelligence. No one really knows how people think, in the broadest sense of that word.

One school of AI theory, led by Stanford's John McCarthy, holds that the key to intelligence is in finding a system that will allow machines to reason most effectively, regardless of whether the reasoning process imitates the workings of the human mind. The language of mathematical logic, they argue, has been developed over centuries and provides a clear path for reasoning from initial facts to inevitable conclusions. A simple logical statement might take the form: If a man lives in Dallas, and Dallas is in Texas, the man is a Texan. By building a chain of logical statements like this, conclusions of surprising accuracy and sophistication can be reached.

At the other end of the AI spectrum, MIT's Marvin Minsky sees imitating the way the human mind works as the more fruitful approach over the long term. This is the basic science element of AI, because it treads on terra incognita—the mechanisms of mind. At the foundation of Minsky's approach is a faith that these mechanisms can be discovered and will, in fact, prove simple enough to be reproducible in a machine. It's as if researchers, blindfolded, are reaching into the mind's tool kit and trying to discern the properties and functions of the objects they feel. From this limited knowledge, programmers make a conjecture about the way people think and then design a computer model that fits their theory. If the model works well enough, they conclude that there is some truth to their conjecture. Minsky asserts that ultimately, no simple way of reproducing human reasoning will succeed because the mind is a collection of many methods and mechanisms that somehow function together.

At a national conference on artificial intelligence in 1982, Minsky and McCarthy debated the advantages of their respective points of view. Minsky sees several problems with using mathematical logic as a basis for machine intelligence. One is the idea that thinking is based on facts, which exist only in the abstract world of mathematics. In the real world facts are fuzzy and can change with different circumstances. For example, is a bird still a bird after it's dead, and if so, how long does it remain a bird before it becomes a skeleton or simply dust? Minsky also objects to the mathematical necessity of reasoning from general principles.

He offers an example: "Consider a fact like, 'Birds can fly.' If you think that common-sense reasoning is like logical reasoning then you believe there are general principles that state, 'If Joe is a bird and birds can fly then Joe can fly.' But we all know that there are exceptions. Suppose Joe is an ostrich or a penguin? Well, we can axiomatize and say if Joe is a bird and Joe is not an ostrich or a penguin, then Joe can fly. But suppose Joe is dead? Or suppose Joe has his feet set in concrete? The problem with logic is that once you deduce something you can't get rid of it. What I'm getting at is that there is a problem with exceptions. It is very hard to find things that are always true."

As an alternative to mathematical logic, Minsky developed a different kind of knowledge structure that he called *frames*. The computer makes use of a frame in the same way humans use stereotypes. For people, stereotypes provide a way of filling in missing information about a situation or thing that isn't fully described.

A program is built up from frame definitions, each of which has an object or activity at its core and a set of typical attributes. To make an example of the bird once again, a frame for "birds" might include such attributes as flying, singing, feathers, wings, and egg-laying. The specific knowledge in the frames is used to guide the reasoning process. Different situations give greater weight to some attributes than to others. It's as if each frame was a sheet of plastic with various attributes printed on it. In building up a chain of reasoning, many sheets are laid on top of one another and some of the attributes are obscured while others stand out clearly. A frame for "birds" laid over a frame for "Antarctica" would stress "feathers," "wings" and "egg-laying," while "flying" and "singing" would be obscured. This kind of approach to matching intelligence, Minsky believes, more closely resembles the human thought process.

RULES OF THOUGHT

Another common way in which people reason uses rules, similar to the heuristics of the chess program. Children are taught to spell not only through memorization and phonetics but by memorizing rules such as "i before e, except after c." Generally, the rules that humans use apply only to a limited domain, which could also be said of the way computers use rules. The problem with more general rules is the abundance of exceptions that seem to crop up like weeds in any field of knowledge. Most logic-based systems rely on rules as their primary method of representing knowledge. Those who favor logic programming for expert systems see the attempt to model human psychological processes as unnecessarily fuzzy and imprecise. Rather, they prefer to look for ways to incorporate an allowance for exceptions into the rules of logic.

Circumscription is the name that McCarthy has given his solution to the problem. The basic idea is to provide the machine with a list of possible exceptions. If none apply, mathematical logic will lead to the correct conclusion. Taking the general rule "birds can fly" as an example, a category called "prevented from flying" would take into account all of the exceptions. That set would include dead birds, birds that are penguins or ostriches, or birds with their feet in concrete. Then the computer would reason: "If Joe is a bird and Joe is not a member of the set 'prevented from flying,' then Joe can fly."

Such an approach can be expensive in terms of the programmer's time and the computer's memory. There are an endless number of exceptions to any rule, some less plausible than others. A dead bird is bound to be a much more common member of the "prevented from flying" set than a bird with its feet in concrete. It's up to the system's programmer to decide where to draw the line. That decision also determines the risk of reaching an incorrect conclusion resulting from an unanticipated exception. Such judgments are common, and necessary, in the development of any expert system.

MACHINE LEARNING

Human beings gain as much from incorrect conclusions as from correct ones—perhaps more, because they can revise their rule sets. In other words, they learn. Machines that learn are one of the primary goals of artificial intelligence researchers for a number of reasons, one of the main ones being the amount of time that is required in programming AI machines. Encoding a single rule in a rule-based expert system requires, on average, an hour. Many such systems contain 2,000 or more rules and the trend is toward ever-larger systems.

One of the earliest programs to demonstrate a rudimentary form of learning was a checkers-playing program devised by Arthur L. Samuel of IBM in about 1960. The machine's learning was analogous to Darwinian natural selection. Two versions of the program battled it out with one another, each one using a slightly different scoring system for evaluating the strength of a position. The winner survived to compete again and from it a slightly altered "mutant" was created to oppose it. This primitive example is still human-aided learning, even though the improvements in the program are the result of random modifications.

More recent programs can expand their capabilities on the basis of experience. A program called Hacker, written by Gerard J. Sussman at MIT, uses a system of planning that starts with the goal to be achieved and works its way backward through a series of subgoals to the initial situation, similar to the General Problem Solver but with a much more limited domain. Hacker was designed to operate in a simplified world consisting entirely of simulated blocks on a simulated table. This keeps its database down to a manageable size. Two features allow the system to learn: *critics*, which note problems in the planning process, and *debuggers*, which formulate new rules that prevent the same mistakes from being made twice. This kind of learning mimics the trial-and-error approach of children. There is some doubt among AI researchers whether similar programs could scale up to encompass larger, more complex worlds.

Some programs are able to create new knowledge in a limited domain. This might be called *conceptual learning*, because it involves reasoning from general principles to specific concepts. One example is AM, an abbreviation of automated mathematics, written by Douglas B. Lenat of Stanford. The program was given a limited set of basic principles in a branch of mathematics called *set theory*. Heuristics guide the formulation of new theorems, which the program then investigates. One of the principles AM investigated was divisors of a number. It discovered that the set of numbers with exactly three divisors were all perfect squares (for example, the divisors of 49 are 1, 7 and 49). It then found that the square root of a number with three divisors is always a number with only two divisors, also known as a prime number. In about an hour of running time, AM went on to reproduce several commonly known conjectures regarding prime numbers and hypothesized that every natural number is the product of a unique set of primes. As it continues to run, however, AM starts conjuring up such computerish impossibilities as numbers that are simultaneously odd and even.

AI researchers have successfully developed programs that mimic several aspects of the human learning process, but none that combines these into an integrated whole. People learn by trial and error, by example, by analogy, by memorization, by reasoning from the general to the specific, and vice versa. With a few exceptions (like those mentioned above), computers learn only with the aid of programmers. A machine has no common sense. It must be taught everything, even the most basic notions, like the fact that an object located in one place can't simultaneously be in another place. Unfortunately, the productivity of the computer's human teachers, unlike that of the machine itself, has increased slowly over the years, increasing only by a factor of two to four in the last 25 years.

The programming of expert systems, often called *knowledge engineering*, is particularly laborious. It requires days-long interviews with a human expert, methodically extracting the accumulated knowledge, methods of operation and tricks of the trade that he has accumulated in years of experience. An initial model of the expert system is programmed and tested against the performance of the expert himself. Often, the initial information is only partially accurate or an embodiment of textbook knowledge that is rarely used in actual practice. A weeks-long process of clarification and testing ensues, which gradually refines the machine's performance until it equals or even surpasses that of the expert. Largely because of the amount of time and effort required in the knowledge engineering phase, the cost of a typical commercial expert system averages $100,000 to $150,000.

The disparity between the increasing efficiency of hardware and the relatively high cost of software means that many potential applications for computers, particularly in the realm of artificial intelligence, are never realized. Some kind of machine learning or automated programming, even if it only provided a rough draft that required human debugging, would significantly improve programming productivity. The complex task of interpreting an expert's statements and devising heuristic principles for problem solving will probably continue to require human intelligence. The development of ever-larger knowledge bases for expert systems, however, might be more amenable to automated learning.

As knowledge bases grow, the problem of search once again becomes paramount. Even with effective heuristics, as in chess-playing programs, the size of the search that a problem requires may still be impractical. At the moment, the smarter a machine gets, the slower it runs. Many expert systems with well-established heuristics are limited in size and scope by hardware considerations. As in the realm of large-scale scientific computing, AI researchers are looking toward parallelism to provide additional speed and memory capacity.

One of several machines being developed specifically for knowledge processing is called DADO. Its creator is Salvatore Stolfo of Columbia University. DADO is a *rule processor*, meaning that its basic unit is not numerical but a two-part statement that has a precondition on one side (if . . .) and a conclusion or inference on the other (then . . .). The problem is broken down into its constituent parts, and the database is searched for rules that might apply. This kind of search can be conducted serially, as well as in parallel, but it's a much slower process. DADO is a tree machine, similar to the Non-Von design also being developed at Columbia, but each of the processors is somewhat more powerful. As with Non-Von, the advantage of the tree is that the speed of the search is proportional to the number of layers in the tree, rather than the number of processors.

The DADO 2 prototype is expected to consist of 1,023 two-chip microprocessors, roughly equivalent to a personal computer, wired together on 32 printed circuit boards. Average cycle times for each processor are relatively slow, about 1.8 microseconds; however, the entire ensemble functioning in parallel should equal the speed and power of a Cray X-MP. But because processing in rule-based systems is relatively slow, instead of 400 megaflops, DADO 2 was clocked in one test at a mere 85 logic calculations per second—about 60 percent faster than a VAX 11/780. Eventually, Stolfo hopes to design a VLSI chip on which several processors of similar power can be incorporated. This would tend to both increase the machine's speed and lower its cost.

KNOWLEDGE IS POWER

Some researchers in this country question whether speed alone will be sufficient to bring revolutionary improvements in the performance of knowledge systems. They point out that few artificial intelligence applications have been limited by the number of logical inferences per second that could be performed. More often, problems have arisen from limitations in the quantity and quality of knowledge available to the machine. They tend to see knowledge as the foundation for effective inference operations. As a result, the American effort has focused less on processing and more on the construction of a database in which knowledge is easily updated and rapidly searched and accessed.

Ultimately, what makes computers seem dumb, in spite of their tremendous processing power, is that they lack common sense. It turns out that common sense is based on an enormous fund of knowledge that humans acquire through years of experience. People tend to approach unfamiliar problems in much the same way that an AI program would. They work out detailed strategies, goals, and subgoals, and then try to muscle through to the solution. But in dealing with the familiar, humans tend not to think at all but to treat a new problem as simply a variation on a theme. By fitting the problem to a familiar pattern, they are able to take a shortcut past the reasoning process and proceed straight to the solution. Humans also have the ability to generalize the method for solving a specific problem to one that is similar. No one has yet developed a machine with that kind of versatility. Machine intelligence is still limited to the realm of the experts, where brilliance is rarely shackled by the fetters of common sense.

Chapter 9

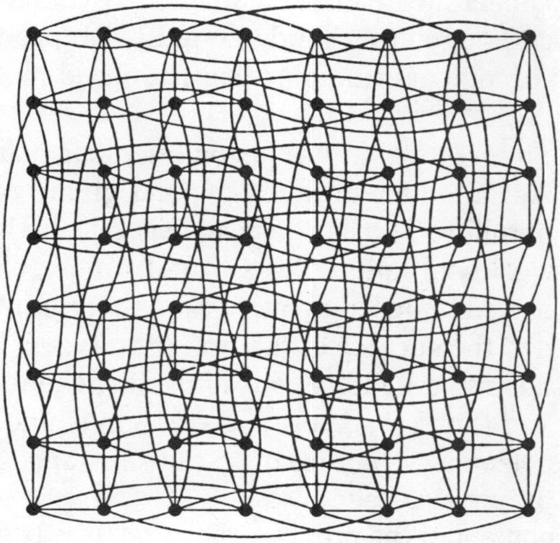

Expert Computers

In the long run, knowledge systems will increase individual and social potential by preserving know-how, distributing knowledge more effectively, and improving performance of tasks that require expertise.

Frederick Hayes-Roth
Cofounder and Chief Scientist
Teknowledge Inc.

As any human expert will tell you, most of what he or she knows can't be found in books. An expert may start out with a head full of facts culled from the printed page, but the winnowing process of daily problem solving soon separates the few useful kernels from the abundance of chaff. The superiority of experience over textbook knowledge is what makes experts so much in demand—and so expensive.

The early years of artificial intelligence research were characterized by a search for grand theories of mind that could be incorporated into machines akin to Simon's General Problem Solver. There was clearly an expectation that the essence of human intelligence could be teased away from the welter of facts, common sense, and experiential memories that clutter the average person's brain. Perhaps because many of the AI pioneers were mathematicians by training, they assumed that thought was fundamentally the product of the same kind of logical principles that governed mathematical reasoning.

By the mid-1960s, it was becoming clear that ten years of effort had failed to do much beyond giving researchers a sense of humility. The backlash against AI's early, euphoric claims and colossal failures was brutal. Interest in systems that emphasized knowledge over grand theories of mind was largely due to the success of the first prototypes. Ed Feigenbaum, author and AI gadfly, was himself one of the principal developers of the first expert system, a machine that could infer the molecular structure of tested substances from data gathered by physical chemists.

Development of the program, Dendral, was begun in 1965 and required years of effort to input the volumes of chemical knowledge required. Different methods for representing that knowledge in the machine were tried, as well as techniques for accessing it effectively. Dendral's kinks were ironed out and it has become a fixture in university and industrial chemical labs worldwide.

It was years before Feigenbaum's approach to AI was widely accepted. The importance of knowledge, which was once regarded as a mass of unnecessary detail, has emerged as paramount. All reasoning, understanding, problem-solving, and even learning is now thought to be built on a foundation of knowledge. Studies of human learning, for instance, have shown that new material is assimilated most effectively when it is presented with concepts that are already understood, so that not more than 25 percent of the material is unfamiliar.

Knowledge-based systems include not only expert systems but those that use information about the world to interpret visual images and understand speech. The distinction is that an expert system's knowledge is concentrated in a single field of human expertise, while language and vision systems are necessarily broader in scope and require extensive preprocessing of raw images and utterances before the stored knowledge becomes useful.

THE KNOWLEDGE INDUSTRY

The number of young graduate students drawn to artificial intelligence research increased dramatically during the 1970s, partly as a result of the renewed interest in real world applications. Increasingly powerful computers and more sophisticated programs stimulated interest not only in the field itself but among the public at large. By 1980, the field was celebrating the first meeting of the American Association for Artificial Intelligence, held at Stanford University. Instead of the several hundred participants that had been anticipated, almost a thousand showed up—including 40 reporters and flocks of venture capitalists. Start-up companies blossomed throughout Silicon Valley, just a few miles south of Stanford, and along Route 128 outside of Boston. Their purpose: to commercialize expert systems.

The commercial appeal of expert systems is based on the provision of a scarce resource—expertise—in a wide variety of situations in which its availability is limited. A classic example is the CATS-1 (Fig. 9-1) expert system developed by General Electric for its diesel locomotive division. GE was faced with the problem that it had only one top locomotive repair expert, David I. Smith, and maintenance problems that needed solutions in repair shops from coast to coast. The expense of flying Smith around the country was considerable, as was the wear and tear on their best mechanic, who was also fast approaching retirement. So GE called in knowledge engineer Francis Lynch and asked him to devise a system that would preserve Smith's expertise and make it widely available to shops around the country. Lynch came up with the CATS-1 system, which not only diagnoses malfunctions but can display parts on a graphics screen and demonstrate repair techniques on a video monitor.

An expert system can also effectively bring together the knowledge of experts in several different fields, building a whole that performs a task beyond the capacity of any one of its parts. Hitachi is working on a Project Risk Assessment System that will aid in the planning of large construction projects. The system brings together the knowledge of individual experts in construction, design, engineering, and project management. Its function is not to replace the human managers of a project but to provide a comprehensive electronic chart of progress and risk that helps in keeping track of the myriad details that are part of any large construction effort.

There are some cases in which expert systems actually

Fig. 9-1. A team of General Electric researchers headed by Piero Bonissone, left, devised the CATS-1 expert system, which enabled them to capture the expertise of top locomotive field service engineer David I. Smith, right.

exceed the performance of their human conterparts. When the problem to be addressed requires the consideration of many different possibilities, a trial and error search for solutions, expert systems are often faster and more thorough in their evaluation.

An example of this is the analysis of failures in steam-driven power plants. The number of possible causes is considerable, and down time for a power plant is extremely costly. In one test of a system designed to diagnose plant malfunctions by analyzing the chemical properties of a plant's steam effluent, the computer did in seconds what it took human experts four days to accomplish. Such rapid analysis of failures can save millions of dollars in just one year. In many cases, the value of an expert system to a company is so great that the payback period for an investment of $100,000 or more is just a few weeks.

Another situation in which computers outperform the experts is in configuring computer architectures. Digital Equipment Corporation manufactures its VAX series of computer systems for business, industry, and university customers, and each order is customized to a certain extent. Various component modules can be assembled in a wide variety of architectures, but the interconnections among them are subject to a thick catalog of constraints and conditions. DEC developed an expert system that can be fed the specifications required for a given system and, working with about 2,500 rules for system design stored in its database, correctly configure the new system 99 percent of the time.

REPRESENTING KNOWLEDGE IN THE MACHINE

Unlike their superpowerful cousins, the big scientific number crunchers, expert systems deal primarily with symbols rather than numbers. A symbol can be just about anything that can stand for an idea, including not only words but pictures. Ultimately, as in all computers, the symbols are stored in memory as machine-language 1's and 0's, but the programmer using a high-level AI language never sees them. There are two main languages in use today for expert systems development. One is LISP, which stands for list-processing language, which is favored by researchers in this country. The other is Prolog, a logic-based language that is preferred

ferred for AI applications in much of Europe and Japan and gaining a following here.

Working in LISP, the programmer endows each object with a list of symbols that represent various significant qualities characteristic of it. A strawberry might include among its list of properties that it is a fruit, has small white flowers, produces red berries, and reproduces by means of runners and seeds. A variety of different operations can be performed on the lists in the database. A simple example is "match," which might be used to find all red-fruited plants or plants that produce small white flowers.

One of the drawbacks of working in LISP is that some of the list operations are beyond the capacity of most small mainframe computers, necessitating the use of a separate program that interprets the LISP instructions and puts them in a form that the computer can understand. The alternative is to spend $50,000 to $100,000 on a LISP work station, which is a powerful personal computer specifically created for AI work using LISP.

Prolog is a logic-based language that provides a form for stating logical propositions in the computer: "All living plants require light, warmth and water; therefore, a plant deprived of water (or warmth or light) for an extended period will die." In examining any member of the set of all living plants, such as the cactus, in an effort to determine proper horticultural practices, an expert system would encounter "light, warmth, and water" as part of the set "needs—all plants." More specific information on the cactus family would form a subset of the set of "needs—all plants" and might detail how much light, warmth, and water was optimal, as well as any other cactus requirements, such as sandy soil and low humidity. Prolog is primarily a descriptive language, used for the creation of data-bases, rather than an operational language like LISP, which includes mechanisms for processing symbols as well as listing them. Many such mechanisms are being introduced to Prolog, however.

Either language can be used to shape a variety of constructs that expert system designers use to represent knowledge in the machine. Perhaps the simplest is a production system, which is merely a set of if-then rules. Suppose, for example, that a household hints expert system is asked the question "How do I remove grease stains from cotton slacks?" The question is first processed semantically, that is, each element is identified as the member of a particular kind of object or condition: "how" might be identified as a request for technique; "remove" as a cleaning action, "grease" as a chemical substance, "stain" as a surface blemish, and "cotton" as a fabric. The program would then search its databases for rules in which any one of these items appeared on the "if . . ." side of the rule. Additional information might be requested, such as whether the cotton is white or colored. Then a chain of all applicable conditions is built: "IF the fabric is cotton AND the blemish is a chemical substance AND the substance is grease AND the cleaning action desired is removal AND the technique requested is how, THEN a paste of corn starch and lemon juice is applied to the stain."

Knowledge can also be represented in a *semantic network,* which is used to codify abstract relationships among objects in a system's domain. The objects are linked together by verb constructs like "is-a." For example, "ivy is-a vine" and "blackberry is-a vine" and "vine is-a plant" and so on. The link is an abbreviated way of saying that an object is part of a larger class. Together, the objects and their links make up a taxonomy.

A semantic network can readily make use of the concept of frames, developed by Minsky and discussed in the previous chapter. A database of this type resembles a tree, with more general objects, such as "vine," closer to the root and more specific objects, "ivy" and "raspberry," making up the numerous subbranches and leaves.

In a semantic network, every object but the root (or roots; there may be more than one) has "parents" above it in the tree and every object but the leaves has "children" below it. "Vine" is the parent of "ivy" and "raspberry," and the child of "plant," which might in turn be the child of the root, something very general like "describable thing." In order to save memory space, objects in the frame can inherit the characteristics of their more general "parents." Some characteristics are variable—a raspberry can either be "red" or "black"—while others are fixed and represent the program's expectations. The latter is the machine equivalent of a stereotype.

Newer expert systems may combine several different methods of knowledge representation. A system might use production rules to define methods for uncovering the characteristics of an object, semantic networks to define the relationships among the objects referenced in the rules, and frames to describe the objects' typical attributes.

SYMBOLIC PROCESSING

The mechanisms used by expert systems to process knowledge superficially resemble human reasoning, but in reality they are dependent on the contents of the database. Two of the most common are mirror images of one another: reasoning forward from the facts to a probable conclusion and reasoning backward from a stated goal to a set of initial conditions or facts. Intuitively, it's easier to grasp forward reasoning, starting with the facts. A millionaire industrialist has been murdered in his study. He was found with a knife in his back, and the door was locked from the inside. The only other exit from the room was through a window above the garden. The butler's footprints were found in the garden, and a bloodstain was discovered on his shoe; therefore, the butler did it.

To get a sense of how backward-chained reasoning works, it's easier to approach the problem as a computer would. In a rule-based system, the program starts with a desired conclusion (supplied most often by a human user) and searches its database for rules that give the conclusion as a result. It then attempts to match the "if . . ." part of the rule against the initial problem description. If the two match, the search is finished. When the match fails, as it most often does, the machine then searches for rules that lead to the rules that lead to the conclusion, and so on until a chain is found that leads from the initial conditions to the desired conclusion.

The hypothetical household hints expert system used backward-chained reasoning to solve the grease stain problem. In that situation, the desired goal was "grease stain removal" and the initial conditions were "a grease stain in cotton slacks." The lemon juice-and-cornmeal method might have been one of several for taking out grease stains, but was the only one that also fit the initial condition "cotton fabric."

Many of the newer systems combine both forward and backward-chained reasoning. The evidence is used to develop a set of initial hypotheses. Each hypothesis then becomes a "goal" and the program works backward to build a chain of reasoning that leads to the initial facts. Often a new item related to the problem is uncovered. This then becomes "evidence" and the machine switches to a forward mode of reasoning, forming new hypotheses.

In most such systems, the logic processor is endowed with some knowledge about its own operations. This allows it to choose the most appropriate method of reasoning for solving a particular problem. This is often referred to in AI circles as *metaknowledge*, because it exists in a realm between the reasoning mechanisms and the knowledge base. In a sense, metaknowledge allows an expert system to find its own way through a problem, giving it much greater flexibility and power.

Another basic feature that distinguishes expert systems from mere computers is their ability to deal with uncertain data and even conflicting information. Even in the physical sciences, complete certainty is a rarity. And in such specialties as medical diagnosis, incomplete information and occasional contradictory test results are the norm. In order to find a path through this shifting landscape, expert systems must have a way of evaluating facts according to their degree of certainty.

As part of the process of providing data to the machine about the circumstances of the problem, the computer may request that the user provide a numerical estimate of the certainty of various pieces of data. These are then incorporated into the machine's calculations, and they allow it to express its conclusions with a numerical estimate of their probable correctness.

In addition to a method for handling uncertainty, a system must also provide an explanation of the reasoning used to reach a conclusion. In AI terminology, such a system is "transparent" to the user. Unlike a computer, which performs its calculations in a realm that's as mysterious to the user as the underworld was to the ancients, an expert system can't be a black box that mysteriously answers questions like the Oracle at Delphi. Its credibility, like that of any expert, depends not simply on coming up with the solution to a problem but on being able to explain the reasoning that led to the solution.

INTERACTING WITH AN EXPERT SYSTEM

A typical exchange with an expert system involves questions on both sides. The program often needs additional information to narrow the scope of its search, while the human may have questions about the machine's line of reasoning. Since expert systems generally communicate in natural language, the interchange between man and machine is deceptively humanlike. In the early 1970s, a program called Eliza, which used natural language and certain psychological keywords, such as "mother" or "depressed" or "sad," to mimic the responses of a clinical psychologist, was written. Eliza was not an expert system in any sense. It was merely endowed with a set of canned responses that could be triggered by the mention of one of its keywords. If a response contained the word "mother," Eliza might reply, "Tell me more about your family." When a subject's statement failed to contain any of the keywords, Eliza would simply turn the statement around and repeat it as a question: "Are you saying . . . ?"

Eliza's creator, Joseph Weizenbaum of MIT, was astounded by the response of fellow researchers and students who had access to the program. All were intimately familiar with computers and the limited nature of machine intelligence in that era, yet many responded to the program as if it were human. They told Eliza their most intimate secrets, as if the machine had the power to heal. His secretary, who had watched him work on the program for months, started conversing with it and moments later asked him to leave the room. Even professionals in the psychiatric community seemed willing, even eager, to use Eliza in the treatment of their mentally disturbed patients.

Weizenbaum was both shocked and perplexed by the response to Eliza. He eventually detailed his observations and reservations in a book about the willingness of people to endow the computer with intelligence and abilities that it didn't possess. In *Computer Power and Human Reason: From Judgment to Calculations,* Weizenbaum argued that computers should be banned from certain particularly human activities, such as psychotherapy and criminal justice.

LIMITED KNOWLEDGE LIMITS EXPERTISE

The Eliza experience points up another reason that expert systems need to be able to explain their reasoning. Even the most sophisticated system has certain limits that may not be readily apparent to the user. In order to keep the size of the knowledge base to a manageable level, it may be necessary to exclude details that in some less-than-common situations prove to be important.

An example can be found in the MYCIN system, which was developed at Stanford in the mid-1970s to aid physicians in the selection of antibiotics for patients with severe infections. In a variety of clinical tests, MYCIN has demonstrated its ability to perform at or near the level of expert physicians. The current system embodies roughly 500 rules. MYCIN first makes a diagnosis based on clinical evidence presented to it by a physician and then recommends antibiotics based on the possible causes of the infection.

One of the rules in MYCIN's database prevents it from recommending the antibiotic tetracycline to patients under 8 years of age. The underlying reason for this rule—that the drug can stain teeth and inhibit bone growth—is not part of the knowledge base because it was deemed an unnecessary detail by MYCIN's developers. In certain severe infections, however, a human physician would prescribe tetracycline despite the cosmetic side effects. MYCIN's recommendations in such a case, taken as gospel, could mean life or death for a young patient.

Any true partisan of the engineering approach to AI would argue that larger, faster systems will soon allow larger knowledge bases to be encoded, reducing the likelihood that important details would be left out. In addition, new systems that employ "deep knowledge" about causality and functional structure are in the development stages. Such systems will be able to function in realms where novel problems are frequent. Current expert systems are said to be "brittle" because they quickly fall apart when questions stray from the heart of their expertise. However, a mechanical engineering expert system using deep knowledge would be able to explain the operation and structure of any device, inferred from information on its physical design and materials.

It should also be pointed out that human experts are fallible. Their judgment is often clouded by issues unrelated to the problem at hand, and sometimes they simply overlook what a computer, in its heavy-footed thoroughness, would never miss.

One company using an expert system called PROSPECTOR to explore for molybdenum ore in the Cascade Mountains of Washington state discovered a deposit that may be worth as much as $100 million. The site was not one that had been identified by the company's human experts and had in fact been used as a dump site for tailings from a nearby dig.

PROSPECTOR was developed by knowledge engineers at SRI International in Palo Alto, who mined the expertise of scientists with the U.S. Geological Survey. The system is used commercially to evaluate the resource potential of an area, identify possible ore deposits and select drilling sites for core sampling. It can be used to hunt for a variety or ores, including copper, lead, zinc, molybdenum, and uranium. There are, however, still a number of economically significant ores that are not included in PROSPECTOR's knowledge base. In tests, the program consistently agreed with the assessments of human geological consultants.

THE MARKET FOR EXPERTISE

Despite the limitations imposed on expert systems, the number of fields in which they are proving their usefulness is already large and still expanding. A 1983 survey turned up more than 80 existing expert systems. The nature of their expertise ranges from diagnosis to design.

Medicine. Perhaps the widest variety of applications can be found in medicine. In addition to MYCIN, there are programs that can diagnose disease based on the symptoms and test results presented. The CADUCEUS system, under development at the University of Pittsburgh, will eventually have a knowledge base that encompasses all of internal medicine, roughly 100,000 disease-symptom associations. Other programs have been designed to determine causal relationships among medical phenomena. Another, called VM, is dedicated to the task of monitoring patient respiration in intensive care units. VM provides a summary of the patient's status, recognizes unusual events, and gives advice on the adjustment of the mechanical ventilator based on an assessment of the patient's progress.

Data Analysis. The first expert system, DENDRAL, falls into this category, as does PROSPECTOR. A system called CHRYSALIS, developed at Stanford, uses crystallographic data to analyze the structure of proteins. Several programs have been devised to assist in the drilling of oil finds, where getting expertise into the field when it's needed is often a problem. As new wells are drilled, core samples are analyzed for the presence of hydrocarbons and to determine how close the drill bit is to oil-bearing rock strata. More importantly, the geologist must ensure that the pressure in the well is sufficient to prevent a costly and dangerous blowout.

Symbolic Analysis. The inputs for these systems are not numerical in a strict sense, though they are often quantified in the same way that MYCIN assigns a numerical certainty to its data. For example, TECH is a system designed by the Rand Corp. for the U.S. Navy that rapidly analyzes enemy threats to a naval task force. The nature of the threat itself is symbolic—a torpedo, say—but the severity of the threat may be quantified and analyzed numerically. Similar systems have been designed for the analysis of digital and electrical circuits. Devices such as resistors and capacitors are symbolic, but the voltages that pass between them are numerical.

Planning. It's a fairly short step from analysis to planning. The Jet Propulsion Laboratory uses data gathered from previous interplanetary flights to plan future flybys with a system called DEVISER. In biology, the MOLGEN expert system helps to guide researchers through the intricate steps of gene splicing and aids in the analysis of an organism's DNA sequence. A particular goal, such as the creation of a bean plant with the vining characteristics of hops, can be fed to MOLGEN, which will then devise one or more hypothetical plans for engineering such a plant. Other systems have been developed to help industries make the most effective use of robotics and to schedule individual jobs in a way that makes optimum use of workers and machinery.

Education. This is one area that's only beginning to be tapped. Artificial intelligence in the pursuit of effective education has the potential to go far beyond the video arcade style programs and simple drills that pass for instructional materials today. Teaching expert systems can make an assessment of a student's progress and guide the presentation of new information accordingly. One of the most active companies in this field is Bolt, Beranek & Newman of Cambridge, Massachusetts. They have developed programs for everything from training electronic trouble-shooters to illuminating the causes of rainfall and teaching steamship pilots how their ship's propulsion system works.

Intelligent Assistant. The computer may someday become everybody's Machine Friday. So far, though, systems have only been designed for situations in which the cost of expertise, and the price of failure, is high. Radiology, nuclear power plant configuration, cancer chemotherapy, and battlefield management have all proven to be fertile fields for expert systems development. Another, surprisingly, is computer sales. The pace of technological development is swift in the computer industry, and competition forces constant price and product adjustments. Because few in the sales force can keep up with all the changes, as many as 25 percent of the orders for large mainframe systems are in error. Salesmen write orders for systems that can't be built or their bids carry a higher price than was necessary. In order to solve such problems, Digital Equipment Corporation, with researchers at Carnegie-Mellon, designed an expert system called XSEL that would check orders at the time they were written. The company estimates that its savings from such a system will amount to $100 million per year.

All expert systems, at least those of the present generation, share certain weaknesses that will continue to limit their use. Perhaps the most significant of these is the amount of time required not only to construct the knowledge base but to maintain it. Knowledge in a particular field changes over time, quite rapidly in some cases. In order to update the system, a knowledge engineer intimately familiar with the structure of the knowledge base must be available, which adds to the cost of the system itself. Some experiments with knowledge acquisition are showing promise as a way of allowing an expert to input knowledge into the machine directly, rather than relying on an AI specialist. But many of these systems are not yet user friendly, and some require a knowledge engineer just to operate them effectively. Properly framing a question and recognizing appropriate responses can be almost as difficult as building the system in the first place.

Some knowledge is next to impossible to represent in a machine. In a rule-based system, for example, not every fact lends itself to expression as an if-then representation of condition and consequence. There is also the difficult necessity of using one of the highly stylized AI languages in describing a problem and interpreting results. Although the programs use natural language in a limited sense, some adjustments on the part of the human user are still required to communicate with the machine. Explanations of the reasoning process can take similarly stylized forms and are often limited by the depth of the knowledge base.

AI researchers have used the word "brittle" to describe expert systems because their reasoning process tends to break down in dealing with problems on the fringe of their areas of expertise. There's no such thing as reasoning by analogy in a machine. It cannot apply the data in its knowledge base to a different, though related, class of problems. This means that the functional domain of a system tends to be quite narrow, or in a few cases such as Caduceus, broad but fairly shallow. In addition, few expert systems have the ability to recognize when a problem is taking them outside their narrow domain. As a result, even some of the best systems come up with wrong answers for problems just outside their scope of knowledge.

FIFTH GENERATION

The Fifth Generation machine that the Japanese hope to build will attempt, in part, to solve the problems that plague expert systems through sheer size and power. They expect to construct knowledge bases at least as large and varied as the Encyclopedia Brittanica and to sort through that information in real time using a parallel logic processing engine 1,000 times faster than any now available. Some kind of intelligent interface, allowing humans to communicate with the machine either orally, in writing, or by means of images or symbols, is also planned. The Japanese also hope to develop a specialized language processor that will translate English to Japanese and vice versa, quickly and accurately. Unlike the monolithic mainframes that are the stereotype of a large computer, the Japanese machine will be built of several different components wired together like a home stereo system.

By mid-1984, the construction of two prototype components had been achieved. The first was a logic processor similar to the American LISP machines but using the Prolog language. The Japanese were the first to extend Prolog in such a way that it could be used as a primary programming language, rather than simply as a descriptive language for knowledge base operations. Processing speeds of 30,000 logical inferences per second (known in computer jargon as *lips*), have been reported for the prototype inference machine, which operates as a sequential computer. To achieve the much higher rates of 100 million to 1 billion lips, some kind of parallel processing will have to be employed. Data-flow and reduction architectures are considered by the Japanese as their primary prospects for parallelism.

The completion of a relational database machine, the other prototype component, marked a significant worldwide achievement, because it was capable of access speeds 100 times greater than any similar machine then available. Part of the additional speed was achieved by hard-wiring much of the software directly into the machine. In essence, a relational database stores information as *relations.* A statement such as "Susan likes hamburgers," would be written as "likes (Susan, hamburgers)." A rule can also be expressed as part of the knowledge base: "Susan likes any object provided it contains cooked beef." The knowledge base can either be searched directly for specific matches, "Does Susan like hamburgers?" or through association, "Who likes hamburgers?"

Because the relationships between objects are stored in the knowledge base, they can be rearranged in new combinations in a wide variety of ways. This kind of associational thinking is characteristic of the human mind, as well, but in the machine it is guided by a complex mathematics called relational algebra. For example, suppose that a database contained information on personnel and payroll at a particular company, and it became necessary to develop a list of all employees who hadn't had a pay raise in the past year. A relational database could prune the search tree to include only that set of employees, while a conventional database would have to search through every employee's record sequentially. For AI applications, this kind of efficient search allows complex logical arguments and inferences to be built from simple facts and rules.

The third component of the Fifth Generation machine, the man-machine interface, had not yet been completed by the time this book went to press. In many ways, it is the most ambitious of the three. Understanding continuous speech and processing visual images has proven to be a much tougher challenge than "thinking." What the Japanese have done so far is to shrink the lead held by the United States in the early part of the decade. From this point on, progress toward their goals will require significant innovations to be delivered on schedule. Vision and speech reveal the subtle processes of mind more clearly than expert "thinking."

The human mind is fluid, mercurial, nonlinear, continuously making new connections and abandoning old ones.

In trying to extract meaning from life's abundance of sensory and factual information, the mind can suddenly reorder its perceptions and achieve deep understanding. It's reasonable to ask whether the expert system will ever be anything more than a sorcerer's apprentice, mimicking the tricks of its master with mixed results. Only time and further research will answer that question definitively, but in the meantime, mankind will gain an effective new set of tools for coping with the complexity of the computer age.

Chapter 10

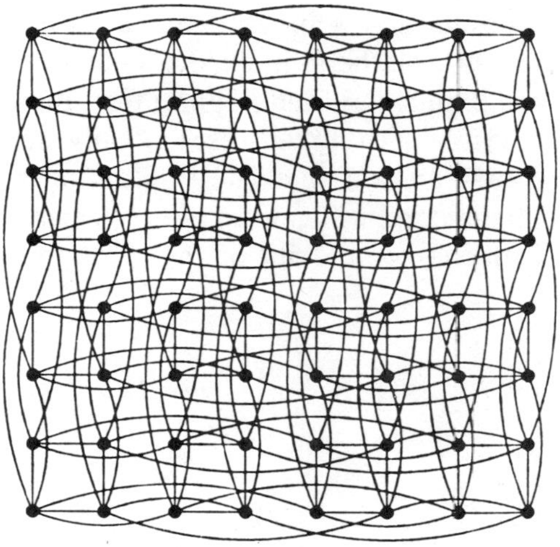

Vision

The irony (of vision) is that the brain is beating out computers with neurons that operate about a million times slower than silicon. The secret, of course, is in the wiring: The neurons are in there doing millions or billions of things simultaneously. Whereas computers, with a few exceptions, are still based on a serial, one-step-at-a-time architecture.

Dr. M. Mitchell Waldrop
in *Science* magazine

One of the oldest stories about the field of artificial intelligence involves vision. In the early 1960s, a professor at MIT (some say it was Minsky) assigned a student the problem of computer vision to solve as his summer project. No one ever relates exactly what happened to the hapless student, but this hoary tale, which has taken on the proportions of legend, is guaranteed to produce a wry smile in anyone who knows even a little about the complexities of vision.

Vision is one of those magical human feats that is performed effortlessly. To ask how it's done is like asking how the heart knows when to beat—it's automatic. The ability to survey a three-dimensional scene, identify objects and colors, notice changes, and extract other kinds of information has evolved over millions of years. For the most part, it's an unconscious process and full of mystery. How is it that a person looking at a picture of a horse knows to equate the image with the real, 3-D creature? Even the barest sketch of a horse can still be recognized. How does the mind know how to "complete the picture" if it is presented with an image of a horse's tail or a hoof? How do humans classify objects, knowing that a straight-back chair, an overstuffed chair, and a rocking chair are all part of the same chair family? Programming a computer to perform any one of these tasks in real time represents the frontier of research into computer vision systems.

The problem is data—not a shortage of it but an overwhelming abundance. Computers see through the eye of a television camera. An individual image is divided into tiny squares called picture elements, or *pixels*. The first step in vision processing is to assign a brightness value for each of these pixels. That, in essence, is the raw material of a digitized image. In a high-resolution system, the computer sees an array of 1,000 by 1,000 numbers, in a medium-resolution system, a 256-by-256 array. A new image flashes across a television screen 30 times a second, so that data from as many as 30 million pixels enter the computer's eye each second. At this stage of the process, the data is nothing but numbers unrelated to the image itself, except as a measure of brightness. The difficulty is in turning this mass of numbers into meaningful information about the objects in a scene.

EARLY ATTEMPTS AT VISION

In the 1950s, the first attempts at a limited form of computer vision were attempted using a technique called *pattern recognition*. The idea was to store in the computer's memory digitized patterns that served as archetypes against which new images were compared. Pattern recognition was essentially a statistical process that depended on numerical analysis of the brightness intensities in an image versus those of the pattern. Each and every pattern, or *template*, in the system's memory had to be compared to the unknown image and its degree of similarity calculated. The pattern that matched most closely was assumed by the machine to be the correct identification.

This approach was fairly successful when the number of patterns was kept to a minimum. A classic example is the optical character reader, which recognizes typed numbers and letters of the alphabet. The problem is that as the complexity of the images intensifies, the number of patterns explodes combinatorially. In addition, for many objects there is no generic pattern that will fit all or even most members of the class, such as rocking chairs, stuffed chairs, and straight chairs. Without first analyzing the data and pruning the search tree, pattern recognition becomes hopelessly bogged down. New techniques and faster processors have improved the effectiveness of pattern matching systems to the point that they are used by the military for target detection, in archeology for the aerial identification of settlement sites, in medicine, and in factories for robot systems and automated quality control.

True computer vision systems which would understand complex scenes weren't attempted until the early 1960s. Seeing was assumed to be as straightforward a problem as thinking. Researchers initially approached vision processing intuitively in the belief that images could readily be separated into their constituent parts, which they termed *features*. A feature could be anything that a machine extracted from the raw data, such as the apparent direction of lighting, an object's reflectivity, and apparent edges. Much early work was devoted to defining object boundaries as a first step toward image understanding. The problem, they discovered, is that an object's boundary is much more a construct of the mind than a piece of physical reality. In many images, the boundary of an object is barely discernible from the background, such as a white sphere against a light-colored background. The fact that human beings see a sphere under such conditions is a result of the same unconscious assumptions that make optical illusions seem so persuasive.

In the 1970s, researchers decided to attack the problem from the opposite end, using knowledge to guide the analysis of an image. Underlying this approach is the assumption that "we see what we expect to see." In other words, learned concepts that are essentially unconscious govern the processing of visual data in the eye. Knowledge about such phenomena as gravity, how objects support one another, or how an object in the foreground can obscure one behind, was programmed into the machine. This enabled researchers to sidestep one of the problems that had plagued the feature extraction model—as the number of features increased, the amount of computation required grew combinatorially. While knowledge-directed vision reduced the need for feature extraction and other forms of image-level computation, it foundered upon two other obstacles. One was the difficulties of representing large bodies of knowledge in a computer. Successful systems had to limit the kinds of images processed to office scenes or simple worlds built of geometric blocks. The other was that the gap between raw brightness values and a conceptual object, like "chair," was often too great to bridge with the techniques then available.

MODELING BIOLOGICAL VISION

The trend in vision processing for the 1980s is toward a more direct modeling of the physiological processes that humans and animals rely on to see. Researchers in the biological sciences are just beginning to understand some of the mechanisms of sight, and others are still unknown. No one knows, for example, just how it is that the brain brings together images from each eye to give an impression of depth. What is known is that vision is an extremely intense problem computationally. It's estimated that the neurons of the visual cortex process data that, in a machine, would require on the order of 10 billion operations per second. The brain accomplishes this task with switches that are at best one-10,000th as fast as the newest silicon switches, making the achievement of vision seem all the more remarkable—and perhaps more remote. If machine vision comparable to that of man can ever be created, parallel computing will be at the core of it.

If any single individual can be said to have served as the von Neumann of vision, it would have to be the late David Marr of MIT. Virtually every paper on the subject cites his work, which was cut short at the age of 33 by leukemia. Marr was in large part responsible for turning the focus of vision research away from the purely cognitive approach and back toward a modeling of animal vision systems. His book, *Vision*, published posthumously in 1982, brought together many of the ideas he and his colleagues had pioneered at MIT in the late 1970s using research results from the neurosciences. The book has been called "an ambitious and exciting attempt to develop an intellectual basis for vision research . . . a coherent theory of animal vision."

Much of Marr's work involved processes that precede the cognitive part of vision, which depends on knowledge of objects and the world. This preunderstanding stage has been called "early vision" by researchers. Work in this area has been based on a reexamination of the biological hardware that carries signals from the eye to the brain. The approach involves treating neurons as a highly specialized kind of electronic device and trying to discover the sequence of steps, or algorithms, that comprise vision. Researchers are well aware of the physical differences between neurons and transistors, but conceptually, in the processing of visual data, certain parallels can be drawn.

For example, the measurement of light intensity in a scene is performed in the human eye by rod cells and cone cells, and the scene is turned upside-down and flattened to a two-dimensional map on the retina. It is the brain that turns the scene right-side up and restores the sense of depth. In a computer, the brightness measurements are made by solid-state electronic sensors. But instead of the 100 million such cells found in the human eye, there are between 50,000 and 1 million pixels in a computer eye.

Researchers have concluded that vision is not the result of a single process but many processes, some working in parallel and others using the results of prior processes in sequence. A completely general vision system would have to incorporate all of those processes. There are roughly five stages of computer vision that are necessary to build an understanding of a particular scene.

—The first might be called the measurement phase, in which the brightness of each pixel is assigned a value and any nonimage noise picked up by the sensor is removed.

—The second phase is two-dimensional analysis. Brightness measurements are contrasted to find edges, where intensity levels change markedly, which may or may not correspond to the boundaries of an object. Other features, such as texture, transparency, and the apparent direction of illumination are calculated. Separate images used to simulate stereo vision are matched and fused.

—The third phase is three-dimensional analysis. Disparities between the fused stereo images are calculated to determine depth. Shape is deduced from shading and texture. The reflectance, or *albedo*, of different parts of the scene is determined. Motion in any part of the scene is identified by comparison with previous images.

—The fourth phase involves grouping different parts of the scene into physically meaningful subsets. This is the stage that immediately precedes object recognition. In essence, the computer groups elements of the scene that seem to go together. Surfaces and volumes are identified in much the same way that an artist sees the human form as an aggregate of cones, cylinders, and other geometric shapes. At this point, the numerical data of previous stages is converted into elementary symbols.

—The final phase is understanding. Objects are identified by name based on programmed knowledge about the world from which the scene is drawn. In addition to simple physical descriptions of objects and environments, knowledge of causality, human intention, and convention is important to achieve the correct interpretation of a scene.

Each of these stages, with the exception of the first, involves significant amounts of computation. Animals nevertheless seem to manage it with a degree of speed and grace that is humbling. One researcher successfully built a robot cart with vision sufficient to allow it to navigate around a room. The machine would determine its position, move forward about three feet, and then stop to recalculate its position—a step that took an average of 15 minutes. It's been estimated that a similar cart moving at walking speed would need to process incoming data at a rate of 1 billion to 10 billion instructions per second. Not only do animals, many of them with fairly simple nervous systems, recognize objects almost instantly, but they react to them quickly in often complex ways. So far, no machine has ever been built that can recognize and interpret images in a completely general way. The amount of computation and knowledge such a system would require has, up to now, been prohibitive.

STEREO VISION

Because of the difficulty in designing a complete vision processing system, researchers have focused on developing subsystems, or modules, of the overall vision process. One of these is stereoscopic vision, which allows depth to be deduced from the slight variations in a pair of two-dimensional images. In animals, the two eyes view the world from slightly different angles. The same point in a given scene appears on the retina of each eye at a slightly different point relative to the center of vision. The brain performs a complex calculation based on this disparity to arrive at a subjective measurement of depth. At first glance, it might seem that the problem could be solved by mathematics no more complicated than trigonometry, but there's a catch.

David Marr and a colleague at MIT, Tomaso Poggio, published a paper in 1979 that sets out in detail their "Computational Theory of Human Stereo Vision." They found that there are basically four steps in the process of deriving depth from a pair of images. First, a particular point is identified in one of the images, and then that same point is found in the other image. Their positions are measured and, based on the disparity between them, the depth of that point in the scene is calculated. The latter part of the problem is a straightforward trigonometric calculation of the kind that computers perform with ease.

Most of the difficulty lies in the first part. All the computer has to work with at this stage is an array of light intensity measurements. Suppose, for example, that a given patch of surface reflects light differently in each image, or that two widely separated points in the image happen to have the same intensity. Both are common situations in the real world, which suggested to Marr and Poggio that another factor was involved.

Rather than simply trying to match intensities, the researchers used mathematical techniques to extract more information, more reliably, from the raw intensity values. They noticed that significant features in an image are often marked by sharp changes in intensity. These are the landmarks in a scene that the eye picks up naturally. Marr and Poggio developed an algorithm that would allow a machine to accomplish the same task. It starts by measuring changes in brightness levels from pixel to pixel across the entire image. Where the change happens sharply, the program locates an *intensity edge*. A second mathematical operation measures how fast the brightness levels change, so that only those areas in which the change occurs most rapidly are emphasized. The effect is to map significant features in each image, making it easier to make the match required for depth calculations.

This approach works best in the laboratory, where the amount of visual "noise" can be carefully kept to a minimum. In the real world, surfaces are often corrupted by dirt or other minor intensity variations. (A houndstooth coat would be disaster.) To solve the problem, Marr and Poggio developed a filtering technique that mimics the function of the cells in the brain that pass signals from the retina to the visual cortex. The filter relies on a complex statistical function that smooths out the image and eliminates most of the noise. The process requires the calculation of a weighted average for each pixel and its neighboring pixels. In the brain a similar process enhances contrast between bright and dark areas in an image.

The filtering performed by Marr and Poggio's algorithm is computationally intense. It requires on average 1,000 operations to be performed for each pixel in an image. In a high-resolution vision system, that would necessitate a computation rate of 30 billion operations per second for real-time processing. Other researchers at MIT have designed a special-purpose machine capable of performing the filter calculations at the rate of about 1 billion per second, but that's still slow compared to the performance of human nerve cells. It also involves only a single subset of the entire vision process, which may require dozens of similarly computation-intensive operations. Marr and Poggio suggested their filtering algorithm as a necessary first step to remove noise and extract key information, providing a basis from which other algorithms, perhaps functioning in parallel, can proceed.

FEATURE EXTRACTION

In most vision systems, before the actual calculations are carried out to determine depth, a process called *feature extraction* takes place. This is still two-dimensional analysis, which is characteristic of the second phase of vision processing. Intensity edges uncovered during the measurement and filtering phase are mapped into the computer's memory, and significant features—surfaces, edges, and shadows, for example—are named and given a value. Marr called this the "primal sketch" because it precedes even the most basic identification of shapes. The goal of this stage is to determine the orientation of objects relative to the light source, which in turn allows contours and textures to be derived.

Further analysis of features leads to the identification of shapes from shading and textures in the primal sketch. The relative depth of points within the image has not yet been computed, so Marr decided to call this stage the 2 1/2-D map.

At this point, all available data about the features in the image—depth, surfaces, patterns, movement, texture, and so on—is combined in an attempt to group them into logically related patterns. These patterns are then matched against the patterns of known objects stored in the computer's knowledge base. Often in actual practice there is considerable interaction between different parts of the process. The grouping of features may be guided by plausible object patterns, which in turn are refined by the grouping algorithm.

Governing the entire vision process are rules that limit the search at each stage. These limits are called *constraints*, and there are some indications that constraints operate in human, as well as computer, vision. For example, when looking at a perspective drawing, it's almost impossible not to perceive depth in it. The eye is constrained to see depth when the lines in a picture all lead off into the distance. Similarly, skillful shading gives a definite sense of volume and shape in three dimensions. The artist M.C. Escher was a master of manipulating the mind's visual constraints to create skillful optical illusions.

Constraints in computer vision provide general rules of perception. In Marr and Poggio's stereo vision algorithm there are two constraints: one, that a given point on a surface has one unique location; and two, that variations in depth are generally smooth. The first constraint allows the machine a degree of certainty in matching points in a pair of binocular images; that is, there's only one correct match. The second constraint enables the computer to distinguish surfaces. Sharp variations in brightness then become indicative of surface boundaries. The effect of these constraints is to simplify the world by eliminating certain exceptions to the rules. It's easy to think of real-world objects that would violate the constraints, like a zebra. But all of the algorithms developed for computer vision have to make use of some kind of constraints.

In deducing shape from an object's shading, the constraints for stereo vision are employed, as well as two others: one, that the brightness of a point on an image corresponds to its position relative to the source of illumination; and two, that the direction of illumination can be determined from information about several points given to the program.

The first constraint limits this algorithm, in effect, to use only in carefully controlled situations. With it a robot might be able to sort parts on an assembly line, but the illumination would have to be ideal and no part could rest on top of another one. Sorting parts in a bin using this algorithm would be impossible. Painted surfaces, shadows, and more than one source of illumination are ruled out by this constraint.

The second constraint provides a starting point for the algorithm, which is based on a process called *relaxation*. It's perhaps easiest to conceive of relaxation in geometric terms. The starting point is a two-dimensional array of brightness measurements in which a few boundary points are known. The goal is to find the best approximation of the object in three dimensions. In concrete terms, the two-dimensional array could be thought of as a piece of plastic film laid over a three-dimensional object such as a pie tin. In this case, all of the points where the plastic touches the tin are given to the computer, all others are unknown. Imagine that the pie tin has been heated, causing the plastic film to gradually melt, or relax, toward a solution in which the plastic conforms to the shape of the tin. In the computer, relaxation involves repeated averaging of brightness values for each pixel and its neighbors, proceeding from knowns to unknowns, just as heat caused the plastic film to relax from the known points, on the edge, to an approximation of the tin's actual three-dimensional shape. Relaxation is also used in analyzing texture, motion, and contours and even in assigning object labels to the elements in a scene. It's a purely local process, lending itself readily to implementation with a large number of processors wired in a nearest-neighbor communication network.

PARALLEL ARCHITECTURES FOR VISION

Computer vision researchers are working on a wide variety of parallel architectures. Another widely used vision processing algorithm that has been developed in parallel as a neural net is the Hough transform. This algorithm dates back to 1962, when P. V. C. Hough patented a device for analyzing tracks photographed in a bubble chamber, a device used for detecting the paths of charged particles through a superheated liquid. The algorithm filtered noise from data using a voting process. Features receiving the most votes are retained. The voting may involve complex interactions among the units in the image, requiring a substantial amount of computation. However, when the complexity of the voting process is expressed as a hard-wired communication network among many processors, all of the voting can be accomplished in a single time sequence.

As research into new architectures and VLSI chip design proceeds, it's inevitable that more efficient vision processors will be developed that will more closely resemble the structure and functional processes of the human vision system. One promising prospect was announced at the National Conference on Artificial Intelligence in 1983, when Scott E. Fahlman and Geoffrey E. Hinton of Carnegie-Mellon and Terrence J. Sejnowski of Johns Hopkins University described their Boltzmann Machine. The machine is named after an Austrian physicist named Ludwig Boltzmann (1844-1906), whose research on gas thermodynamics led to the field of statistical mechanics. The connection the researchers discerned between the behavior of gases, processors, and neurons inspired them to name their machine after Boltzmann.

The design resembles the structure of the brain in the sense that it is comprised of a large number of simple processors, each of which is connected to hundreds of others. A neuron, by comparison, may be connected to as many as 10,000 other neurons. Each processor is either on or off at any given moment. The communication links between processors are assigned positive or negative numerical weights. A change of state in a processor, from on to off or vice versa, can occur when the sum of the weighted inputs from all other active processors exceeds a specified threshold level. A similar phenomenon occurs in neurons, which fire only when stimulated beyond a threshold point. In dim light, for example, fewer neurons fire (and those at a slower rate) than in bright light.

The Boltzmann machine is also unique in that it operates with uncertainty. Just because a threshold is passed, there's no guarantee that a processor will change its state. A probabilistic decision rule is applied: If the sum is exactly equal to the threshold, the processor will change its state half the time; if it is above the threshold, it will probably, but not always, change state; if it is below the threshold it will probably not change state. Studies of the brain have shown a similar absence of programmed certainty. In a typical computer, by contrast, the switching of each transistor is determined—directly or indirectly—by the programmer.

The probabilistic behavior of the processors in the

Boltzmann machine provides the connection to its namesake. The switching of the network as a whole can be analyzed with the same statistical formulas that describe the thermodynamic motion of gases. In studying the behavior of a machine with thousands of processors, it's no longer important to know whether any individual processor is on or off. Instead, the state of the system as a whole can be determined and represented by a number that behaves like potential energy in a physical system. Potential energy is a concept that physicists use to describe stored energy. A flashlight battery contains potential energy, as do gasoline, a tightly wound spring, and a piece of uranium ore. Even a ball at the top of a ramp has potential energy, which would be turned into kinetic energy in rolling down the ramp.

The operation of a Boltzmann machine in processing images can be compared to dropping a carton of ping-pong balls onto an uneven floor to determine its shape. Each processor in the machine is represented by a ping-pong ball. First, the machine randomizes its state—i.e., the bottom of the carton opens and the ping-pong balls are falling freely. As the balls hit the floor, they interact with its irregularities and with each other. In the machine, processors are summing the weights of their interconnections, trying to decide whether to turn off or on. As the motion of the ping-pong balls subsides, the potential energy of the system reaches a minimum. The summing of values in the machine is complete, and the image is expressed as an array of 1's and 0's (on and off processors) and the weights between them. The weights represent the position of each ball relative to its neighbors. Knowing the position of any one ball is useless, but all of them together form a good approximation of the floor's uneven pattern. Similarly, all of the processors together with their weighted interconnections provide a numerical pattern that closely approximates an image and identifies key features.

The machine then tries to match the image pattern against others stored in its memory, similar to a pattern recognition system but with one important difference. The weighted connections between processors act as constraints on the system, signaling the relative importance of features in a scene and their relation to one another. In trying to match a particular pattern, the machine adds together the current state of all processors (1's and 0's) and the interprocessor weights and compares the sum to that of the original image.

The difference between the two sums corresponds to the machine's potential energy. Processing proceeds until the pattern stored in memory is found that best matches the input image, meaning that the machine's potential energy is again at a minimum.

This kind of distributed memory resembles more closely the organization of the brain. No particular neuron, or processor, is critical. It also enables the machine to identify a horse, say, from only a part of the pattern, such as an image of a horse's head. It can also solve another problem that has baffled other vision systems, that of extracting a part from the whole, such as distinguishing the horse from its rider. Even if there are several patterns that more or less fit the weighted combination of features, the machine settles on the best of them.

The researchers believe that their machine, which is still in the early stages of development, has a natural capacity for learning. When input signals don't match the pattern that is already represented in memory, the weights and unit states can be modified slightly to make a better fit with the outside world.

The brain makes use of this kind of learning in the process of generalization. As repeated examples of an object are presented, each slightly different from the others, a sense of the essential characteristics of that object develops. In other words, the constraints are gradually refined into a more and more general stereotype. An arch, for example, may be rounded in the Byzantine manner, peaked in the Gothic style, or squared off in the ancient Greek fashion. In analyzing each of these, a human observer quickly grasps that the shape of the area enclosed by an arch is less relevant than the fact that it consists of two vertical elements somehow capped or brought together at the top.

The biggest problem facing the researchers in developing the hardware for the Boltzmann machine is wiring. While a single neuron has as many as 10,000 connections to other neurons, a state-of-the-art microprocessor is limited to about 64 connections. To a certain extent, the problem could be solved by etching the wires directly onto a silicon wafer, but the difficulties of wafer-scale integration are still too formidable for economical manufacturing. It remains to be seen just how many processing units are needed for a vision system based on the Boltzmann design.

Commercial vision systems have reached the point where they can guide robots through limited tasks, such as spot welding or parts sorting, in carefully illuminated environments. As robotics technology develops, no doubt vision systems will be refined to better enable them to perform a variety of tasks. The military has commissioned the development of an unmanned robot scout with vision processing capabilities sufficient for it to navigate in unfamiliar territory at a speed of 40 mph. There's also a strong military demand for systems capable of interpreting satellite photographs and other visual data that come flooding in to various U.S. intelligence agencies from around the globe.

It seems likely that as computers evolve from number crunchers into knowledge systems, their ability to interpret image data will improve as well. Because the processing of images is so computer-intensive, it's probable that machines will be designed purely for vision and used as an adjunct to a more generalized parallel machine. New ways of thinking about the vision process may lead to more efficient algorithms that will require less computer power to operate effectively. But whether a machine with the visual acuity of the human eye will be developed within this century is an open question. It may turn out that keen vision, rather than reason or language, proves to be one of the key factors distinguishing man from machine.

Chapter 11

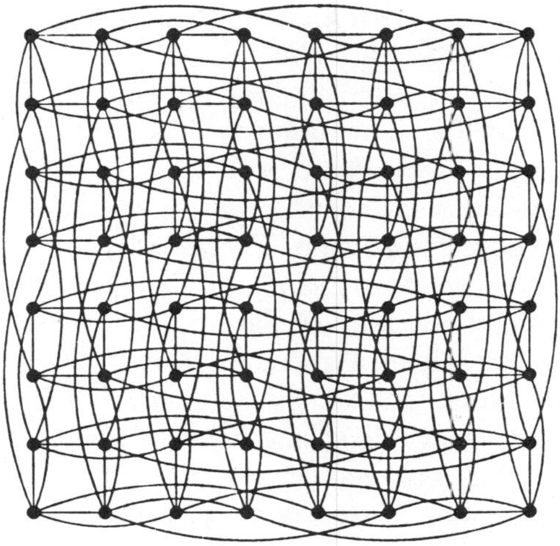

Understanding Language

The medium for human interaction with computers is often called a language, but programming computers to understand ordinary natural language is one of the most difficult challenges now facing the discipline of artificial intelligence.

David L. Waltz
in *Scientific American*

The problem of programming computers to understand spoken language has proven as difficult a problem as vision. Some progress has been made in processing sounds into digital patterns that are intelligible to the machine, but a genuine understanding of language remains elusive. Like vision, language is inextricably bound to the inner workings of the human mind, both conscious and unconscious. There is much that is still a mystery about the way people acquire and use language, which makes programming a machine to do the same that much more difficult. But unlike vision, in which the difficulty arises in sorting through an overabundance of data, the processing of speech suffers from the opposite problem.

LIMITED SUCCESSES

The goal of computer researchers in the field of speech processing is a machine that can carry on a conversation with anyone on any topic. That they haven't even come close to succeeding despite more than 30 years of effort is an indication of the complexity of the task. Limited success has been achieved by training a program to understand the speech patterns of a particular individual. But whenever someone new uses this type of system, it must be retrained. Such systems are said to be *speaker dependent*, and most commercially available speech recognition devices fall into this category. A few are designed to function independently of an individual's prestored speech patterns, but because the search needed for each word is more extensive, these are limited to small vocabularies of 100 words or less.

An additional crutch is required by most current systems. Between each word, a speaker must insert a small but definite pause. This helps the computer to distinguish between the end of one word and the beginning of the next. Without it a pair of phrases like, "He rows" and "Heroes" can't be distinguished by their patterns. The insertion of a tiny moment of silence between words marks the difference between *isolated word recognition* and *continuous speech recognition* systems. The former is easier for the computer but can seem cumbersome to a user. Try reading aloud at a normal pace, being careful to insert short pauses between words. Not easy, is it? Continuous speech slurs words together, often producing strikingly different sound patterns for the same word in different contexts.

PROCESSING STRATEGIES

The task of understanding speech can be divided into two distinct processes, similar to those required for vision. The first stage is signal processing. A word or phrase is spoken into a microphone, which produces an analog electrical signal. The analog signal is digitized, converted into binary 1's and 0's, and fed into the computer. Often some preprocessing of the signal, such as filtering out noise, is required. Then the binary strings are broken into smaller subunits that can be matched against sound patterns stored in the machine's memory. The subunits may be based on phonemes, syllables, or entire words. A problem arises in the fact that even the most basic elements of language, phonemes, are partially based on perception. For example, English-speaking people make a small puff of air when pronouncing a word like "pin," but not when saying "spin." The distinction is ignored by a human listener, but the two sounds generate different patterns in the computer. The machine has to have a way of coping with variation, not only between speakers but between sounds spoken differently by the same speaker. A second stage of processing, based on knowledge, is required.

Various strategies for second-stage processing have been devised over the past two decades. The pattern-matching process may be guided by grammatical rules, by knowledge of word meanings and word order, by real-world scripts, or by all three. What's clear is that signal processing and pattern matching are insufficient tools for understanding language. Context can make all the difference. When a casual acquaintance says, "Let's have lunch sometime," it may mean something entirely different than when a close friend says the same thing. Distinguishing among homonyms—words like "there," "they're," and "their"—is impossible without some reference to meaning. Similarly, a word like "potted" can mean something completely different when applied to a human instead of a plant.

No one knows the precise process that humans use to comprehend language. Studies of how children acquire language have led to several different hypotheses but little in the way of consensus. As with the study of artificial intelligence in general, the field of speech understanding has divided into two camps: the scientists and the engineers. The engineers are satisfied with a functional definition of language understanding that requires only that a machine make an appropriate response. The scientists, less interested in immediate results, are searching for the mechanisms of mind that are involved in language in the hope that they will shed light on the nature of human intelligence.

LANGUAGE AS CODE

When researchers first set out to design programs that could understand language, it was assumed that words were little different from the codes of the Enigma machine that the competitor Colossus was used to crack. In 1949, the director of natural science for the Rockefeller Foundation, Warren Weaver, proposed that computers be used for "the solution of worldwide translation problems." Weaver compared his efforts in translating Russian into English to the process of decoding a message encrypted in "strange symbols." He suggested that a computer could be programmed as an automated dictionary, a translation machine, in effect. Each word of the language to be "decoded" would be translated into an equivalent English word, and then the words would be rearranged into the proper order for English grammar. Naturally, Weaver was aware that some words are idiomatic, essentially untranslatable, and that the meaning of others varies according to context, but those words were considered exceptions to the rule.

By 1954 the field had matured to the point that a journal, *MT* (for Machine Translation) was founded and reports of breakthroughs began to appear in the press. This was during AI's first golden age, when everything seemed possible. It soon became clear, however, that the results of machine translation often needed more translation than the original. A. G. Oettinger wrote the first Russian-English translation program in the mid-1950s. For words that couldn't be translated directly, it offered a variety of possible choices, set here in parentheses: "(In, At, Into, To, For, On) (last, latter, new, latest, lowest, worst) (time, tense) for analysis and synthesis relay-contact electrical (circuit, diagram, scheme) parallel- (series, successive, consecutive, consistent) (connection, junction, combination) (with, from) (success, luck) (to be utilize, to be take advantage of) apparatus Boolean algebra."

The original: "In recent times Boolean algebra has been successfully employed in the analysis of relay networks of the series-parallel type."

Another AI legend that has circulated for many years but has no recorded source involves a machine translation from English to Russian and then back to English. The original phrase was "The spirit is willing but the flesh is weak." After a double dose of machine translation, the result was said to have been, "The vodka is good but the meat is rotten."

Ten years of intensive effort brought little improvement. By 1966, the National Research Council's Automatic Language Processing Advisory Committee recommended that virtually all funding for research on machine translation be withdrawn. As with problem solving and vision processing, it was becoming clear that knowledge was the key to language. Understanding was not simply a matter of knowing word definitions, it required an awareness of the world and of human purposes and emotions.

TEMPLATE MATCHING

At about this same time, Joseph Weizenbaum's program ELIZA was busy psychoanalyzing people at MIT. The success of ELIZA was not a result of any particular intelligence. The program just gave its patients a beguiling sense of being able to understand and communicate. ELIZA relied on a technique called *template matching* , which it used to recognize certain words. The inputs to both ELIZA and the translation machines were entered via teletype, rather than being spoken, but template matching has also been used in virtually all commercial spoken language systems.

Template matching is at the heart of efforts to develop a commercial voicewriter, essentially a dictation machine, that could accurately transcribe speech, provided the speaker pauses between words, as fast as the words can be spoken. The problem is to extract as much information as possible from the acoustic signal. A spoken word offers little more in the way of data than a measurement of sounds produced at frequencies between 300 and 3,000 hertz. Consonants tend to produce sounds in the upper frequency ranges, while vowel sounds are lower. The duration of each is also a factor. But basically the features that can be extracted are limited in their power to describe unique words. Variations in volume, pitch, and speed can affect the sound patterns produced by a spoken word. And even a small amount of noise can throw the system off, resulting in misidentification.

The first step in template matching is finding the silences that mark the beginning and end of each word. The next step is called *segmentation*. Each word is chopped up into as many as 100 smaller sound chunks. These chunks are then mapped onto a stored sound template that can be thought of as a curve on a graph. This mapping process allows the program to work around differences in sound, pitch, and speed that may influence the sound pattern. The distance between the curve representing the trial sound and that of the stored sound is measured and compared with the results of other template comparisons. The closest match is considered the correct word.

IBM has developed an isolated word recognition prototype system that is capable of distinguishing among 5,000 words in a business-oriented vocabulary with 95 to 97 percent accuracy. The system is speaker dependent. Training is relatively painless, however, requiring only that a speaker spend about 20 minutes repeating 100 specially prepared sentences. From the sentences, the machine extracts an individual's unique way of pronouncing roughly 200 *sound labels* that are the basic alphabet of sounds that the system uses.

Developed by the Speech Recognition Group under the direction of Frederick Jelinek, the system can process words as fast as they are spoken. The computational requirements are large, however. In order to perform the matching process, the system uses a small mainframe computer and three specialized array processors. IBM denies any plans to develop the system into a commercial product, but that could change. Jelinek says a PC-sized system could be feasible within five years. In the meantime, Jelinek and his colleagues plan to expand the system's vocabulary to 20,000 words and are hoping to improve its accuracy and reduce its vulnerability to noise.

CONTINUOUS SPEECH

A few continuous speech recognition systems have been developed commercially, but their vocabularies encompass fewer than 200 words. The problem with continuous speech is determining where one word ends and another begins. With a pair of words like "gas station," there's no distinguishable pause that separates the two words. These systems still rely on pattern matching, but each segment of the spoken phrase must be looked upon as a possible starting point for a new template, a new word. Each time a particular sound chunk matches the beginning of a template, the possible match must be recorded. When the entire phrase has been analyzed once all the way through, the machine goes back and compares templates chunk by chunk to determine which set of templates best matches the entire phrase. Because the number of possible matches turned up the first time through is large, the machine's vocabulary is limited.

As yet, no one has discovered algorithms in human language understanding, like those for vision, that can be used to guide the early stages of continuous speech processing. Even locating the end of one word and the beginning of another seems to require knowledge. People listening to an unknown foreign language have as much difficulty as computers in separating words. But just how much knowledge is needed and what kind is still a mystery. Children, for example, often start using words before they understand their meaning. A four-year-old child will often say that a green frog is some other color because the concept of "color" hasn't yet been understood. The child nevertheless uses color words like green, yellow, and red and is aware that they describe a certain attribute of surfaces.

The first major effort to coordinate the processing of sounds and knowledge for understanding continuous speech started in 1971 under the sponsorship of DARPA. The goal was a machine with a 1,000-word vocabulary that had a 10-percent error rate in processing speech over an extended period of time. Funding for the project was discontinued in 1976, but several demonstration systems were built. A system developed at Carnegie-Mellon, called Hearsay II, achieved the original goals but with certain restrictions. Sentences to be analyzed by the system could only come from a limited set that was stored as sound patterns in the machine's memory. Recognition was then accomplished with nearly the same matching techniques as those used to identify isolated words.

Since 1976, research on continuous speech recognition has been all but abandoned in this country. Only IBM is still sponsoring work on the problem at any significant level. Even that is being gradually phased out, however, in favor of the voicewriter prototype.

WAVES OF UNDERSTANDING

New work in the field of neuroscience may revive research into continuous speech processing. In a departure from the "feature extraction" model that has dominated for the past two decades, a small group of researchers has begun to analyze the patterns of electromagnetic waves produced in the brain. Instead of studying the behavior of individual neurons, brain-wave research emphasizes the cooperative action among millions of neurons. It's like the difference between listening to the entire orchestra and a single instrument. What these researchers have uncovered is a direct link between neuronal activity and cognition.

Robert M. Chapman and his colleagues at the University of Rochester reported in 1980 that spoken words with similar meanings produced similar brain-wave patterns—even if the words themselves had very different sound characteristics. Chapman also found that there were recognizable similarities in the patterns produced by a particular word in different test subjects. Other researchers have since determined that a verb, like "(he) rose," and a noun that sound the same, like "rose," produce strikingly different brain-wave patterns.

The implication of these results is that there may be a physiologically measurable component to what psychologists term associative thinking. Humans often use reasoning by analogy to put the unfamiliar in a familiar context. It's much easier, for example, to think of the functioning of the brain as an orchestra than to picture a 4-pound blob of neurons sending signals to one another. When the sound patterns for word stimulate the brain's auditory neurons, their response might be compared to a musical chord played by an orchestra. A word like "great" might cause the neuronal orchestra to strike an A-sharp minor chord that emphasizes the woodwinds. A synonym, like "good," would strike the same chord but emphasize the strings or brass instruments. In the brain, the word "great" produces a particular wave pattern. Synonyms like "good" and "fine" generate similar patterns that vary only in certain details. The individual neurons that are involved in the process of comprehending the word "good" may also be stimulated by "great" and "fine," but in a slightly different sequence or to a different degree. It remains to be seen whether this kind of processing can be modeled effectively in computer hardware or software.

UNDERSTANDING NATURAL LANGUAGE

Most of the work on the cognitive aspect of language understanding, as opposed to simple acoustic processing, has not involved speech as such but written language. Eliminating the ambiguities inherent in the spoken word is one way to simplify and clarify the problem; another is to simplify the world that a system must work within.

A world bounded by laboratory walls closely limits the amount of knowledge that a system must possess in order to respond to language. In other words, common sense—a simple phrase that encompasses an encyclopedia of real-world knowledge—is not a requirement in such a world. One of the first systems to embody this concept was SHRDLU, named after the 7th through the 12th most frequent letters in English. SHRDLU was written by Terry Winograd of Stanford for his doctoral thesis at MIT. Its universe was a simulated tabletop populated by simulated blocks. The machine could manipulate the blocks on the table using its simulated robot arm. It had a vocabulary of only 200 words.

SHRDLU was an expert system, in a sense, but its field of expertise extended only as far as an imaginary tabletop. It was an experiment not just in language understanding but in machine intelligence. The program used natural language to answer questions about its reasoning process put to it by the programmer. SHRDLU proved to be capable of explaining its actions, clarifying ambiguous questions,and dealing with human caprice. When asked for the fourth time during one trial why it performed a particular sequence of moves, the machine responded: "Because you asked me to." Language, reasoning ability, and knowledge were intimately linked in SHRDLU, and within its domain, the program performed extremely well. Unfortunately, enlarging SHRDLU's world required ever-greater amounts of processing power.

Most current expert systems are designed to use natural language in the manner of SHRDLU, which uses a fairly simple set of rules to parse, or diagram, sentences and assemble its responses in the proper order. One of the first so-called *parsing engines* was the Augmented Transition Network developed in the early 1970s at Bolt, Beranek & Newman. The system was designed to tease apart text and determine key relationships among words and sentences, as if grammar was a kind of code that could be unlocked by the machine.

One of the primary goals of researchers working on the problem of language understanding has been to find meaning apart from specific knowledge. A completely general language processing system that relies on knowledge of the world to achieve meaning would require enormous processing power and memory capacity. It's estimated that the human brain can hold the equivalent of 100 trillion bits of data in a lifetime. In children, language ability and world knowledge develop together, each stimulating the other. Linguistic researchers have found, however, that the process of acquiring and using language seems to have a definite set of rules independent of culture. AI researchers are working on the theory that a conceptual framework for computer language programs can be created that will limit the need for knowledge.

DEEP GRAMMAR

Noam Chomsky, a linguist at MIT, was one of the first to develop a deep grammar of formal, quasi-mathematical rules that govern word order, tenses, and word endings. His theories, published in the late 1950s, brought an unprecedented degree of precision to linguistics. They have since been at least partially discredited by subsequent observations of the way humans use language. Chomsky's theories were tried as the basis for various language processing programs. Their rigid formalism proved too cumbersome for practical use, however. In some ways, Chomsky's theories may have been too precise, leaving little leeway for the creativity that humans bring to language. What the theories gained in terms of precision was achieved at the expense of psychological realism.

More recent attempts to formalize grammar into a language comprehensible to computers have focused on the functional roles of words in a sentence. Lexical Functional Grammar, known as LFG, was developed by Ronald Kaplan and Joan Bresnan at the Xerox Palo Alto Research Center. Instead of creating precise formulae for word order and phrase structure, LFG identifies each word in terms of its role as part of a sentence's subject, predicate, modifying clause, and so on. Its language representations can nevertheless be manipulated mathematically. The Japanese have designated LFG as a prime candidate for use in the language processing component of their Fifth Generation machine.

Yet another approach to language understanding was pioneered in the early 1970s by Roger Schank of Yale University. Underlying this approach is the conviction that the deep structure of language is not simply a matter of grammar, but of ideas. Schank's model of language is built around a structure of general concepts called *semantic primitives.* In computer terminology, a primitive is akin to a sketch, defined only in its outlines. It's a kind of generalization. For example, one of Schank's semantic primitives is an ACT called PTRANS, and it includes all words that involve changing the physical location of an object: "walk," "lift," "move," etc. Other primitives are MTRANS, which includes all actions involving a transfer of mental information; ATRANS, all actions in which there is a transfer of possession of an object; and ATTEND, for actions involving the senses.

The database references these primitives in terms of what Schank calls *conceptual dependencies.* Their effect is to organize the processing of sentences according to certain expectations. For example, after analyzing a portion of a sentence as "Joe lifted," the program would expect to find an object named somewhere in the remainder of the sentence. Because the processing of a sentence is organized on the basis of meaning, rather than grammar, two differently structured sentences that mean the same thing are analyzed in a similar manner. By categorizing knowledge about motion, sensing, giving and receiving, and other actions into generalized primitives, Schank was able to reduce the total amount of knowledge that his program required.

LANGUAGE: A TOP-DOWN PROCESS

Schank's work suggests that human language understanding is at least partially a top-down process. Words serve as cues for retrieving stereotypes from memory and as evidence confirming or refuting the stereotype. This is in direct opposition to the early supposition of machine translation researchers that understanding was a result of the combination of word meanings according to grammatical rules. Taking Schank's work one step further, his colleagues at Yale have developed language processing programs based on Minsky's concept of frames and a similar notion, scripts. Both are more explicit statements of the relationships among objects and actions.

A *script* is actually a special kind of frame that outlines the background expectations most people have about a particular activity. Often in speaking, people use a kind of conceptual shorthand that omits a lot of background details that the listener is expected to know. For example, a person might tell a story like this: "Bill was on his way to work last Monday when he ran out of gas. He was an hour late, so the boss fired him." A person listening to this story, in order to make any sense out if it, would have to know that driving a car is one way of getting to work, that running out of gas stops the car and causes a delay, and that being an hour late can result in one's getting fired. A program interpreting the same story might consult a script involving transportation by car and another involving events in the workplace.

A program called FRUMP, written by Gerald F. DeJong II while a student at Yale, makes use of scripts in summarizing news stories transmitted by United Press International. FRUMP's database includes scripts for a wide variety of news events, such as accidents, earthquakes, elections, and diplomatic exchanges. DeJong has since moved to the University of Illinois at Urbana-Champaign, where he has been working to enable FRUMP to write its own scripts in response to novel situations, in effect, to learn. Suppose, for example, that the program was analyzing a story about an arson-for-hire scheme. Without a stored script relating directly to this kind of fraud, the program would consult a script on arson and another on insurance fraud. Linking the two, FRUMP develops an essentially new script that can then be stored for future reference.

PLAUSIBILITY, EMOTION, AND HUMOR

Even the best language understanding programs falter in interpreting certain kinds of expression. Lies, exaggeration, understatement, metaphor, and humor all depend on an ability to judge plausibility. Poetry and emotional language depend on knowledge and interpretive capacity far beyond that of any computer. In "Computer Power and Human Reasoning," Weizenbaum writes:

> "It may be possible, following Schank's procedures, to construct a conceptual structure that corresponds to the meaning of the sentence, 'Will you come to dinner with me this evening?' But it is hard to see—and I know this is not an impossibility argument—how Schank-like schemes could possibly understand that same sentence to mean a shy young man's desperate longing for love?"

Once again the question of machine intelligence boils down to this: Will additional knowledge alone be sufficient to create machines with near-human intelligence or will it be necessary to discover new methods and new models for language, vision, and problem solving before general purpose AI machines can be developed? There are fundamental differences at the physical level. The brain sends analog signals relatively slowly from neuron to neuron in a massively parallel, highly interconnected network of cells. The computer sends digital signals at blinding speeds through processor networks that are only beginning to exploit parallelism. Processing in the machine is essentially mathematical, while in the brain there is evidence of dozens of applications-specific processes that are far more efficient than any computer algorithm.

Knowledge of brain function at the cellular level is still sketchy and incomplete. Some studies have indicated, for example, that the brain "rewires" itself in response to new information. Even more vague is the connection between neuronal activity and "mind." As more is learned about the way the brain processes information, it's reasonable to assume that more efficient analogs will follow. The computer will also no doubt continue to provide a useful proving ground for the discovery and testing of general principles of intelligence.

If knowledge alone is the key to machine intelligence, the question becomes one of whether computers can be developed with the capacity to store and sort the trillions of bits of information that occupy human heads. Clearly this will require machines orders of magnitude faster and memories far larger than even the next generation of supercomputers.

Chapter 12

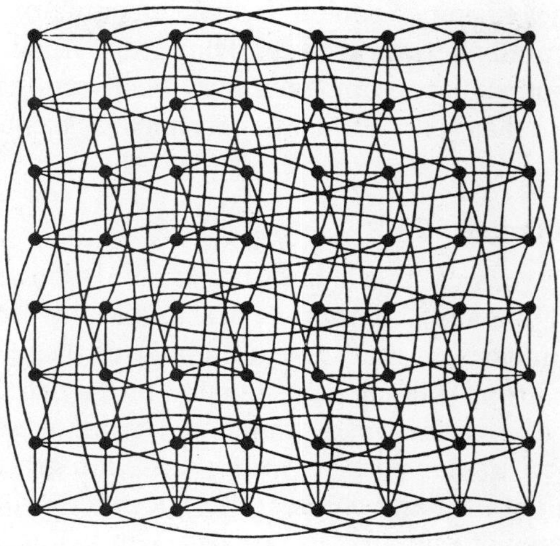

Technologies for the 21st Century

If we could provide biological inputs for digital computers, we would be marrying the best features of biology and electronics, carrying bionics to a logical end.

F. Eugene Yates
Director, Crump Institute for Medical Engineering, UCLA

In searching for new ways to make the computer smaller, faster and smarter, researchers have begun investigating exotic new materials and technologies, some of which may not find practical application until the next century, if ever. Machines that use beams of light, instead of electric current, to carry data; sensors made from living bacteria; memory units based on spectral holes that can store 1,500 volumes of the Encyclopedia Brittanica in an area the size of a fingernail; and computers with switches made from organic molecules are all seen as promising possibilities for the long-term future.

Two other technologies that were once considered promising and had actually proved workable in prototype have been pushed into an indefinite future by the success of parallelism in improving the performance of high-speed computers. The manufacture of machines based on wafer-scale integration and super-cooled Josephson junction switches seemed virtually certain as recently as 1984. Major research and development programs were drastically cut back in the latter part of that year, but neither technology has been abandoned completely.

WAVERING WAFERS

Of the two, wafer-scale integration (WSI) shows the most promise. Typically, computers are assembled from chips packaged in carriers that have a number of pins protruding from the bottom. The pins are pushed into a printed circuit board that carries the wiring connection from one chip to another in a particular pattern. Wafer-scale integration allows the equivalent of many chips, up to 100 microprocessors or 20 megabytes of memory, to be placed on a single sliver of silicon 4 to 8 inches in diameter. The number of pins, which tend to be a source of device failure due to both mechanical breakage and electrostatic discharge, is significantly reduced by WSI, improving system reliability. Also, the wasted space and long wires needed to interconnect chips on a circuit board are eliminated.

Commercial development of WSI has been inhibited by several problems that appear to have no ready solutions. One company, Trilogy Systems Corp., suspended its efforts to build a mainframe computer based on WSI circuits after the expenditure of more than $200 million on development. Even though the company succeeded in making functioning wafers, they could not be made at a price competitive with alternative technologies. Before WSI circuits can begin to replace smaller chip designs on a broad scale, several hurdles will have to be overcome:

Heat Dissipation. Because its circuits are so densely packed, a single wafer may generate 1,000 watts of heat. IBM and Trilogy have designed packages capable of that kind of high-efficiency cooling, but the number of wafer layers that can be interconnected is sharply limited. Both packaging systems are air-tight and use helium gas to draw heat away from the wafer to metal heat sinks. Some researchers have suggested that WSI circuits could be immersed in liquid nitrogen, at a temperature of 270 degrees Fahrenheit below zero. Such supercooled circuits must be protected against thermal shock, which could shatter a wafer.

Signal Quality, Noise and Power Distribution. The WSI circuit designed by Trilogy measured 6 centimeters on a side and had 2,000 pins distributed over its surface to provide both power and data access to the wafer's surface. Density here is also the key factor. If wires are spaced too closely, signals running down one can be induced in the other, creating a false signal (that is, noise). Similarly, too much power in too small an area leads to a phenomemon called *electromigration*, which causes the atomic structure of metal wires to deteriorate over a relatively short period of time.

Yield. In manufacturing smaller integrated circuits, defective chips can simply be discarded. But a wafer is too expensive to be thrown away, so some method of repairing defects has to be incorporated into the manufacturing process. It was the yield problem that ended Trilogy's WSI program. The company's early wafers had a low yield due to defects and short circuits. A number of good wafers were made, but they would have cost too much after factoring in the cost of the wafers that didn't work. The wafers were redesigned with a large number of redundant wires that could be used to avoid defects, thus raising the yield. Unfortunately, the long lines took up area on the wafer, resulting in longer signal paths that made the circuits too slow. Curing the problem would have taken more money and time than the company felt it could afford to invest.

Despite Trilogy's failure, other U.S. companies and several university laboratories are still involved in WSI development on a lesser scale, and several Japanese companies have introduced commercial products. NTT Musashino Electrical Communication Laboratory in Tokyo has introduced a 4-megabit read-only memory (ROM) wafer that holds the entire Kanji alphabet of more than 20,000 Japanese characters. For a variety of reasons, memory wafers appear to be the most attractive initial applications for WSI. Compared to logic circuits, memory requires only a few pins for data, control, and timing signals. The president of one U.S. firm involved in WSI circuit development, appropriately named Wafer Scale Integration Inc., believes that wafer memories might displace slower hard-disk memories for certain applications, providing a sizeable market.

JOSEPHSON JUNCTION JITTERS

The other technology that had once shown great promise for computers of the 1980s and beyond is the Josephson junction. This superfast, superconducting switch was named after British physicist Brian Josephson of Cambridge University, who received the Nobel Prize in Physics for his discovery. In the mid-1960s a technique for using the phenomenon discovered by Josephson to make a transistor-like switch was demonstrated. Josephson junctions looked good enough in the later 1970s that IBM had as many as 115 researchers working to develop a high-speed, general-purpose computer based on them. A small, working prototype was built with a 3.7 nanosecond cycle time—three times faster than the Cray 1—and there was talk of a machine with a 1 nanosecond clock. But by 1983, the team's progress had slowed to the point that IBM decided to sharply reduce its effort. Only a sixth of the original team continues to work on the use of superconductors in computers.

Two characteristics of the Josephson junction made it particularly appealing. One was its ultrafast switching time. Logic delays as small as 10 picoseconds (trillionths of a second) have been attained, which is 50 times faster than the fastest silicon transistor. Perhaps more significant, however, is its low power consumption and heat dissipation. Josephson junctions emit only one-thousandth as much heat as semiconductor transistors, which means that they can be packed more densely into a given area.

A Josephson junction is not a semiconductor transistor like those on silicon or gallium arsenide chips. Semiconductor transistors switch on or off based on an applied current that, above a certain threshold, changes the material from an insulator to a conductor. Josephson junctions are based on a phenomenon called *electron tunneling*. Two strips of a metallic superconductor, like lead, are separated from one another by a layer of insulating material. At the junction, the insulator thins to just a few nanometers (billionths of a meter). When the circuit is cooled to the temperature of liquid nitrogen, about −270 degrees Fahrenheit, a superconducting current of electrons will tunnel across the insulator with no voltage. Above a certain critical current, a voltage arises across the insulator, and it is no longer superconducting. A magnetic field generated by a current in an adjacent superconducting strip is used to switch the Josephson junction between its non-zero voltage and zero voltage states. This basic switching action can be used as the basis for logic and memory circuits.

Cooling electronic circuitry to near absolute zero has the advantage of allowing signals to travel at close to the speed of light. At room temperature, the fastest a signal can travel in a conductor is about one-fourth the speed of light. Even with instantaneous switching, a computer can only be as fast as the time it takes for a signal to travel the longest wire in the machine. However, supercooling circuitry places stresses on the materials that increase the likelihood of failure. Every time a device fails, the machine must be warmed to room temperature, repaired, and then cooled again. If in the process of cooling another device fails, the cycle has to be repeated, risking still another failure. To solve this problem, IBM switched from the lead alloy it had been using to make the bottom superconductor to another metal, niobium, which was more mechanically stable under the stress of repeated warming and cooling.

It was ultimately economics, not technological problems, that ended IBM's Josephson junction computer project. The rapid advance of silicon VLSI circuits, and the promise gallium arsenide holds for additional speed, trimmed the advantage of Josephson junction technology. IBM estimated that by the time a commercial computer could be built from Josephson junctions it would not be far enough ahead of its semiconductor competition.

Two other U.S. companies have significantly cut back on Josephson junction research. The Sperry Corp. closed a research center in Sudbury, Massachusetts, although some work on Josephson junctions is continuing at the company's Computer Systems Division in St. Paul, Minnesota. And Bell Laboratories cut back its program from a dozen to two or three researchers. However, the Japanese still have two large research programs devoted to the development of Josephson junction computers.

THE OPTICAL COMPUTER

Even more exotic, and faster, than a Josephson junction computer is a machine that uses beams of laser light to transmit signals and switch a device called a *transphasor*, a light-activated transistor. The only part of the machine that's ever been built and tested is the optical transistor. But by one estimate, a computer built of optical transistors would be capable of performing at the rate of a trillion operations a second.

Researchers at Heriot-Watt University in England have built a working transphasor using small crystals of a semiconductor material called indium antimonide. When light from a laser is shined on one side of the crystal, the light that passes out of the other side is either near zero or close to the intensity of the original beam. These two states are analogous to the on-off switching of a conventional transistor.

The behavior of the transphasor is based on a device invented in 1896 by two French physicists, Charles Fabry and Alfred Perot. In its most basic form, the device was made

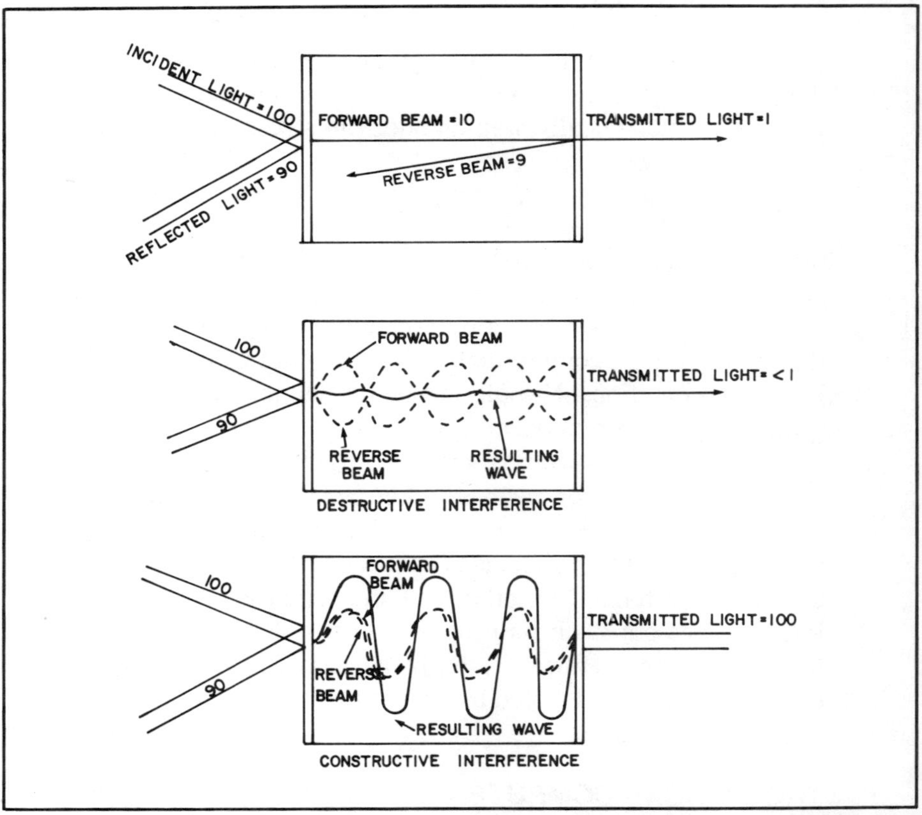

Fig. 12-1. The diagrams above show the effects of interference on a Fabry-Perot interferometer. Typically, only 10 percent of the light striking a side of the interferometer passes through, while the remainder is reflected. When the crests and troughs of beams reflected within the interferometer occur at opposite points, destructive interference virtually eliminates any transmitted light. But when the crests and troughs coincide, constructive interference leads to a transmitted beam equal in strength to the incident beam. In a transphasor, the kind of interference that results is determined by the intensity of the incident beam, rather than its wavelength.

by placing two flat mirrors parallel and facing each other with a space between. The Fabry-Perot interferometer, as the device is now known, was originally used to measure the wavelengths of various colors of light. Its usefulness in the making of optical transistors has to do with the interaction of light waves within the walls of the device.

In a transphasor, the walls of the crystal act as the mirrors. A beam of light hitting one side of the crystal is mostly reflected, but a small amount of light gets through to the interior. Inside the crystal, the light is reflected back and forth between its two interior walls. The effect is a bit like standing between two mirrors, with reflections within reflections within reflections off into infinity. An even smaller amount of light passes from the interior through the far wall; in most cases it's a fraction of a fraction of the original beam.

In certain circumstances, however, the reflected beams within the crystal combine, and the transmitted beam is equal in intensity to the original. This effect is the result of *constructive interference* among the light waves bouncing back and forth in the crystal. The crests and troughs of the light waves traveling in both directions in the crystal line up, producing an interior wave that can be up to 10 times the intensity of the original beam. Similarly, *destructive interference* causes the forward and backward beams to cancel each other out.

In the original Fabry-Perot interferometer, the interaction of the reflected light waves within the device was determined by the wavelength of the light and by the distance between the sides of the device. The difference between the interferometer and a transphasor is that the interaction of the light waves is determined by the intensity of the beam striking it. Unlike the interferometer, the transphasor has a special material between its two sides that changes its response to light according to the intensity of the beam striking it. The British researchers made use of indium antimonide, but other materials, like gallium aluminum arsenide and special dyes, have been used. The result is a device that can switch between two stable, readily distinguishable states.

In addition to speed, a computer built with transphasors would have two other distinct advantages over its electronic counterpart. One is that more than a single beam can be passed through a single transphasor. This kind of parallel processing at the device level is impossible with transistors, which can have only one input and one output. Another possibility is computers with more than two logical states. It's been demonstrated that transphasors made from certain materials will produce successively higher levels of transmitted light intensity as the beam striking the device increases in intensity. Instead of just yes or no, true or false, optical computers might be able to take in more of the shades of gray that constitute the real world.

STORING BITS IN HOLES

Laser beams and supercold temperatures are combined to create yet another computer technology that is under development for the 21st century. Researchers at IBM's research laboratory in San Jose, California, are using lasers to create spectral holes in a crystal. The holes store information not just as micron-size spots but in color, allowing as many as 1,000 different colored holes to be created, each holding a single bit of data, in the same physical space. The colors correspond to different wavelengths of laser light.

IBM researchers estimate that a spectral hole storage unit the size of a refrigerator, including lasers and apparatus for cooling the crystal to −270° F., could store all the books in the Library of Congress—approximately 5 billion pages of text. It would require as many as 1,000 of today's largest disk drives to store that much information.

The basic idea behind the technology, which IBM patented in 1978, is to dope a crystal with molecules that absorb light. When laser light of a specific color, or frequency, strikes these molecules, they seem to disappear. A hole is born. What happens in actuality is that the molecules become invisible to light of that color. The adjective "spectral" applied to the holes comes from the role color plays in making the molecules vanish.

Under ordinary circumstances, spectral holes are extremely delicate. The vibration of molecules in a crystal at room temperature is sufficient to destroy them. But scientists discovered that by supercooling the crystal to near absolute zero it remained quiescent enough for the holes to persist.

Another curiosity about spectral holes is that their size is only a tiny fraction of the wavelength of the laser light. Typically, a laser produces light with a wavelength of about

1 micron, but the holes are only a few molecules across with a diameter measuring about one-hundredth of a micron. Hitting just a few molecules with a laser is like shooting the wings off flies with a cannon. Normally, the beam would interact with millions of molecules in its path. But tiny variations in the crystal cause variations in the way individual molecules react to light. Points of stress form in the crystal where atoms, or a row of atoms, are missing, or where the wrong type of atom is present. When the dopant molecules are added, these local tensions cause each one to react to light in a slightly different way.

IBM's researchers have demonstrated that spectral holes can be used to store information. A system based on the technology would use variations in the intensity of a laser beam to encode either a 1, bright light, or a 0, dim light. The bright light creates a spectral hole, while the dim light does not. Then without moving the beam, its frequency is changed to the next step up or down the spectrum, and the process is repeated until all 1,000 frequencies have been used. Reading the stored data is accomplished by keeping the intensity of the beam constant, stepping through the frequency spectrum and measuring the amount of light transmitted through the material, interpreting it either as a 1 or 0.

The biggest problem with spectral hole storage is that it's slow. At present, data can be stored at the snail-like pace of 1,000 to 2,000 bits per second. Even the slowest floppy disk storage units are faster than that. The goal of the researchers at IBM is to create a system that can store 30 million bits per second, but there's no certainty that such a goal can be achieved.

ORGANIC TRANSISTORS

Beyond the supercold and superfast, researchers are investigating the supersmall for possible use in machines of the future. Specifically, organic molecules have shown promise as minuscule switches a thousand times smaller than the tiniest silicon switches. Instead of just 200 of the smallest silicon switches, it would be theoretically possible to line up 200,000 molecular switches across the width of a period. These tiny devices have been termed *nanocircuits* because their size is measured in nanometers (billionths of a meter).

Building circuits with pieces as small as molecules is naturally no easy task, nor is it clear that the necessary switching functions can be carried out by individual molecules. No one has ever built a functioning molecular electronic circuit, although the design for a diode made from two organic molecules was conceived and patented by IBM researchers in the mid-1970s. A diode is a device that allows current to flow in one direction only. In the case of a molecular diode, two organic substances, abbreviated TTF and TCNQ, are separated by an insulating bridge of urethane. When the molecule is placed between two metal electrodes a few nanometers apart and a current is induced, electrons flow readily, tunneling from the TCNQ complex to the TTF complex through the insulator. But when a reverse voltage is applied, the flow of electrons is negligible. This asymmetry forms the basis for a diode, a basic element in many kinds of electronic circuitry.

Another approach to molecular circuitry combines this concept with optical computing methods to produce a *soliton switch*. An ultra-thin, polycrystalline film made of TCNQ and either copper or silver was found to exhibit switch-like behavior in experiments at the Applied Physics Laboratory at Johns Hopkins University. Beams of laser light directed at the film cause the level of resistance to electric current flow to be reduced by a factor of 10,000. When the light is removed, the high resistivity state is restored. The researchers, led by Richard Potember, have speculated that the cause of the switching is not the light itself but the electric field produced by the laser.

In addition to the change in resistivity, Potember and his colleagues found that there were also changes in the optical properties of the material. A focused laser beam producing light in the infrared part of the spectrum can write patterns into the film, which can also be erased by a second beam. This capacity has suggested the possibility of information storage devices that could pack far more data into a given area than current magnetic storage disks. Similar optical storage disks that are read by lasers are also beginning to find widespread use, but unlike the soliton films, these cannot be erased.

In order to make molecular chips, it will be necessary to build up successive layers of molecular switches into arrays that would form the machine's basic calculating engine. Depositing molecule-thick layers on a substrate material like glass is a relatively old technique that dates from the 1930s.

The molecules are prepared with water-loving and water-repelling ends and then lined up across a water surface. A barrier is used to compress the molecules so that their hydrophobic ends all point upward. When a glass slide is immersed in the water and then pulled out, it is covered with a single layer of molecules all lined up and pointing the same direction.

By incorporating light-emitting and light-absorbing dyes into the films, one West German researcher has found that primitive optical switches can be constructed. Generally, however, the electronic properties of the films laid down in this way don't readily lend themselves to the construction of computer logic circuits. One group of researchers in Britain is working on multilayered chips built up from derivatives of two organic semiconductors that might have potential as the raw material for electronic devices. Circuits might be constructed using wires made of the one-dimensional polymer trans-polyacetylene, which can carry a current of either electrons or the vibrational pulses called solitons. By combining special-purpose molecules with molecular wires, just about any kind of circuit element needed for a computer could be constructed. Molecules, like transphasors, also exhibit a talent for switching among more than just two logical, on-off states.

A researcher at the Genex Corporation in Gaithersburg, Maryland, has proposed making molecular computers essentially by growing them. Kevin Ulmer calls his idea, an extension of genetic engineering, *protein engineering*. By altering the genes that control the structure and function of natural proteins, it might be possible to learn how to engineer cells that can produce molecules capable of performing the functions of a computer. The machine would assemble itself, and perhaps even reproduce—von Neumann's cellular automata in a petri dish.

The possible applications for molecular computers have a definite ring of science fiction. Forrest L. Carter, a chemist at the Naval Research Laboratory and organizer of a workshop on molecular devices, imagines a computer the size of a sugar cube with the calculating power of a Cray 1. Such a machine might be implanted in the human brain, where it could serve as a sort of second brain, for performing complex calculations and processing volumes of data.

Scientists at a company called EMV Associates foresee the possibility of restoring sight to the blind with molecular computers. A small television camera mounted on a pair of eyeglasses would send image data to a molecular computer connected directly to neurons in the visual cortex. Current pulses would be sent to an array of tiny electrodes. The electrodes would be coated with protein and cultured nerve cells, which would grow and form connections with the brain's natural cells.

Implanted molecular computers could go artificial intelligence machines one better by feeding complex data directly into the brain. Current military research is focused on the development of an intelligent pilot's assistant that keeps him informed of instrument readings and significant data from the plane's on-board electronics. The data would be displayed holographically across the pilot's field of vision or communicated verbally. But a molecular computer might be capable of sending data directly to the brain, making the pilot and his aircraft, in effect, a single machine. Similar monitoring of complex machinery, like nuclear power reactors, might be achieved with direct links between man and machine.

Others believe the initial step toward molecular electronics should involve the use of biological organisms, like bacteria, as sensors. F. Eugene Yates of UCLA's Crump Institute for Medical Engineering envisions using genetically engineered E. coli bacteria as a bioelectronic sensor. The behavior of E. coli is determined by its pursuit of nutrients. In seeking a supply of nutrient, the bacterium processes information about its chemical environment. Among 20 or more distinct chemical substances, the bacterium is able to pick out a single nutrient. It swims not just in the direction of more nutrient, but toward the densest concentration of nutrient. By genetically engineering the bacteria, its preference for different substances (and therefore its range as a sensor) could theoretically by altered to suit the needs of researchers.

ARE COMPUTERS ALIVE?

Successful development of molecular computers, or even the combination of biological and electronic components, will blur the distinction between computers and living organisms. At least one computer expert is prepared to say that computers have already become an emerging life form. Geoff Simons, chief editor for the National Computing Centre in England, presented his ideas in a book entitled *Are Computers*

Alive? published in 1983. His premise is that computers exhibit all the functional characteristics associated with life forms, and therefore, they are in some sense alive. Simons suggests that growth, metabolism, movement, information processing, reproduction, ingestion of chemicals, and the development of survival strategies are the essential qualities of life.

It's clear that computers engage in information processing and, via robotics, are capable of movement. It could be argued that the electricity a computer consumes can at least be derived from chemicals, and the conversion of electrical energy to digital signals and heat could be called metabolism. Growth, reproduction, and survival all require that the definition be stretched enough to include human beings as the beneficent partner in a symbiotic relationship. Simons argues that computers at least "involve themselves in the generation of new computers" via computer-aided design of microcircuits and so on. Their actual reproduction, however, must be aided by humans in a manner similar to the way the bee aids in the reproduction of clover. He even goes so far as to assert that computers are "cultivating allies" for survival by making themselves indispensable to such powerful institutions as banks, multinational companies, the armed forces, and police agencies. Many will no doubt find Simons' arguments sophistic, but they do raise important questions.

If a computer made of organic molecules and using artificial intelligence software were created, would this not in fact be a form of intelligent life? If people are willing to ascribe a high degree of knowledge and authority to a simple program like ELIZA, how would they react to a "living" machine that can converse with them in their own language but with far superior knowledge? Though the computer's internal processes might be limited and somewhat mechanistic, wouldn't they have to be recognized as a form of consciousness? How much individual autonomy and decision making responsibility would people be willing to give such a machine?

Chapter 13

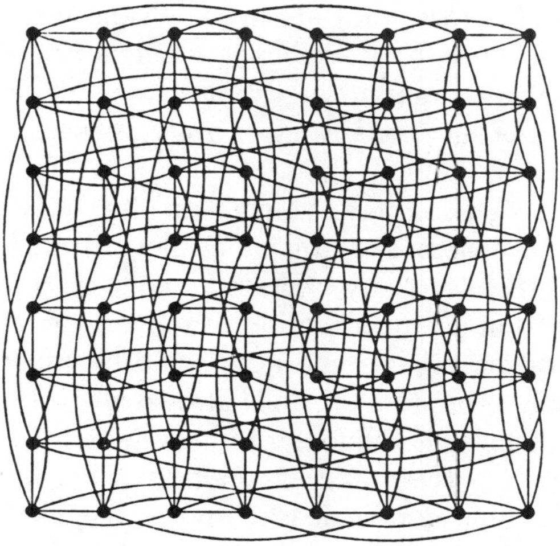

Litany for Luddites

When evaluating a technology, and seeking to articulate the way it changes the circumstances of existence, we must always consider the worst possible use of that technology.

Jerry Mander
The Whole Earth Review
Special Issue: "Computers as Poison"

As the computer prepares to take yet another quantum leap forward in its evolution, many people are beginning to wonder just who is writing the program. Like any tool, the computer augments the power of those who wield it. It has the potential for both good and evil, just as an automobile, a handgun, or nuclear power does. But there are few tools that combine the power and versatility that can be found in a supercomputer. When the processing might of such a computer is combined with robotics and with artificial intelligence software, as will happen in the coming decade, the result is a machine with unmatched potential for executing the will of its masters.

THE ALL-KNOWING MACHINE

Information is the currency of the new age, and more powerful computers make it easier to gather information of all kinds, including data on individuals. Invasion of privacy is a form of burglary in an Information Age. Already the paper trail left by an average person going about his business is extensive and can provide information on purchasing habits, income, and property ownership, all compiled legally from public records. As more powerful computers are linked together in ever-expanding networks, the task of compiling this information is made easier. And as computers are used for new kinds of transactions, additional data will be added to an individual's paper—or electronic—trail. Political groups, private companies and law enforcement agencies use computers to compile dossiers on individuals by taking bits of information from such sources as telephone directories, voter registration lists, drivers license information, vehicle registrations, land ownership records, and birth, marriage, and death certificates. Ultimately, this information may be used for purposes far different from those for which it was gathered.

For example, the Internal Revenue Service is collecting data from the states, compiling lists of individuals who register expensive cars, obtain plumber's licenses, or provide other indications of additional, possibly unreported, income. The IRS is also experimenting with commercially compiled mailing lists used by businesses to direct advertising to specific income groups. If an individual's name appears on the mailing list but not on the federal tax rolls, an inquiry is made that could lead to an audit.

A major clothing firm seeking the names and addresses of petite women used a list of 63 million licensed drivers to identify women from 21 to 40 years of age who were less than 5 feet 3 inches tall and weighed less than 120 pounds.

Using commercially compiled data on the socio-economic class of people living in particular census tracts, the Natural Gas Supply Association was able to create an instant lobby in support of the deregulation of natural gas.

A sociologist at Yale University, Scott A. Boorman, asserts that a few major corporations are using computers to gather and compile seemingly trivial data to detect the flow of communication within their organization. Information on which executives receive copies of internal memoranda, eat lunch together, or converse on the company's internal phone system is stored in computer data files.

One of the main sources of personal information is the telephone. Starting with the names and addresses listed in the phone directory, a computer is used to assign each name to a census tract. This allows the creation of a list of every household in the country that includes estimated incomes, average numbers of children, and median ages. When access is gained to the list of toll calls billed to a particular phone, either legally by law enforcement agencies or illegally, then a nearly complete picture of one's activities and associates emerges.

The federal Office of Management and Budget sparked a chorus of alarm with its proposal to use a computer to monitor government employees' use of the telephone. A record of every call made and the name and number of the person receiving the call are stored by the computer, ostensibly for the purpose of billing workers for personal calls. One congressman who was informed about the plan feared that it would stifle whistle blowing by employees who become aware of unethical or illegal acts on the part of superiors. And though the OMB has offered assurances that the information gathered will only be used for its intended purpose, that's the only guarantee of privacy the employees have. As the technology for speech recognition matures, it's conceivable that powerful computers could be programmed to pluck certain key phrases from among millions of irrelevant telephone conversations—in effect, bugging a nation's entire phone system.

Some argue that if a person has done nothing wrong, he has no need to worry about a computer keeping track of his telephone calls or any other activity. But the computer's power to record and compile the trivial facts of life takes this argument to the point of logical absurdity. A professor of philosophy at Bentley College in Massachusetts, Jerry Samet, offers this example:

> We consider it a violation of privacy to look in someone else's window, but the reverse, looking out one's own window is no problem. Suppose, however, that an individual sat all day and all night recording everything that he observed out his window about passersby: their clothing, where they

were headed, their apparent mood, the packages they were carrying. It still doesn't seem a threat to privacy. But if every person in a neighborhood did the same thing, and they compared notes, they would have a detailed personal profile of everyone who walked through the neighborhood. If every move that a person made in public were recorded, the veil of anonymity that protects one's public privacy would be torn away. Even if such records were never used, they would certainly change the way people act in public.

COMPUTER SECURITY: FAR FROM FAILSAFE

If legal access to information were the only threat to privacy, it would still be a formidable one, but on top of that is the all-too-common problem of computer break-ins. While most breaches in computer security are the work of young hackers who see it more as a Gordian knot just waiting to be cut, others are the means to more devious ends.

One of the most notorious break-ins was the French government's raid on the computers of the famed banks of Switzerland. Out of concern that a growing percentage of French tax revenues were being diverted to numbered Swiss bank accounts, the French government enlisted the help of a group of teen-age hackers to help them crack the Swiss banking system. The youngsters made random calls to certain prefixes in Switzerland and within days had turned up direct lines to computers at several banks. After several weeks of effort, the hackers gained electronic access to the accounts of people with addresses in France. Not long afterward, thousands of tax notices went out to citizens who had made cash deposits in what they had believed were secure, numbered Swiss accounts.

The nation's largest credit information data bank, run by the information services division of TRW, holds credit histories on more than 120 million consumers. Information pirates raid the company's computers using access codes stolen from the banks, stores, and finance companies that are its customers. The company has said that it cannot secure the system against unauthorized entry when a few of its customers are careless with their passwords. Credit card numbers pilfered from the data bank are sometimes used fraudulently to make illegal purchases.

In one case reported widely in 1984, a reporter for Newsweek magazine was told that his VISA card number had been posted on an electronic bulletin board in West Virginia. The reporter, Richard Sandza, had written an article exposing some of the computer mischief caused by hackers, and this was their form of retaliation. The card number had been obtained illegally from the TRW data banks.

Unauthorized access to computer systems was not a crime in many states until a few years ago, but it's now a felony in most. Computer break-ins used to be considered fairly minor crimes in a league with vandalism and other childish pranks usually perpetrated by juveniles. As information has come to be seen more as a form of property, however, that view is changing. But securing computers against break-ins is no easy task, in part because they are meant to be user-friendly.

Hackers almost always penetrate systems from a remote location using personal computers and a device called a *modem*, which links two computers via conventional telephone lines. In essence, what the device does is convert binary digits to high and low tones, analog signals that the phone lines can carry, at one end, and at the other end, another modem reconverts the tones to binary digits. Any computer can communicate with any other in this way, which means that any machine hooked up to a telephone is vulnerable to unauthorized entry.

The list of computer systems that have been invaded by hackers is a long one. It includes systems at Los Alamos National Laboratory, where much of the government's research on nuclear weaponry is carried out; Memorial Sloan-Kettering Cancer Center in New York, where patient files were ransacked; and various university and corporate computers. The success of teen-agers at gaining access to sensitive information stored in computers all around the country has raised questions about how to provide ready access to legitimate users while keeping unauthorized users out.

One of the most commonly used—and easily broken—security measures is the password. Changed daily, passwords can make it more difficult to gain entry and can limit the extent of damage if unauthorized entry is made. The problem is in getting the necessary passwords to users without also communicating them to others outside an organization.

Security is usually compromised for convenience, and the passwords are changed monthly, or not at all. This allows a hacker trying to break into a system by trying random passwords more time to work, and magnifies the rewards of success. The security system at one major West Coast university was so lax that, after someone tried three incorrect passwords, it offered help on gaining access to its files.

CRYPTIC BUT CRACKABLE CODES

Another way of securing information in a system that remains readily accessible is by encrypting it in a code of some kind. Computers have always been adept at creating complex codes for data—and at cracking codes, as well. One cryptographic system that looked promising as a way of encoding data in open systems was for eight years deemed unbreakable, until the power of a new parallel supercomputer was brought to bear on it. The system was based on a simple concept, using a mathematical procedure that is easy to compute but nearly impossible to reverse without special information. It's called a *public key cryptosystem* because one of the two keys needed, the encryption key used by the sender, is published openly. The key used by the receiver, which is essential to decoding the message, is kept secret.

In late 1983, however, an IBM researcher named Donald Coppersmith discovered a peculiarity about the public key system that allows it to be broken in a matter of hours. The peculiarity is grounded in the fact that in binary arithmetic $1 + 1 = 0$, not 2. When two binary numbers are added together and squared, $(x + y)^2$, the result is a much simpler expression than it is in decimal notation. Instead of $x^2 + 2xy + y^2$, the equation becomes $x^2 + y^2$, the sum of the squares of the two numbers. The first step in cracking the code is generating a huge database, which takes about an hour on a mainframe computer, and the second step is finding specific keys, which takes only a few seconds. The only way to make the code more secure is to increase the key size from the present 127 binary digits to 241 or even 1,000. With the larger keys, however, the time required to encode and decode messages grows from a few minutes to several hours.

Early in 1984, Israeli scientists published a paper announcing a new unbreakable code, but they have published no details of how it works. Whether the new system will actually prove to be unbreakable, which the public key system was once thought to be, remains to be seen.

THE ONLY REAL SECURITY

With password and encryption systems vulnerable to determined efforts to crack them and still more powerful computers on the way, it's becoming clear that the only sure way of securing a system is by closely limiting physical access to it. Computers at military installations and those used for secret research at government laboratories are linked together by networks outside the telephone system. The Department of Defense uses the World Wide Military Command and Control System, while National Security Agency and Central Intelligence Agency computers are linked in the Community On-line Intelligence Network System, or COINS. Machines in these networks can't be reached by dialing from outside telephones. Furthermore, they can only be used in closely guarded areas so tightly secured that no electromagnetic radiation can be detected outside the computer room. The concern is that the radiation could be read by special equipment to reveal what kind of data the computers are processing.

Corporations are beginning to take similar steps to secure computers that may contain sensitive corporate information. At AT&T, for example, computers with data the company wants to protect have no connections to the outside world. For its Bell Labs subsidiary, AT&T hired a professional hacker who is specifically authorized to try and break into the computers there. Password systems are also being made more sophisticated. Some allow only a few incorrect guesses, then break the connection. Others will allow an unauthorized user into the system and feed him false information while security personnel trace the call.

The need for computer security has spawned a small legion of start-up companies and new products. One security system, ingenious in its simplicity, protects a computer by calling outside users back. A caller gives an identification code to the main computer and hangs up. The computer then calls back using the telephone number that is assigned to that ID code. Another system uses a laser scanner to read a user's fingerprint. The computer asks for an ID number and instructs the user to place his finger on the scanner. If the fingerprint matches the print stored in memory, access to the computer is granted.

INFORMATION FLOW: NO LONGER FREE

While the protection of data stored in computer memories is important to the protection of individual and corporate rights, carried to an extreme it can interrupt the free flow of information. In fact, "free" may be an inappropriate word to describe the flow of information in the future. Although it's true that almost any kind of information is available (witness the Princeton undergrad who designed his own atomic bomb), getting it requires one of two precious resources: labor or money. A simple example is investment information. A lot of investment advice and data on individual companies can be obtained free in libraries from books, magazines and the Wall Street Journal. For the price of a stamp, most companies will mail out a prospectus or an annual report. Sorting through the facts and figures takes time and a certain amount of expertise, which is in itself information.

The alternative is to hire someone to perform the service of information gathering. Stockbrokers will provide advice and information and are compensated by a commission based on the value of an investment. Investment newsletters range in price from as little as $60 per year to $1,200 and more. And for the truly affluent, special investment detectives will, for $100 a day plus expenses, perform a thorough check of high-risk, high-return investment opportunities. All of these vendors use their knowledge and skills as capital to provide a product, information.

Computers add an unprecedented degree of efficiency to the information gathering, but good tools don't come cheap. The price of entering the Information Age—a computer, modem and necessary software—is beyond the reach of many in the United States. Once the basic equipment has been acquired, the cost of accessing databases is still substantial. Obtaining investment information on line can cost up to $102 per hour of computer time, more if special newsletter databases are accessed, plus long-distance phone charges in many cases. There may also be initial membership charges of up to $200 and monthly dues of $50 or more. Some databases also charge a per-search fee of up to $18.

HAVES AND HAVE-NOTS

Some fear that the computer may be dividing society into

information haves and have-nots. A certain amount of education is required to make profitable use of information, and using a computer effectively calls for even more training. Yet only 22 percent of those in the key 25-to-29 age group in 1980 had graduated from college. Students who don't finish college once had the option of doing a variety of semi-skilled factory and clerical jobs, but that is precisely the area that next generation computers and computer-guided robots are moving into the fastest. Learning a particular trade is no longer a guarantee of lifetime income. Even programmers may face the threat of losing their jobs to intelligent, automated programming systems before the century is out.

The trend toward using robots for manufacturing and AI software for many office tasks tends to reduce the overall skill level required for many jobs. A secretary who uses a word processor that automatically corrects spelling, grammar, and syntax needs fewer skills than a secretary using a regular typewriter. And when speech recognition systems become more accurate and less expensive, the role of secretary may be reduced to that of a receptionist, with an accompanying reduction in salary.

According to labor statistics compiled by the U.S. Department of Labor, the ranks of the low-skilled are expected to grow dramatically during the 1980s. Though the fastest rates of growth are predicted for high technology jobs, the actual number of new jobs will be relatively small. A growth rate of 74 percent to 148 percent was forecast for computer programmers and technicians, as compared to a 22 percent growth rate for all jobs. The total number of new jobs in this area, however, is expected to be about 150,000, while some 1.3 million new jobs are expected for janitors, nurse's aides, and orderlies. Data processing machine mechanics are the fastest growing job category, but their 148 percent increase amounts to only 100,000 new jobs. By comparison, 800,000 new jobs for fast food workers and kitchen helpers are projected. Overall, only 7 percent of the jobs created by 1990 are expected to be in the high technology field.

The statistics, reported in a study by Stanford University researchers Henry Levin and Russell W. Rumberger, led the authors to conclude that "the new technologies provide opportunities to further simplify and routinize work tasks and to reduce the opportunities for worker individuality and judgment." Computers also invite abuse of their power to monitor worker performance, measuring a typist's output in keystrokes or a programmer's work in lines encoded per hour.

MIT's Professor Weizenbaum, participating, ironically, in a computer-linked roundtable discussion organized by IEEE Spectrum magazine, sees the computer's power eroding the inner psychological resources of the semi-skilled, nibbling away at their autonomy, their humanness. "We will have an information society populated by those whose lives are characterized by their plastic, machine-readable cards. Great masses of people will live out their lives alternating between obeying the imperatives of machines at their work, and in their free time, suckling at the breast of the great bitch entertainment."

ELECTRONIC WARFARE

As faster, more intelligent computers become ubiquitous in business, law enforcement, defense, education, and other fields, a society becomes vulnerable to a new kind of terrorism: electronic warfare. Because of their tendency to centralize information storage and processing in a single location, computers are an easy target in terms of the amount of damage that could be done to an organization in one attack. Although radical anticomputer sentiment remains diffuse and largely unspoken in this country, it has begun to surface in Europe, particularly in France, as a justification for violence. At least two dozen bombings of computer facilities in Europe have been reported since 1978. One organization involved claims that its members are data processing workers opposed to the "current and future dangers" of computerization. Its name, translated from the French, is Committee for Liquidating or Detouring Computers. The Red Brigades have also apparently had inside help in attacking computer facilities.

Perhaps the most vulnerable spot in a country's soft electronic underbelly is its banking system. In the United States, roughly $400 billion is transferred daily from bank to bank through the Electronic Funds Transfer network, and another $200 billion is sent overseas. Already individuals have demonstrated that gaining access to that network is possible, but their purposes were usually criminal rather than political. Some of the largest thefts in history have involved bank computers. In 1976, an alienated young computer technician named Stanley Mark Rifkin succeeded in transferring

$10 million from Security Pacific Bank in Los Angeles to a numbered Swiss bank account. He was eventually apprehended by the FBI, but only because he returned to the United States with a sackful of Russian diamonds purchased in Switzerland. In another case, an officer of Wells Fargo Bank in Los Angeles used the bank's interbranch computer account-settlement system to produce fake deposits over a period of two years, from 1979 through 1980, ultimately defrauding the bank of $21.3 million.

Using the banking system to achieve political ends might involve different tactics. One of the leading experts on computer security, Donn Parker, a consultant and researcher at SRI International in Palo Alto, California, believes that a thief would have to get away with $160 billion in order to cause nationwide economic disruption on the scale of a Great Depression. Instead, it would be easier for a well-organized group of computer guerrillas to, in effect, hold the banking system hostage.

The Federal Reserve relies on about a dozen large computers in various locations throughout the country. Once a terrorist group had gained access to even one of those machines, it would theoretically be possible to encode the data it contained, withholding the key until certain demands were met. Without the key, it could take months to crack the code, even using the fastest supercomputers. Parker also envisions more subtle and sophisticated forms of electronic warfare being used to disrupt commodities markets or control the nationwide distribution of energy by deliberately introducing small but significant errors into a system's database.

A 1981 report by the Office of Technology Assessment underscores Parker's impressions. The report also asserts that even a simple malfunction could snowball into a catastrophic breakdown with equally disastrous results: "Banks or brokerage houses could be ruined in a matter of minutes, long before it was discovered that the system had failed. The potential victims would be the owners of a failed system, individuals with accounts, correspondent organizations, and, were the failure to cascade through other institutions, even all of society."

THE COMPUTER'S ACHILLES' HEEL

The OTA report also stressed that computer calamities

need not be induced by outside agents but can occur as a result of a failure in the system itself. It pointed to an incident involving the research network set up by the Department of Defense, ARPANET, which provides communications links between a variety of government and civilian laboratories doing work under contract to DOD. The designers of the system recognized that individual components would fail from time to time, so they designed the network's traffic control software to isolate such a failure. No single failure would take down the whole network.

What ARPANET's designers hadn't anticipated was a failure in the traffic control software itself. According to the report, "bad data in one processor was rapidly and systematically propagated throughout the network, bringing traffic to a standstill . . . Thus the network's primary shield against failure proved to be its Achilles' heel."

The Pentagon is working to ensure that computers don't turn out to be the United States' Achilles' heel, but serious problems with the hardware, particularly microcircuitry, used in hundreds of weapons systems have been discovered in recent years. As many as 100 million chips that were manufactured for the military between 1977 and 1983 by a Texas Instruments plant in Taiwan were not properly tested, according to one Defense Department official. How many of those are actually defective may never be determined, and DOD is naturally reluctant to advertise a potential for failure in U.S. weapons systems.

The National Aeronautics and Space Agency, however, used microchips assembled at the same TI plant in several computers aboard the space shuttles Challenger and Discovery. NASA traced the failure of two of the computers aboard Challenger in December 1983 to short circuits caused by loose silicon or metallic particles inside two TI chips. The failure of another computer in June 1984 was also traced to a TI circuit, this time contaminated by either saliva or perspiration. Further testing of 13 additional TI chips slated for use aboard the shuttle fleet revealed that all were contaminated.

Altogether nearly 10,000 different types of microcircuits are involved. They've been installed in such major weapons systems as Trident submarines, B-1 and B-52 bombers, F-15, F-4, F-111, A-6 and A-7 aircraft, and HARM and Harpoon missiles, among others. Because of the huge number of chips involved, testing of individual circuits is almost impossible. The only solution is simply to wait for the weapons systems to fail. A senior DOD engineer quoted in a report on the controversy in Science magazine said, "We don't have absolute, across-the-board evidence that indicates TI circuits are failing more often than they should. But if you go out and look at these weapons systems, there are plenty of malfunctions—even more than we anticipated. The sorry news is that TI parts may not be better or worse than any others and still be pretty bad."

With the number of computers in use by the military doubling every two years, the vulnerability of the nation's security to sabotage and malfunction must also be growing rapidly. This is especially true relative to the Soviet Union, which generally produces less sophisticated weapons in much greater quantities than the United States. Once again, it's a case of the computer generating its own complexity, which threatens to engulf the ability of institutions to manage it. The software required to run the military's computer systems is estimated to total 50 million lines of code, written in dozens of different and incompatible programming languages, representing an $85 billion investment. Finding bugs in those programs is a never-ending task, but national survival might depend on it. Ultimately, the computer's Achilles' heel is man.

THE HALO EFFECT

Dependence on computers for a wider variety of tasks, and the increasing speed and power of next-generation machines, may magnify the false sense of security created in many people by the seeming efficiency and competence of computers. When they are also capable of communicating in natural English, reasoning, and offering explanations for their reasoning, it may be tempting to turn over much of the responsibility for decision making to computers. Already that trend is evident in organizations where decisions are made and ratified within the relative anonymity of a committee. How much easier it would be to blame a bad decision on a machine. This becomes all the more likely as expert systems become more user-friendly and thus can be freed of the need for operators who are aware of their limitations.

Computerized psychological testing is one area where the computer's halo effect has prompted particular concern. The proliferation of personal computers has enabled employers, counselors, educators, and others with little expertise to use psychological testing software outside the clinical setting for which it was developed. The tests usually require a subject to answer several hundred psychologically oriented questions. The answers are fed into the computer, which spits out up to 50 pages of "evaluation" describing the subject's personality traits, disposition, temperament, vocational interests, intellectual abilities, potential for suicide or drug addiction, and a host of other personal details. When the same evaluation is given by a human examiner, experiments have shown that it is given less credence than when its source is perceived to be a computer. The machine gives the whole process a false air of objectivity and infallibility.

NEO-LUDDISM

Faced with the catalog of the computer's frailties and its inarguable potential for evil, it may seem like the world would have been better off if it had never been invented. In his article, "Six Grave Doubts About Computers," Jerry Mander says as much, writing: "People interested in decentralized political solutions would be better off if computers were never introduced into society." Similar doubts were expressed about factory machines at the beginning of the industrial revolution. A group of textile workers in Nottinghamshire, England, blaming machines for unemployment and low wages, entered factories and destroyed knitting machines in 1811. The following year, the rioting spread to other parts of the country and was harshly suppressed by the government. Those involved in this loose-knit movement claimed to be followers of an imaginary figure named Ned Ludd and were called "Luddites."

As with the early textile machines, the computer's capacity for disruption is derived not from the device itself but from the way in which it's used. It seems odd now to argue that the world would have been better off if the knitting machine, the cotton power loom, or the wool carding machine had never been invented. That argument, carried to its extreme, would have people huddled in caves, hunting wild animals, and gathering berries for sustenance. Even if a small, dedicated band of fanatics tried to purge the world of computers, it's doubtful they would succeed. The Red Brigades and the Committee for Liquidating or Detouring Computers probably have about as much chance of halting the computer revolution as the Luddites did of stopping its industrial predecessor. If computers are indeed a fact of life, the question then becomes: How do we make the best use of them?

Chapter 14

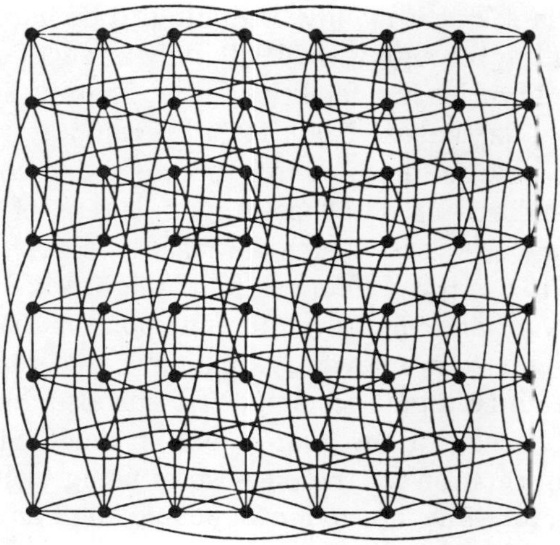

Into the Information Age

The machine's power will introduce further complexity at the same time it helps us deal with complexity. For symbol systems, from language to mathematics, have always accelerated and amplified our intellectual grasp, and the computer is the symbol processor par excellence.

Pamela McCorduck
in *Science 84*

The world that existed before computers is already long buried. Layer upon layer of data, facts, knowledge, and information, like silt after a flood, has been laid down by this new machine. And still the torrent of new information continues, stronger and faster than ever before. A study of the flow of information by Ithiel de Sola Pool, a professor of political science at MIT, showed that the number of words made available in all media to Americans over the age of 10 grew three times faster from 1960 to 1977 than the rate at which people were able to absorb them. People are almost literally drowning in information.

NEW INFORMATION STRATEGIES

The computer has played a major role in generating this ocean of data, but it is only beginning to be used as a tool for navigating through it. In 1980, only a few of the largest university libraries had facilities for performing searches of commercial databases. Now, for a fee ranging from $25 to $50 plus a charge for computer time, one can choose from among hundreds of databases covering tens of thousands of sources. Choosing which database to search and what keywords to use is a skill in itself and might someday be the inspiration for an expert system. The point is that information is being used in a new way. In many cases it has become a resource to be mined for a specific purpose, like iron ore for making steel, rather than an end in itself. Simply consuming information for the purpose of being well-informed is almost a full-time job, and most people don't have the time for it.

New strategies are required to use information effectively, and fortunately, the computer is ideally equipped to implement those strategies. The electronic equivalent of scanning the headlines is already available from television news broadcasts, but television is a passive media. One has to sit through irrelevant items to get to those of interest. The computer makes it possible to customize information retrieval.

Suppose you're particularly interested in news about Belize. Only rarely does anything about that tiny Central American country show up on the evening news, the front page of the newspaper, or the weekly news magazines. Searching the back pages of the newspaper every day is time consuming, and you're just as likely to miss an article as notice it. Taking the time to look up Belize in various indexes at the library would turn up some information, but the most recent articles indexed would probably be three months old. Using a computer and modem attachment, it would be relatively easy to keep track of current events in Belize. There are several databases offering current news from dozens of wire services and hundreds of magazines and newspapers. The computer can be instructed to monitor a database for articles containing a specific word, like "Belize," and to compile a list of those articles.

MAN-MACHINE COEVOLUTION

If all the next generation of computers had to offer was

a convenient way of accessing data, its impact wouldn't be any more revolutionary than that of the electric toothbrush. The next step is part of an evolution, but it is man's evolution rather than the machine's. All the pieces aren't quite in place yet, but soon it will be possible to quickly and (relatively) inexpensively retrieve any knowledge now stored in the world's great libraries. In effect, the capacity of the human memory will have increased a billion times over. The creation of this vast network will mark a new epoch in human evolution. Just as written language expanded the boundaries of knowledge beyond what could be contained in a single individual's memory, or that of a generation, the development of a worldwide electronic nervous system will allow the mind to transcend both physical and temporal barriers to the spread of knowledge.

Of course, it will still be necessary to sit at a terminal and by trial and error locate specific bits of data, but the speed and ease with which this task can be done will make it seem almost effortless. The physical barriers to knowledge acquisition—distant libraries, books that are checked out or missing—will be minimized. And as computers acquire an intelligence of their own, temporal barriers imposed by the sheer volume of available knowledge—not knowing where to look for information or how to sift through hundreds of possible sources—will be minimized, as well.

At present, methods for entering data into computer memory are still primitive, which has limited the amount of information available on-line. Optical character readers can be used in some cases, but their adaptability to unusual type faces and symbols is narrow, and in many cases data must be keyed into the computer by hand.

At Oxford University, a $10 million project is under way to computerize the Oxford English Dictionary. It's a huge undertaking, in part because the OED's 20,000 pages, containing more than 500,000 entries, must be typed manually into the computer. Once that is done, every part of each entry must be identified and indexed, so that etymological history and literary allusions can be cross-referenced in various ways. For example, medical historians will be able to retrieve the origins of terms limited to a little known specialty; musicians can find the first literary references to certain instruments; or lawyers can search out the relationships between terms rooted in English common law. The OED has existed for decades as a static catalog of the language, resistant to revision by virtue of its immensity. The first seven volumes have not been updated since the 19th century. Maintained on computer, the OED will become a living document charting the progress of the English language.

A similar effort at Bar Ilan University in Tel Aviv, Israel, is dedicated toward putting the entirety of Jewish law and religious thought on computer. Much of the rabbinical tradition in Judaism is recorded in large volumes of *responsa*, questions and answers on religious matters. Already 250 volumes, totaling more than 50 million words, have been stored in the database. The 50,000 questions and rabbinical judgments also offer scholars an intimate look at Jewish life in Europe and North Africa from the Middle Ages to the 20th Century. In addition, the Hebrew Bible, the Babylonian Talmud commentaries on the Bible, and modern Hebrew novels based on religious themes have been stored on disk. Terminals have been installed in several locations in the United States and Europe that allow scholars to access the database directly. The Responsa Project, as it's known, has established a kind of communal memory for the Jewish people of the world.

These two projects are just a beginning. New storage media based on the same kind of laser technology used in home videodisc players will make it possible to pack vast amounts of data into a small physical space. The entire Oxford English Dictionary would fit on a pair of disks a little more than 5 inches in diameter. A laser reads the topography of the disk as a series of 1's and 0's, which of course are the computer's raw material. Pictures can be stored, as well as text, and they can be combined with music or spoken language to create a kind of talking book. Imagine, for example, studying medieval musical instruments and being able to see them in pictures and hear their sound, or reading about Abraham Lincoln and seeing the handwritten text of the Gettysburg Address.

THE ELECTRONIC SOCIETY

Memory is just one part of a computerized nervous system that may someday link the elements of an electronic society. Japan is one of the leaders in fostering this new technology, which it calls the Information Network System. The goal is to provide a digital network for the entire country that integrates telephone, telex, facsimile, teletext, computer data and video transmission systems by the year 2000. It would enable a wide variety of activities to be carried out from the home, but the estimated cost of the basic investment in capital equipment required for the network dwarfs even the most grandiose United States military projects—$150 billion.

Construction has begun on a model system in the Mitaka suburb of Tokyo that will serve 2,000 homes at a cost of $100 million. That amounts to $50,000 per household, but it will allow most of the terminal equipment that may be in every home in the 21st century to be tried out now. The equipment will include videophones that allow two or more people to meet face to face on the video screen. There will also be a service that allows video cameras to be operated remotely, so that, for example, the progress of construction on a building site could be monitored from an office. Another device transmits manuscripts and hand-drawn diagrams telephonically. Initially, these "sketchphones" will be used primarily by the deaf.

The model network will also offer a variety of new information services to consumers. Rather than calling a dozen friends to invite them to a party, it would be possible to store your message and the telephone numbers in a central voice accumulation device that would complete the calls. The same facility can also be used to transmit facsimiles, although it's doubtful that such social niceties as New Year cards (a Japanese tradition) will be amenable to computerization. Messages can also be left for callers who can then leave messages themselves, similar to an answering machine.

Videotext will also be a part of the network's services, but unlike current systems, it will also allow the transmission of still and moving pictures, diagrams with voice instructions on how to use the system, and devices to turn the transmission into hard copy. As of mid-1984, more than 300 companies had signed up to provide services to customers on the network. Banks and financial service companies make up almost 25 percent, but a variety of retail businesses have also decided to give the system a try. Department stores plan to offer an electronic catalog. Rail and transport companies want to provide timetables and route maps. Travel agents are considering conducting potential clients on pictorial tours of countries overseas. The local utility is looking into the possibility of transmitting monthly bills straight into customers' homes. One company is even offering a fortune-telling service.

Critics of the system believe its main weakness is a lack of intelligence, not on the part of the designers but the machines themselves. The system's search capabilities are limited. Often a user has to call up screen after screen of text to find a particular item. Because of the relatively high cost of accessing information by computer, the quality of that information needs to be higher in terms of its usefulness to the consumer. That means that the machine must more accurately define what's being sought, making it as complete and concise as possible. A system similar to the INS, though more primitive, was tried in Britain in 1979. It failed, in part because it wasn't useful enough to justify its cost.

ENABLING THE HANDICAPPED

There is one group of people who find the kind of services provided by the INS system not only useful but essential—the handicapped. Advanced microprocessors are being used to control increasingly sophisticated artificial limbs that can be manipulated by nerve signals. Quadriplegics are able to work without ever leaving home, communicating with work via a computer and modem. Optical character readers free the blind from dependence on braille texts and may someday provide limited sight. Voice synthesizers allow the deaf to communicate over regular telephone lines. In this country alone, there are an estimated 2 million people with hearing, visual, speech, motor, or learning disabilities that could become more productive with the aid of computerized assistants.

In his book *Personal Computers and the Disabled*, Peter A. McWilliams tells the story of a college professor who had lost all speech and motor control to a disease called amyotrophic lateral sclerosis, but his mental strength was left intact. Using the muscles of one eyebrow to control a single switch, he communicates to the world through a computer. The computer allows him to talk to his family, tell jokes, and write and receive letters. Similar stories could be told about hundreds of handicapped people whose lives are immeasurably improved by the computer. Making these machines more powerful, more intelligent, and more portable could enable many of the handicapped to live normal, productive lives.

Improving access to computers for the handicapped is one by-product of the same process that reduces the skill level required for certain kinds of jobs. A machine that can understand spoken language would allow a quadriplegic to operate a computer without the difficult necessity of using a mouth stick to hit keys. But that same machine would also effectively eliminate the need for secretaries to possess typing skills. There are probably several thousand secretaries for every quadriplegic, but how do you help one without hurting the other? Banning the use of speech understanding systems by nonquadriplegics is one answer, but an intrusive one. Another answer is to provide secretaries with new skills that the computer can't match.

As the full capabilities of AI software, parallel computers, and robotics begin to be realized in actual use, no doubt dozens of different kinds of jobs will be lost to automation or modified to the point that an entirely new set of skills is required. But the same machine that is making old skills obsolete is also the ideal tool for learning new, more marketable ones.

THE COMPUTER REVOLUTION IN EDUCATION

Though it's slow in coming, the computer revolution in education is inevitable. Consider that the personal computer is barely 10 years old, and already many school systems have one for each classroom. Most colleges and universities have established computer centers where dozens of terminals provide access to a mainframe machine, and others, most notably the Air Force Academy, are insisting that new students come to school with a personal computer or not at all. Several major universities have pooled their resources to establish new centers where students and researchers will have access to the latest, most powerful supercomputers. But most of the effort, especially in the development of learning software, is directed toward the largest potential market—schoolchildren. But that may change as the need for adult retraining grows.

Most learning software is now used either for drill or for enabling a student to learn standard material at an individualized pace. Computers are ideal for drill because mindless repetition happens to be what they do best. As Stewart Brand points out in the Whole Earth Software Review, computers "don't drum their fingers or roll their eyes or breathe audibly through their noses while you take a long slow time coming up with the wrong answer to something." They also will track a student's pace, administering tests and providing tutorial help at appropriate points.

A small number of educational programs that employ some of the rudiments of artificial intelligence are available. Their method of teaching is essentially the Socratic dialog. The computer asks a series of questions that are intended to lead a student to an understanding of the subject matter. Programs are supplied with sentence parsing features that allow them to interpret a variety of responses. Instructional dialogs are like primitive expert systems, but the intelligence reflected in a program is not embodied in specific knowledge but in the questions used to guide the learning process. Each correct answer allows the student to continue along the main question sequence. An incorrect answer causes the program to branch off to a remedial sequence designed to clarify the misconception that led to the error.

Needless to say, programs at this level of sophistication are expensive to develop. They require hundreds of hours to write and debug. The dialog's sequence of questions is modeled after real person-to-person dialog in covering the same material. Certain key words and phrases are recorded and used in the sentence parsing subsystem. Then the system is put through a series of trial runs to turn up previously unanticipated answers, which are collected and added to the program. A dialog usually ends with a test composed of a series of questions selected at random from a large bank of stored test questions.

The future development of instructional dialogs will depend on progress in natural language understanding and expert systems development. At present, each dialog is a custom creation specifically tailored to a body of knowledge. If a standardized shell or framework can be developed that allows knowledge to be "plugged in," as is happening with some expert systems, the cost of instructional dialogs could fall dramatically.

Demand for instruction and training at all levels is expected to increase as jobs continue to migrate from other sectors of the economy to the information sector. A Department of Commerce study published in 1982 indicates that the information sector grew from 5 percent of the work force in 1870 to 33 percent in 1950 to 50 percent of all employees in 1980. The percentage of workers involved in the production of goods—agriculture, manufacturing, mining, and construction—has fallen from 54 percent of the workforce in 1940 to 32 percent in 1980. The main factor in that decline has been the loss of agricultural jobs, which fell from 18 percent of the workforce in 1940 to a mere 3 percent in 1980.

ROBOT WORKERS AND MACHINES WHO THINK

Up to now, agricultural work has been more easily adapted to mechanization than manufacturing. But as the nation's robot population increases, the number of jobs in manufacturing could drop substantially. A single robot can usually replace several human workers. For example, at a Chrysler plant in East Detroit, Michigan, 50 robot welders have taken the jobs of 200 humans. They work so well that the plant's output increased after one year by 20 percent. At a McDonnell-Douglas factory in St. Louis, where sheets of graphite are sliced up by laser to make brake assemblies for military jets, two human workers using robot cutters now do the job once performed by 30. Often the cost of a robot can be recovered in less than one year, which is one reason why many companies are investing heavily in robotics. General Motors alone is planning to increase its robot work force from 1,600 to 16,000 by 1990.

Similarly high rates of return have been recorded for investment in expert systems. The Digital Equipment Corporation reports annual savings of $10 million from its R1 expert system for configuring VAX computers, suggesting a payback period of less than a month. The number of potential applications for expert systems is unknown, but the economic incentive is there to encourage experimentation.

Frederick Hayes-Roth, chief scientist at Teknowledge Inc., which manufactures expert systems, sees three trends growing out of the commercialization of expert systems. Writing in *Computer* magazine, Hayes-Roth predicted that the new technology would spawn a wide variety of new consumer products as entrepreneurs try to meet old needs in new ways. Systems designed to help with a job search, improve personal finances, or do something as frivolous as selecting colors for a new wardrobe might strike a responsive chord among consumers.

A second trend Hayes-Roth sees is the widespread use

of expert systems by a growing number of commercial and industrial concerns. Systems for automotive and equipment repair, planning and control systems for industrial automation, design systems that make use of specialized knowledge, aids to management planning, and scientific instruments and sensors that can interpret their own readings. The key is improved performance. Hayes-Roth estimates that the typical expert system now in use has increased the efficiency of the task it performs by a factor of two to 10, saving millions of dollars.

The third trend is an increasing integration of data processing and AI systems; in other words, the creation of intelligent databases. Increasingly, knowledge will be required to manipulate information and make the most efficient use of it. Already the data produced by orbiting satellites far exceeds the human resources devoted to analyzing it. Expert systems can be programmed to search for patterns in the data, which could then become subjects for human analysis. A wide variety of applications, particularly military intelligence and earth resources exploration, stand to benefit.

As the next generation of parallel supercomputers reaches the market, the knowledge explosion will surely accelerate by yet another order of magnitude. Problems that had not been amenable to computation by current supercomputers may be solved by those on the horizon. Computer models with a degree of complexity never before possible may open up new phenomena to the eyes of science. New methods of investigation in physiology, genetics, and the behavioral sciences may deepen our understanding of mind and man. As with any fundamental change in the circumstances of life, the next generation of more powerful, more intelligent machines will strain the fabric of social order. But the computer, alone among man's inventions, has the capacity to solve many of the problems it creates.

Index